Children's
Encyclopedia

First published in the UK in 2013 by Chancellor Press,
an imprint of Bounty Books,
a division of Octopus Publishing Group Ltd.
Endeavour House
189 Shaftesbury Avenue,
London WC2H 8JY
www.octopusbooks.co.uk

An Hachette UK Company
www.hachette.co.uk

Produced by Brown Bear Books Limited
First Floor
9–17 St Albans Place
London N1 0NX, UK

ISBN: 978-0-753724-27-9

Managing Editor: Tim Harris
Designer: Jerry Udall
Picture Manager: Sophie Mortimer
Art Director: Jeni Child
Production Director: Alastair Gourlay
Editorial Director: Lindsey Lowe
Children's Publisher: Anne O'Daly
Contributors: Tim Harris, Ian Graham, Paul Sterry and Andrew Langley

A CIP catalogue record for this book is available from the British Library.

Printed and bound in China

Key: TP = Title Page, IF = Inside Flap, t = top, b = bottom, l = left, c = centre, r = right

Inside: Alamy: Art Archive 124tr, cbimges 96tr, Steven Frame 121t, Mira 217b, Stuart Pearce 224tl, Paul Risdale 197t;
Michael Barnes: 125t; **Corbis:** Macduff Everton 40b; Patrick Giadomo 188tr, **FLPA:** Gary K. Smith 49tr; **Fotolibra:** 207tl;
Bernard Gagnon: 141b; **Getty Images:** National Geographic 229t; **Brad Hall:** 235tr; **AJ Haverkamp:** 105b;
NP Holmes: 157b; **iStockphoto:** Tim Mosenfelder 193b, Andrew Howe 92t; **Ceska Kralove:** 64b;
Museum of Mankind: 146tl; **NASA:** 23cr, 38cr, APOD/NOAO/AURA/NSF 4tr, Apollo Gallery 16r, 17t, 17b, 19tr, Blue Marble 29, Earth Observatory 22bl, ESA 24cl, GRIN 24b, 36tl, JPL 12tl, 13cr, 28tl, 69b, Mt Palomar Observatory 7r, NIX 4/5, 6cl, 6br, 7l, 8tl, 12b, 16tl, 21tr, 21b, 24tl, 25; **Natural Visions:** Peter David 81t; **Public Domain:** 65b, 76tl, 101t, 133tl, 145tr, 149tr, 240tr; **Robert Hunt Library:** 153t, 157t, 160bl, 161tl, 161tr, 162tr, 162cl, 240tl; **Charles Marion Russell:** 148b; **Science Photo Library:** Anthony Mercienca 172br, Frank Morgan 219br, Philippe Psaila 173t; **Shutterstock:** 9b, 36b, 40cr, 41tr, 44bl, 49b, 56tl, 56r, 60tl, 61bl, 68tl, 69t, 72r, 80b, 100tl, 108tl, 109tl, 112b, 113b, 116tl, 129t, 172tl, 185tl, 185b, 196t, 202tr, 205tr, 212tl, 216b, 220tr, 221b, 225b, 232tr, 232b, 233t, 238tl, 248tr, Jacqueline Abromeit 236tl, Alphaspirit 184t, Eti Ammos 152b, Yuri Arcurs 204tr, Anton Balazh 52tl, Andrey N Bannov 208b, Mark Beckwith 96tl, Giovanni Benintende 9t, Stephane Bidouze 44r, Blend Images 216tr, Goran Bogicevic 248b, Ryan M Bolton 60b, Darryl Brooks 200tr, Gregor Buir 133tr, Rich Carey 80tl, 172b, 228t, John Carnemolia 52b, Hung Chung Chih 97t, Chrislofoto 160br, Marcel Clemens 5tr, Colin Edwards Photography 104tr, Tom Curtis 156b, Chantal DeBruijne 181t, Dirk Ercken 84tl, Gregory Fer 184b, FloridaStock 232tl, Fotocrisis 204b, Chris Fourie 97b, Natali Glado 112tr, Tatiana Gladskikh 164b, Volodymyr Goinyk 37b, Laurence Gough 136b, Shane Gross 81b, GW Images 109tr, Levente Gyori 225tr, Gyuszkofoto 217t, Claude Huot 92b, Javarman 249t, Gregory Johnston 89b, Panos Karapanagiotis 128tl, Kenneth Keifer 45b, Andrew Kerr 233b, Herbert Kratky 44tl, Ivan Kuzmin 193t, Andy Lim 57t, Don Long 105t, Torsten Lorenz 173b, Xavier Marchant 100b, Mikhail Markovskiy 52tr, Jens Metschurat 48b, Joyce Michaud 189t, Byron W Moore 13t, Berna Namoglu 112tl, Pete Niesen 28bl, Pedro Nogueira 61r, Boris Pamikov 73b, Christopher Parypa 213b, Tomasz Parys 212tr, Nick Pavlakis 129b, Photobank Kiev 32tl, Adam Przezak 237b, Dr. Morley Read 48tr, Jeremy Richards, 57b, Pedro Salaverria 176b, Pete Saloutos 165t, Adrin Shamsudin 205b, Dwight Smith 148tl, Sportgraphic 164tl, Tim Hester Photography 48tl, Richard Thornton 236tr, Emilia Ungur 33cl, Pippa West 137b, Paul Wilkinson 80tr, Kim Worrell 93t, Vasyl Yakobchuk 201b, Gary Yim 53, Jurgen Ziewe 8tr; **Thinkstock:** Ablestock 88b, 245b, Comstock 177t, 201t, 209, Creatas 225tl, Design Pics 84tr, FAE 20bl, Goodshoot 37t, Hemera 20tl, 28/29, 32b, 89t, 113t, 120tr, 120b, 144tl, 168tl, 224br, 224b, 237t, Ingram Publishing 45t, iStockphoto 4tl, 33tl, 40t, 64tl, 64tr, 73t, 76r, 77b, 85t, 88tl, 88tr, 93c, 96b, 100tr, 104tl, 104b, 108tr, 116b, 125b, 144tr, 145tl, 145b, 149tl, 153b, 160tl, 169t, 180b, 185tr, 188tl, 206tr, 208tl, 213t, 216tl, 219tl, 220tl, 235cr, 244t, 244b, 249b, Photodisc 136tl, 212b, 241t, Photos.com 20r, 41tl, 60tr, 84b, 101b, 108b, 117t, 124tl, 140tl, 140tr, 140b, 141t, 152tl, 156tr, Pixland 168b, Stockbyte 72tl, 85b, 208tr, 241b, 248tl, Top Foto Group 149b, Zoonar 176tr;
TopFoto: Granger Collection 229b; **U.S. Fish & Wildlife Service:** 117b.

All artworks Brown Bear Books Ltd.

CONTENTS

THE UNIVERSE

The Universe is thought to be about 13.7 billion years old, the result of a massive explosion called the Big Bang.

KEY FACTS

Age: 13.7 billion years
Age of stars: began to form when the Universe was about 400 million years old; they are still forming today
Biggest star: Canis Majoris is the largest known

Scientists still do not know how big the Universe really is – but they do know that it is expanding. The Universe contains vast numbers of stars, planets, comets and smaller icy and rocky debris. It also contains large quantities of gases, especially hydrogen and helium.

Stars

Most of the objects in space that we can see are stars. A star is a mass of gas held together by its own gravity. The centre of a star is very hot and gives out heat and light. Stars are fuelled by nuclear fusion reactions, which change hydrogen to helium.

Stars come in different sizes, colours and temperatures. Our Sun is a star and it is classed as a yellow star. The hottest stars (for example, Zeta Orionis) shine with a bluish light, and the biggest are red supergiants. Canis Majoris, which is 2,000 times further across than the Sun, is classed as a red supergiant.

Galaxies

Stars are usually grouped into galaxies, and there are probably more than 80 billion galaxies in the observable Universe. Each is made up of many stars, from 10 million in dwarf galaxies to 1 trillion in big galaxies, making an estimated total

▲ The Carina Nebula is a vast area of gas and stars, including some very large stars.

of 3×10^{23} stars. Our own Solar System is a tiny part of the huge Milky Way galaxy.

▶ Our own galaxy, the Milky Way, is visible on a clear night. It contains 200 to 400 billion stars.

material left over may form planets and other rocky bodies.

▲ Halley's Comet comes close to Earth every 75 years.

Nebulae

The Universe also contains nebulae. These vast clouds of dust and gas are places where stars are made. Dust and gas join together to form bigger and bigger bodies. Eventually these may be big enough to make stars, and the

Planets

Since planets do not give off light and are relatively small, we probably know of only a tiny fraction of the total. Smaller fragments of ice, dust and rocky particles orbit our Sun – sometimes forming comets and meteors – and probably exist in other galaxies.

Black holes

Black holes form in places where stars have collapsed in on themselves. There, the gravitational pull is so strong that nothing can escape – not even light. There is a giant black hole at the centre of the Milky Way. Scientists still have a lot to learn about black holes.

GENERAL INFORMATION

- Our own galaxy, the Milky Way, measures about 100,000 light-years across.
- It has been estimated that there are 3×10^{23} stars in the Universe.
- Three-quarters of the atoms in space are hydrogen.

See also:

The Moon, The Planets, Solar System

THE UNIVERSE

Q How did the Sun and planets form?

A Nobody knows for certain. Most scientists think that the Sun, Earth and other planets (the Solar System) were formed from a mass of dust and gas. Nearly 5 billion years ago, this mass started to shrink, and then spin and flatten into a disc. The centre of the disc spun fastest. This became the Sun. The rest of the material turned into the planets (below).

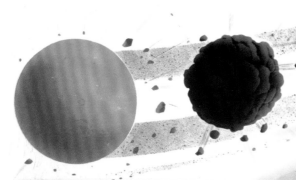

Q What is a nebula?

A A nebula is a cloud of dust and gas in space. Some of the clouds block out the light from the stars behind. These are called dark nebulae. One of the best known is the Horsehead Nebula (right). Other dust clouds reflect the light from the stars and shine brightly. These are called bright nebulae.

Q What is a meteor?

A A meteor is a sudden streak of light in the sky (above). It is caused by a piece of rock from outer space entering the Earth's atmosphere. The friction causes it to burn up.

Q What is a black hole?

A Sometimes – no one knows why – stars collapse in on themselves. This increases their gravity (a force that pulls everything inwards). Nothing escapes – not even light. These very dense bodies are called black holes (below).

Q What is a galaxy?

A A galaxy (below) is a huge spinning mass of stars in outer space. There are millions of galaxies, each containing millions or billions of stars as well as gas and dust. Our galaxy, the Milky Way, contains 200 to 400 billion stars.

Q How did the Universe begin?

A Many scientists believe that all the material of the Universe was once crammed together in one place. Then, about 13.7 billion years ago, an explosion or 'Big Bang' occurred. The material of the Universe flew out in all directions, forming galaxies and other bodies, mainly gas and dust. The effects of this explosion are still continuing, causing the Universe to expand (right). The galaxies still seem to be rushing away from each other.

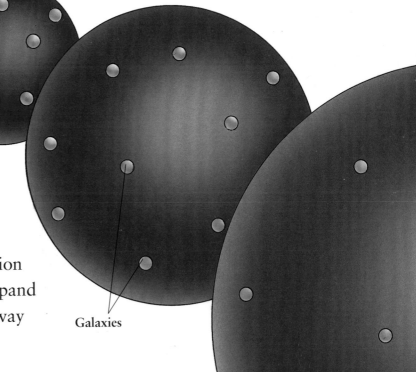

Galaxies

SOLAR SYSTEM

The Solar System is made up of the Sun, the eight planets – including Earth – that move around it and millions of smaller objects such as asteroids.

KEY FACTS

Age: the Sun probably started to form 4.5 billion years ago

Planets: eight planets circle the Sun

Moons: there are 169 or more moons in the Solar System

Rings: the outer planets have rings

Our Solar System is just one of many in our galaxy, the Milky Way. The Sun is at the centre of the Solar System. It is a giant ball of gas, 1.32 million kilometres across.

The inner planets

The planets nearest the Sun are the terrestrial planets. They are Mercury, Venus, Earth and Mars.

These planets are made mainly of rocks and metals. None of the inner planets has rings, and only Mars and Earth have moons. Earth is the largest of the inner planets, and Mercury the smallest.

The outer planets

The outer planets are the gas giants Jupiter, Saturn, Uranus and Neptune. They are much bigger

▲ Our Solar System includes the Sun and the planets that orbit around it. *Solar* means 'of the Sun'.

than the terrestrial planets. Jupiter is large enough to swallow all the other planets, having a diameter of about 143,000 kilometres. Its mass is more than 300 times greater than that of Earth, though its density is much less.

DISTANCE FROM THE SUN

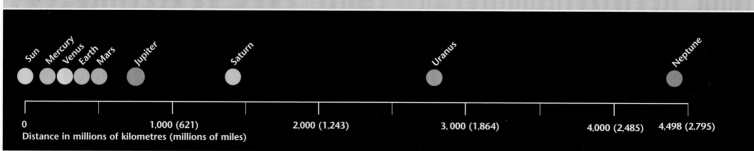

| 0 | 1,000 (621) | 2,000 (1,243) | 3,000 (1,864) | 4,000 (2,485) 4,498 (2,795) |

Distance in millions of kilometres (millions of miles)

Ganymede, one of Jupiter's moons, and Titan, one of Saturn's, are larger than the planet closest to the Sun, Mercury.

Comets

Astronomers know of more than 4,000 comets, but it is almost certain that there are many, many more in the Solar System. Comets are made of ice and dust. As they enter the inner Solar System, the ice begins to turn to gas, forming a distinctive tail, or coma. The orbits

of comets are highly variable, but all take a long time to complete. Some may last less than 200 years, and others may take thousands of years to complete their orbit.

Asteroids

Asteroids are relatively small bodies of rock and ice or metal and rock that orbit the Sun. Most are in the asteroid belt between Mars and

▼ When meteorites smash into Earth, they leave holes or craters. Some measure more than a kilometre across.

Jupiter. Some are very small but an asteroid called Ceres has a diameter of more than 975 kilometres. It is sometimes called a dwarf planet.

◄ A comet blazes across the night sky. The bright head and tail of a comet form when it gets close to the Sun.

GENERAL INFORMATION

- The largest planet is Jupiter, and the smallest is Mercury.
- Venus is the hottest planet, and Neptune is the coldest.
- It takes Neptune 165 years to complete an orbit of the Sun.
- The Sun is composed mostly of hydrogen gas.
- There may be 1 trillion comets in the Solar System.

See also:

The Moon, The Planets, The Universe

METEORITIES

Meteorites are natural objects from outer space that strike Earth's surface. As they pass through Earth's atmosphere they become very hot and give off light. In the night sky they are visible as shooting stars. Depending on what they are made of, meteorites may be stony, iron or stony-iron.

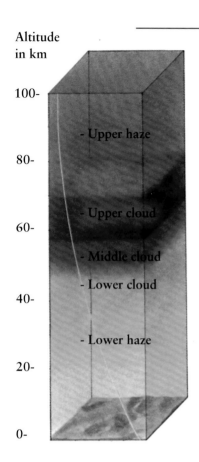

Altitude in km

100 - Upper haze

80 -

60 - Upper cloud

- Middle cloud

40 - Lower cloud

- Lower haze

20 -

0 -

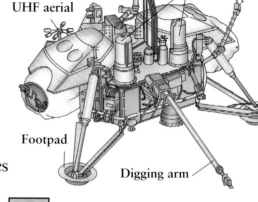

Dish aerial

Cameras

UHF aerial

Footpad

Digging arm

Q Which is the hottest planet?

A Venus. It is the second planet from the Sun. Venus is completely covered in dense clouds (left). These act like a giant greenhouse, raising temperatures to 462°C. Several probes have landed on Venus but none has survived.

Q Which planets have rings?

A Jupiter, Saturn, Uranus and Neptune have rings. The rings are actually tiny pieces of rock covered with ice. Rings may be fragments of moons that were destroyed, or they may have been part of the planets.

Q Is there life on Mars?

A In 1976 two Viking probes (above) landed on Mars and sent pictures of the rocky surface back to Earth. There were no astronauts aboard the Viking probes, so automatic soil samplers tested the red, dry soil for any sign of life. None was found.

Q How large is our Sun?

A The Sun (below) has a diameter of 1,320,000 kilometres. Its volume is approximately 1.3 million times larger than the Earth's. However, the Sun is only a medium-sized star; many stars are much bigger. By comparison, the biggest planet in our Solar System is Jupiter (142,984 km diameter), and the smallest is Mercury (4,879 km diameter).

Jupiter

Mercury

Venus

Earth

Mars

Sun

Q How hot is the Sun?

A The Sun is a vast ball of glowing gas (right). At the heart of the Sun, temperatures are thought to be 15,000,000°C! The heat is created in the core, or centre, by the nuclear fusion of hydrogen atoms. This is similar to the process that occurs in an exploding hydrogen bomb. Marks on the Sun, called sunspots, appear dark only because they are 1,200°C cooler than the surrounding gas. Solar flares are great tongues of gas. All life on Earth is dependent upon the light and heat from the Sun.

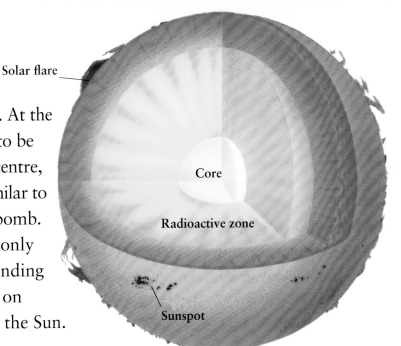

Solar flare

Core

Radioactive zone

Sunspot

Q How do we know so much about the planets?

A Space probes travel through the Solar System sending information back to Earth. Space probes carry cameras to take pictures, as well as equipment to detect the presence of radio waves and magnetic fields.

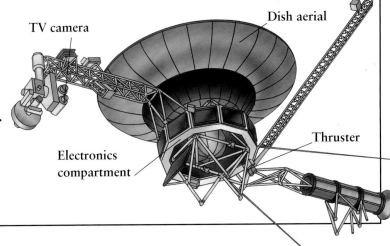

TV camera

Dish aerial

Electronics compartment

Thruster

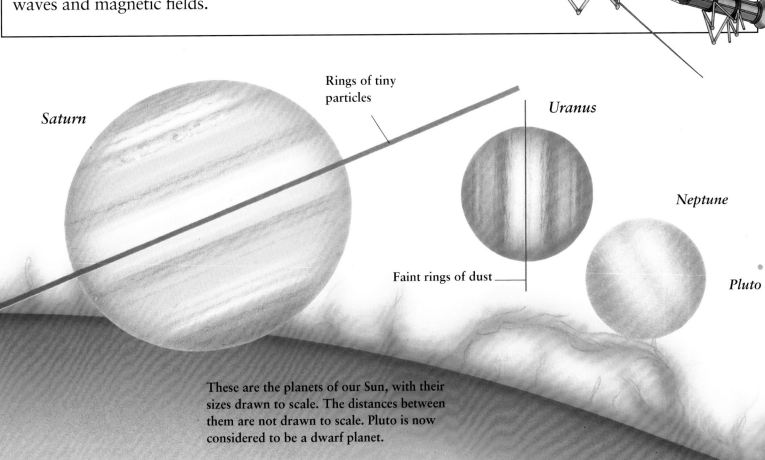

Saturn

Rings of tiny particles

Uranus

Neptune

Faint rings of dust

Pluto

These are the planets of our Sun, with their sizes drawn to scale. The distances between them are not drawn to scale. Pluto is now considered to be a dwarf planet.

THE PLANETS

There are eight planets in our Solar System: the rocky Mercury, Venus, Earth and Mars, and the gas giants Jupiter, Saturn, Uranus and Neptune.

KEY FACTS

Smallest: Mercury, diameter 4,879 km
Largest: Jupiter, diameter 142,984 km
Lightest: Mercury, 5.5 per cent of Earth's mass
Heaviest: Jupiter, 318 times Earth's mass

All the planets follow elliptical (oval-shaped) orbits (paths) around the Sun. Mercury is the closest planet to the Sun. At its nearest, Mercury's orbit brings it to within 46 million kilometres of the Sun. Mercury is the smallest of the true planets. Its diameter is only 4,879 kilometres, half that of Earth's. Mercury has little atmosphere and its gravity is just one-third that of Earth's. When the Sun is above the horizon the ground temperature rises to a scorching 370°C.

Venus, the second planet from the Sun, is similar in size to Earth and is covered by thick clouds of sulphuric acid. The atmosphere is extremely hot and there is a lot of volcanic activity.

Earth is the third planet from the Sun. Mars is the last of the terrestrial (rocky) planets. Intermediate between Mercury and Earth in size, Mars has only a thin atmosphere, and less gravity

▼ This robotic rover operated on the surface of Mars, the 'red planet', between 2004 and 2010.

▲ Jupiter is the biggest planet in the Solar System. The Great Red Spot atmospheric storm is visible near the bottom of the image.

than Earth. The surface of Mars is a freezing desert with dry and bitterly cold weather.

The gas giants

The largest of the planets is the gas giant Jupiter, which has a diameter more than 10 times that of Earth (142,984 kilometres) and huge gravity. It takes nearly 12 years for Jupiter to orbit the Sun. The planet does not have a solid surface. Below an atmospheric mix of hydrogen and other chemicals is a zone of purer hydrogen gas. This merges gradually into an ocean of liquid hydrogen and helium. No one knows for certain what is inside Jupiter's core.

Saturn is huge, though not as enormous as Jupiter, and is the least dense of the planets. Being 10 times further from the Sun than Earth, it takes 30 years to complete one orbit. Saturn is best known for its rings. These are bands of millions of lumps of rock and ice. The planet has a small rocky core, surrounded by hydrogen gas and liquid hydrogen and helium. Saturn's surface is racked by constant storms. Although Saturn's

PLUTO

For many years Pluto was the ninth planet in the Solar System. In 2006, scientists agreed to rename it a 'dwarf planet'. Pluto is much smaller than the other planets, even smaller than our Moon. Its orbit is tilted compared with those of the other planets.

surface is much colder than anywhere on Earth, its core may be as hot as the surface of the Sun.

The most distant true planets – Uranus and Neptune – are sometimes called ice giants. They are about the same size and mostly made of hydrogen and helium, with some methane. Each one has a solid core; Neptune's is hotter than that of Uranus.

▲ An artist's impression of one of Saturn's rings, seen close up.

GENERAL INFORMATION

- Mercury's orbit is the most elliptical, ranging from 46 million km to 70 million km from the Sun.
- Although it is further from the Sun than Mercury, the hottest surface temperatures are found on Venus.
- The temperature on the surface of Neptune falls to –200°C, making it the coldest planet.

See also:

The Moon, Solar System, The Universe

THE PLANETS

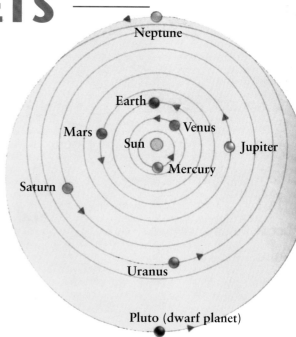

Q What are planets made of?

A The planets that are closest to the Sun, from Mercury to Mars, are small, rocky worlds. They have a metal centre, or core, surrounded by a thick mantle of rock with a thin, rocky crust on the surface. The outer planets are very different. Jupiter and Saturn are made mostly of hydrogen. Uranus and Neptune have a rock core surrounded by ice and hydrogen and helium (below).

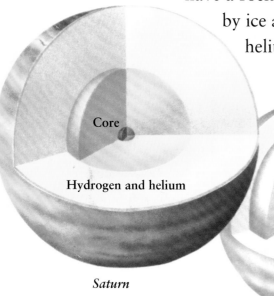

Core

Hydrogen and helium

Saturn

Core

Hydrogen, helium and ice

Uranus

Q How do the planets orbit the Sun?

A All the planets in the Solar System travel in the same anti-clockwise direction around the Sun (above). Their paths are slightly flattened circles called ellipses. Mercury's orbit is the most elliptical.

Q What are planets?

A Planets are worlds that orbit the Sun. The word 'planet' comes from a Greek word meaning 'wanderer', because of the wandering paths they appear to have when seen from Earth. The eight planets (right) are Mercury, Venus, Earth, Mars, Jupiter, Saturn, Uranus and Neptune. Pluto is now described as a dwarf planet.

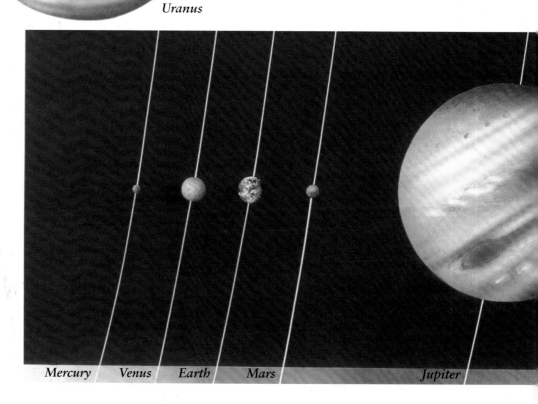

Mercury   *Venus*   *Earth*   *Mars*   *Jupiter*

Q What is the Great Red Spot?

A Jupiter's Great Red Spot (below) is a swirling storm 30,000 kilometres across. It was first seen in 1664. Storms on Earth last a few weeks at most. The Great Red Spot has lasted for centuries because Jupiter has no solid surface to slow the storm down.

Great Red Spot

Q Which planets have moons?

A Only Mercury and Venus do not have moons. Earth has one moon. Mars has two (above). Jupiter has 64 moons. One of them, Ganymede, is larger than the planet Mercury. Saturn has 62 moons, Uranus 27 and Neptune 13.

Q What are the canals of Mars?

A Over the centuries, astronomers thought that the dark lines and patches on the surface of Mars might be canals, built by an ancient civilisation for carrying water. However, none of these so-called canals is visible in photographs taken by probes sent from Earth to Mars. Therefore scientists now believe that the canals are probably an optical illusion.

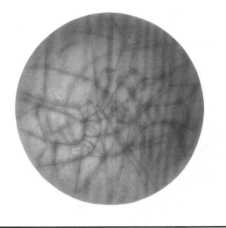

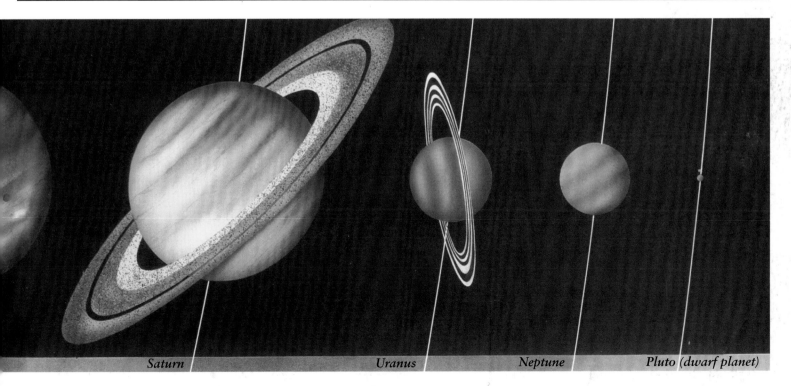

Saturn *Uranus* *Neptune* *Pluto (dwarf planet)*

THE MOON

With a radius of 1,737 kilometres, the Moon – Earth's only natural satellite – is the fifth biggest moon in the Solar System.

The Moon has hardly any atmosphere, has no weather and shows no evidence of recent geological activity. Because it has no protective atmosphere, surface temperatures range enormously, according to whether there is direct sunlight or not. At the Moon's equator temperatures range from −173°C to 117°C. It is colder at high latitudes; the temperature near the poles ranges from −203°C to −43°C.

The Moon's gravitational force is much weaker than Earth's, though it is still strong enough to exert a pull on Earth's oceans. This causes the tides. Its magnetic field is also much weaker than Earth's.

KEY FACTS

Age: 4.5 billion years
Radius: 1,737 km
Earth orbit: 27.32 days
Solar orbit: 365.26 days

▲ The far side of the Moon, which cannot be seen from Earth. It is sometimes called its 'dark side' but it is not always dark.

Lunar orbit

The Moon's orbit takes it as close as 356,400 kilometres from Earth and as far as 406,700 kilometres. The Moon takes just over 27 days to orbit Earth and always shows the same face to its parent planet.

Because of the changing angle of direct light from the Sun, the Moon passes through several phases during the course of its

ECLIPSES

A lunar eclipse only takes place when the Sun, Earth and the Moon are perfectly aligned and Earth is between the other two bodies. Earth's shadow prevents sunlight reaching the Moon so its luminous disc is extinguished. A solar eclipse is very different. It happens when the Moon is perfectly aligned between the Sun and Earth, blocking out the Sun's light. From Earth, the Sun then partially or wholly disappears.

THE MOON

27-day orbit: new moon, waxing crescent, first quarter, waxing gibbous, full moon, waning gibbous, last quarter and waning crescent. These phases have been known since ancient times and the first calendars were based on them, thousands of years ago.

The Moon's origin

The Moon has an inner and outer core, a mantle and a crust about 50–60 kilometres thick.

It is now thought that the Moon formed from the debris resulting from a collision between two planets about 4.5 billion years ago.

▼ Neil Armstrong was the first person to set foot on the Moon, in July 1969.

The surface

The Moon's surface has many craters. With no protective atmosphere, the Moon has been hit by lots of meteorites. At least 300,000 large impact craters pepper the surface. There are also lunar plains (maria), formed from pools of solidified lava.

◀ Earth rising over the Moon's horizon. The Moon is the only body in the Solar System that people have visited. There were six manned lunar landings between 1969 and 1972.

GENERAL INFORMATION

- Because of the way it orbits, the same face of the Moon always faces Earth. It was only when astronauts were able to orbit the Moon in the 1960s that the far side of the Moon was seen.
- The centre of the Moon is made of a solid inner core of iron-rich rock.

See also:

Planet Earth, The Planets, Solar System

THE MOON

Q **Why does the Moon seem to change shape?**

A The Moon shines because it reflects light from the Sun. However, as it travels around the Earth, we see more or less of its surface, making it appear to change in shape. The different shapes are called phases (below).

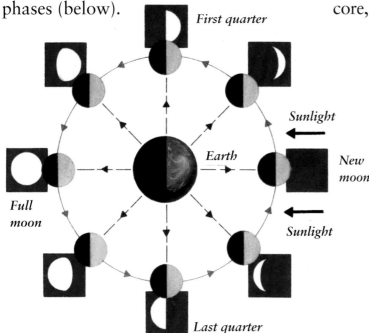

First quarter

Sunlight

Earth

New moon

Full moon

Sunlight

Last quarter

Q **What is inside the Moon?**

A No one has ever examined the inside of the Moon (below). Its outside looks very different from the Earth, but inside it is probably similar. Beneath the thin outer crust is a mantle of solid rock. Under this is a thinner layer of molten rock, and at the centre is the core, about 1,410 kilometres from the surface.

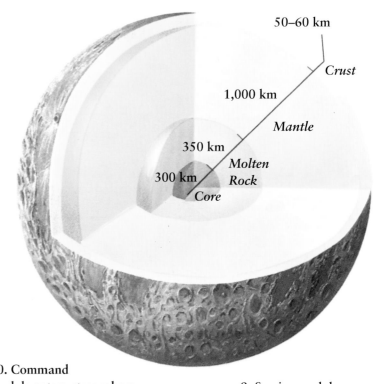

50–60 km

Crust

1,000 km

Mantle

350 km

Molten Rock

300 km

Core

Q **When did people first land on the Moon?**

A The *Apollo 11* spacecraft (right) took off in July 1969. It was carried by a huge Saturn rocket for the first stage of its journey. Shooting out of Earth's orbit, *Apollo* travelled to the Moon. The lunar module separated and landed on the Moon's surface. Two of the crew, Neil Armstrong and Edwin Aldrin, became the first people to walk on the Moon.

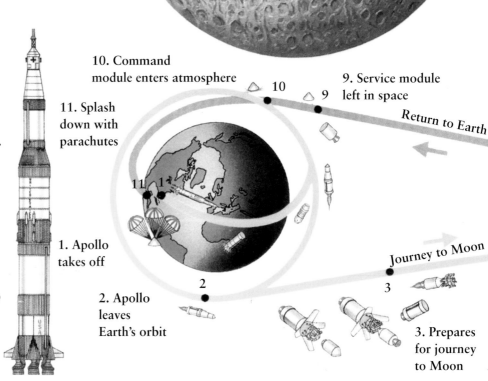

10. Command module enters atmosphere

11. Splash down with parachutes

9. Service module left in space

Return to Earth

1. Apollo takes off

2. Apollo leaves Earth's orbit

Journey to Moon

3. Prepares for journey to Moon

Q What is on the surface of the Moon?

A The Moon's surface (right) is covered with dust and rocks that have been smashed to pieces by showers of rock-like objects called meteorites. It is pitted with craters, also caused by meteorites. Most are just tiny dents, but some are hundreds of kilometres wide. Some areas of the Moon look dark. People once thought these areas were seas. They were formed when meteorites cracked the Moon's surface. Molten rock bubbled up from below and grew hard. There are also many high mountains and deep valleys.

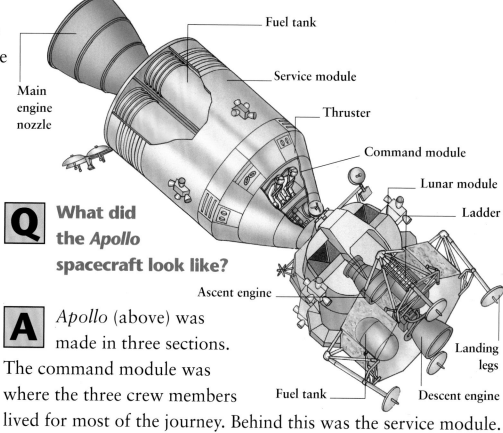

Main engine nozzle

Fuel tank

Service module

Thruster

Command module

Lunar module

Ladder

Ascent engine

Fuel tank

Landing legs

Descent engine

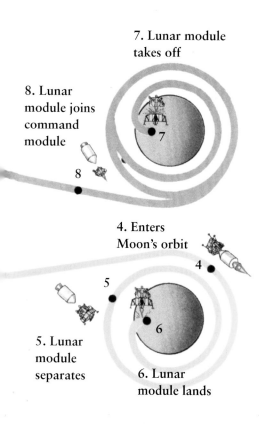

7. Lunar module takes off

8. Lunar module joins command module

4. Enters Moon's orbit

5. Lunar module separates

6. Lunar module lands

Q What did the *Apollo* spacecraft look like?

A *Apollo* (above) was made in three sections. The command module was where the three crew members lived for most of the journey. Behind this was the service module. This contained the rocket engine and tanks for fuel and oxygen. The lunar module was used for landing on the Moon. It had four legs that spread out to support it on the Moon's surface. The lunar module and service module were left behind in space. Only the command module returned to splash down in the Pacific Ocean.

EXPLORING THE HEAVENS

For thousands of years people have been fascinated by the night sky. Until recently our knowledge depended on observations from Earth.

▲ The 7th-century B.C. Venus tablet of Ammisaduqa details Assyrian observations of that planet.

▲ Galileo Galilei demonstrates his telescope in Venice, Italy, in 1609.

The ancient Babylonians, Egyptians and Greeks made surprisingly thorough observations. Priests took a particular interest in astronomy, believing that movements of the 'celestial bodies' (planets and stars) were signs from the gods.

In the 3rd millennium B.C. the ancient Egyptians built pyramids to align with the Sun. Astronomy was an important part of their religion. They recorded the phases of the Sun, Moon and stars.

The Sumerians (who lived in present-day Iraq) had noted Venus by 1500 B.C., and not long afterwards ancient Babylonian stargazers observed, described and predicted the movements of Venus, Mercury, Mars, Jupiter and Saturn. These were the only known planets until the invention of the telescope.

Earth at the centre?

Early people thought that Earth was at the centre of the Universe and the stars and planets moved around it. In the 3rd century B.C. the ancient Greek Aristarchus of Samos (310–230 B.C.) was probably the first person to suggest a heliocentric model of the Solar

System. This meant that the Sun, not Earth, was at its centre. The heliocentric model was not generally accepted for many centuries. Most people still believed that Earth was at the centre of the Universe until the idea was challenged in the 16th century.

KEPLER SPACE OBSERVATORY

This observatory orbits high above Earth. When it was launched in 2009, its aim was to search for planets outside our own Solar System (exoplanets) that could support life. As of early 2012 nearly 1,000 of these had been found. Several of them were in 'habitable zones' where there was the potential for life. There could be 160 billion exoplanets in the Milky Way galaxy.

Renaissance discovery

Our understanding of the Solar System grew during the Renaissance of the 15th–17th centuries. Copernicus (1473–1543) argued for a heliocentric system for the Solar System in 1543. Galileo Galilei (1564–1642) used a telescope to discover the four largest moons orbiting Jupiter.

Expanding Universe

The work of theoretical physicists such as Albert Einstein (1879–1955) helped scientists understand how the Universe is changing.

In the late 20th century giant telescopes allowed people to see more distant objects. The European Very Large Telescope Array at Cerro Paranal, Chile, has tracked the movement of stars orbiting the huge black hole at the centre of the Milky Way galaxy.

▲ An unmanned space probe is launched on a rocket. Space probes now have powerful telescopes to view the Universe.

The *Voyager* probes sent to the outer limits of the Solar System have added to our knowledge.

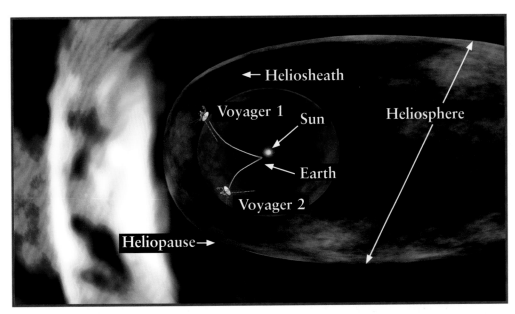

▲ The routes of *Voyagers 1* and *2* as they pass through the outer region of our Solar System, the heliosheath, and approach its edge, the heliopause.

GENERAL INFORMATION

- Galileo supported the heliocentric model of the Solar System. At the time, this went against the teachings of the Catholic Church, and Galileo spent years under house arrest.
- In 2012 the space probes *Voyager 1* and *Voyager 2* were 17 billion and 14 billion km from Earth.

See also:

The Planets, Solar System, The Universe

EXPLORING THE HEAVENS

Q How did early astronomers study the heavens?

A Astronomers studied the sky with the naked eye until the 17th century. In 1609 the Italian astronomer Galileo Galilei (above) became the first person to study the sky with a telescope.

Q What did Giotto tell us about comets?

A In 1986, the *Giotto* space probe (below) studied Halley's Comet. A comet consists of a lump of rock and ice called the nucleus, inside a cloud of gas and dust called the coma (inset). It also has a bright tail. *Giotto*'s photographs show a nucleus measuring 8 kilometres by 12 kilometres. Its instruments found that the coma and tail are made of dust and water vapour.

Q How does a modern telescope work?

A There are two types of telescope. A refractor uses a lens to form an image. A reflector uses a curved mirror. Most modern telescopes used in astronomy are reflectors. The telescope is finely balanced and turns slowly to keep the image steady as the Earth moves. A Schmidt telescope (right) is used to photograph large areas of the sky.

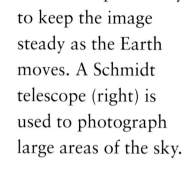

Schmidt telescope gathering light from the stars

Counterbalance

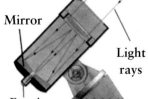

Inside the telescope

Mirror

Light rays

Eyepiece

Q Why is the Hubble Telescope in space?

A Light from distant stars passes through the Earth's atmosphere before it reaches a telescope on the ground. The swirling atmosphere makes the stars twinkle. Modern telescopes are usually built on top of mountains, where the atmosphere is thinner, to reduce this effect. The Hubble Space Telescope (below) can see more clearly than any telescope on Earth because it is above the atmosphere.

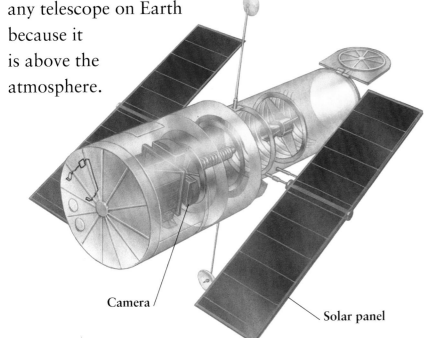

Camera

Solar panel

Q How did the *Pioneer* space probes work?

A *Pioneer 10* and *11* (right) were the first spacecraft to visit the outer Solar System. They were designed to find out if a spacecraft could travel through the asteroid belt, a swarm of rocks orbiting the Sun between Mars and Jupiter. Most spacecraft use solar cells to make electricity from sunlight. *Pioneer 10* and *11* travelled so far from the Sun that solar cells would not work. Instead, they carried nuclear power generators to make electricity.

Thruster

Cosmic ray telescope

Nuclear power generator

Q Where did the *Voyager* space probes go?

A *Voyager 1* and *2* were launched in 1977. The pull of gravity from the outer planets guided the spacecraft from one planet to the next. *Voyager 1* flew past Jupiter in 1979 (below) and Saturn in 1980. *Voyager 2* flew past Jupiter (1979), Saturn (1981), Uranus (1986) and Neptune (1989). Their cameras and instruments studied each planet. All the information was sent back to Earth by radio.

Pioneer 11

SPACE TRAVEL

Space travel was the dream of science fiction writers before the rocket technology developed in World War II began to make it a reality.

American scientists used German V2 rocket designs to launch rockets into the upper levels of Earth's atmosphere. One rocket reached 400 kilometres high in 1950.

The space race

The 1950s and 1960s were dominated by the 'space race' – furious competition between the former Soviet Union and the United States. The Soviet Union scored the first successes. *Sputnik 1*, launched in 1957, was the first humanmade object to orbit Earth. Soon after, the Soviets put the first animal – Laika the dog – into orbit. In 1961 Russian cosmonaut Yuri Gagarin (1934–1968) became the first person to go into space, completing a full orbit around Earth. Four years later Alexey

▲ In 1961 the Russian astronaut Yuri Gagarin was the first person to complete a full orbit of Earth.

Leonov (b. 1934) performed the first walk in space.

The Apollo missions

From the mid-1960s the United States' Apollo programme was very successful. The *Apollo 8* mission was the first to orbit the Moon, then on 20 July 1969 *Apollo 11* landed astronauts Neil Armstrong (1930–2012) and Edwin 'Buzz' Aldrin (b. 1930) on its surface. However, after six missions to take people to the Moon, the manned programme was ended.

Going further afield

The emphasis switched to unmanned probes and space stations. The American space

▼ One of the American space shuttles lands after a mission to the International Space Station.

KEY DATES
First manned space flight:
12 April 1961, Yuri Gagarin
First space walk:
18 March 1965, Alexey Leonov
First manned orbit of the Moon:
24 December 1968, Borman, Lovell and Anders
First person on the Moon:
21 July 1969, Neil Armstrong and Edwin 'Buzz' Aldrin

THE SPACE STATION

The International Space Station (ISS) is a collaboration between the US, Russia, Europe, Japan and Canada. The American space agency NASA used five space shuttles – the first reusable spacecraft – to get astronauts there and back between 1981 and 2011. The ISS will operate until 2020 at least. In its first 10 years of orbit the ISS travelled 2.4 billion kilometres – 57,361 orbits around Earth.

agency NASA's Mariner, Pioneer and Voyager probes made many discoveries. Flybys of the planets began in 1962 when *Mariner 2* passed Venus, and *Mariner 4* approached Mars in 1965. The pace then picked up: *Pioneer 10*

passed close to Jupiter in 1973, *Mariner 10* did a flyby of Mercury in 1974 and *Pioneer 11* approached Saturn in 1979.

More distant planets

Much more recently the *Cassiana* spacecraft went into orbit around Saturn in 2004, and a lander craft has sent back information from the surface of Titan, one of its moons.

The *Voyager 1* and *Voyager 2* unmanned probes have now gone far beyond Neptune. In early 2012 the probes were travelling at great speed through the distant reaches of the Solar System.

Commercial space travel started in 2001. Since then, small numbers of space tourists have been able to visit the International Space Station, but the flights are very expensive.

▲ Scientists in the International Space Station, which orbits Earth at a height of 330 to 410 kilometres. The station's crew comes from different countries.

GENERAL INFORMATION

- The American Apollo programme ran from 1961 to 1972. Its goal was 'landing a man on the Moon and returning him safely to Earth'. This happened in 1969. The programme cost $24 billion.
- Teams of astronauts have occupied the International Space Station (ISS) continuously since November 2000. During that time more than 200 individuals of 10 nationalities have visited.

See also:

The Moon, The Planets

SPACE TRAVEL

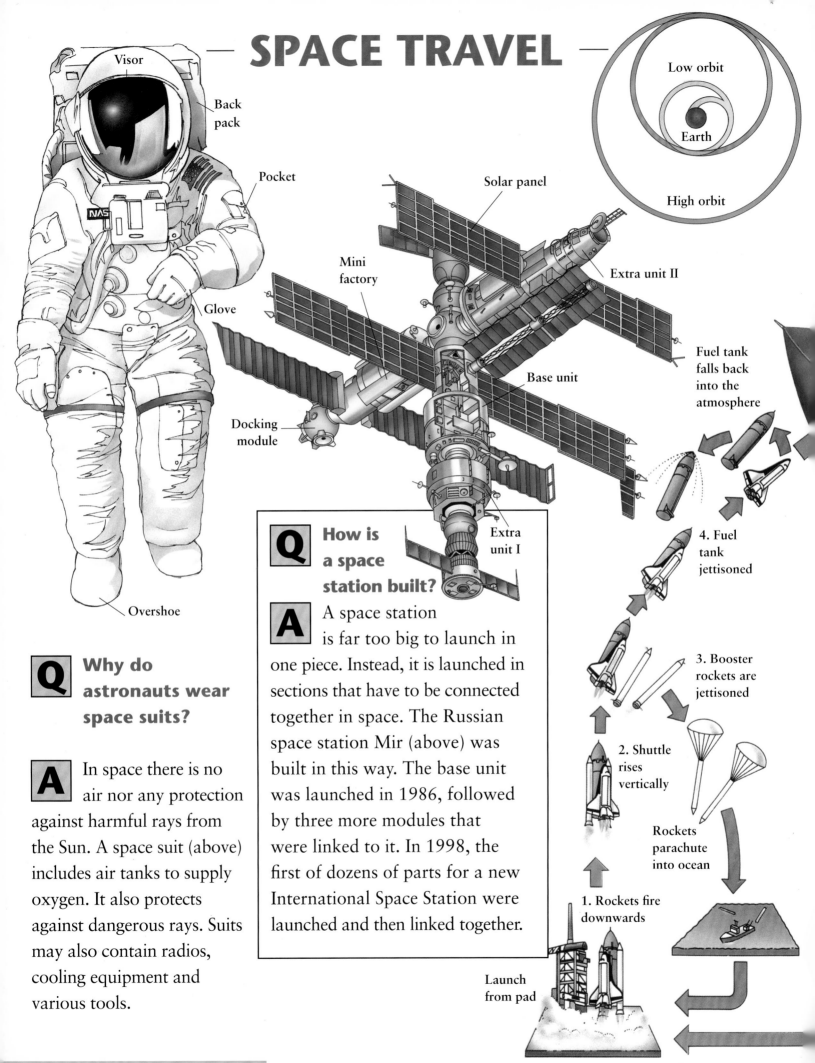

Visor

Back pack

Pocket

Glove

Overshoe

Solar panel

Mini factory

Docking module

Base unit

Extra unit II

Extra unit I

Low orbit

Earth

High orbit

Fuel tank falls back into the atmosphere

4. Fuel tank jettisoned

3. Booster rockets are jettisoned

2. Shuttle rises vertically

Rockets parachute into ocean

1. Rockets fire downwards

Launch from pad

Q Why do astronauts wear space suits?

A In space there is no air nor any protection against harmful rays from the Sun. A space suit (above) includes air tanks to supply oxygen. It also protects against dangerous rays. Suits may also contain radios, cooling equipment and various tools.

Q How is a space station built?

A A space station is far too big to launch in one piece. Instead, it is launched in sections that have to be connected together in space. The Russian space station Mir (above) was built in this way. The base unit was launched in 1986, followed by three more modules that were linked to it. In 1998, the first of dozens of parts for a new International Space Station were launched and then linked together.

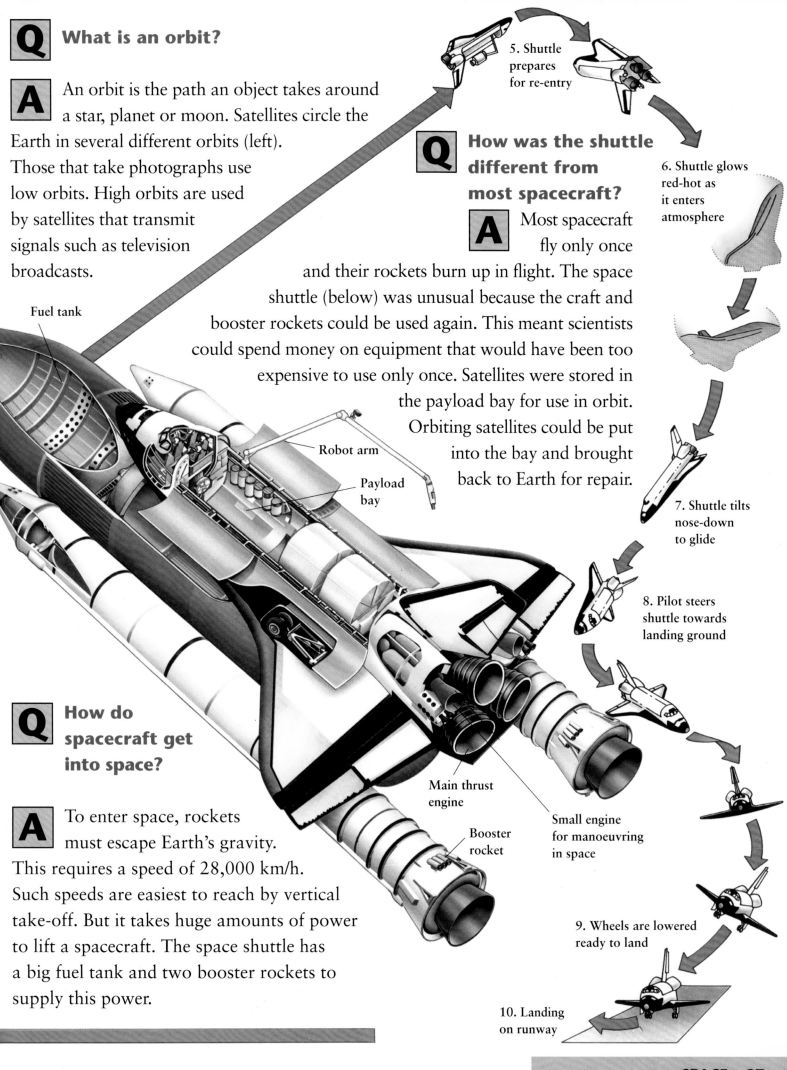

Q What is an orbit?

A An orbit is the path an object takes around
a star, planet or moon. Satellites circle the
Earth in several different orbits (left).
Those that take photographs use
low orbits. High orbits are used
by satellites that transmit
signals such as television
broadcasts.

Fuel tank

Robot arm

Payload
bay

Q How do
spacecraft get
into space?

A To enter space, rockets
must escape Earth's gravity.
This requires a speed of 28,000 km/h.
Such speeds are easiest to reach by vertical
take-off. But it takes huge amounts of power
to lift a spacecraft. The space shuttle has
a big fuel tank and two booster rockets to
supply this power.

Main thrust
engine

Booster
rocket

Small engine
for manoeuvring
in space

5. Shuttle
prepares
for re-entry

Q How was the shuttle
different from
most spacecraft?

A Most spacecraft
fly only once
and their rockets burn up in flight. The space
shuttle (below) was unusual because the craft and
booster rockets could be used again. This meant scientists
could spend money on equipment that would have been too
expensive to use only once. Satellites were stored in
the payload bay for use in orbit.
Orbiting satellites could be put
into the bay and brought
back to Earth for repair.

6. Shuttle glows
red-hot as
it enters
atmosphere

7. Shuttle tilts
nose-down
to glide

8. Pilot steers
shuttle towards
landing ground

9. Wheels are lowered
ready to land

10. Landing
on runway

PLANET EARTH

Earth is the only planet in the Solar System that supports life. It takes just over 365 days to make one complete orbit of the Sun. Earth spins on its axis every 24 hours.

Earth's axis is tilted at 23 degrees and this tilt gives our planet its seasons. Earth has a core at the centre, a solid mantle and a thin crust. Its chemical make-up is mostly iron, oxygen, silicon and magnesium. The core is mostly iron and is very hot – the temperature in the inner core is probably about 5,430°C.

Earth's outer shell is made of individual plates, called tectonic plates. These are made from the crust and the topmost part of the mantle. As the mantle material slowly moves, so do the plates. When two plates move apart, molten rock rises from below, filling the gap. The continents are stuck on the plates, so as the plates move, the continents move with them. Volcanic activity, earthquakes and mountain building all happen when two plates come together.

Above the surface

Much of the surface of Earth (71 per cent) is covered by water – in the oceans, freshwater lakes and frozen polar regions. Together, these are described as the hydrosphere. The Earth has a well-developed atmosphere, composed

KEY FACTS
Age: 4.5 billion years
Radius at equator: 6,384 km
Radius at poles: 6,353 km
Speed of orbit around Sun:
108,000 km/h

HIGHEST AND LOWEST
The highest point on Earth's surface is Mount Everest in the Himalaya mountain chain. It rises to 8,848 metres above sea level. The Himalayas formed from the collision of the Indian and Eurasian tectonic plates. The lowest point on the crust is Challenger Deep, in the Marianas Trench of the western Pacific Ocean. This trench-like valley in the ocean floor is 10,190 metres deep – deeper than Everest is tall.

▲ The Great Barrier Reef runs for 2,600 kilometres along the north-east coast of Australia.

▲ The East Africa Rift Valley runs along the edge of the Somali and Nubian tectonic plates.

mostly of nitrogen (78 per cent) and oxygen (21 per cent). Three-quarters of the atmosphere's mass is concentrated in a layer just 11 kilometres deep; it extends much

▲ Earth, showing the continents of South and North America and the Pacific and Atlantic oceans.

is closer. Earth's tilt varies the length of day and night and the amount of sunlight reaching different latitudes.

Earth has a strong magnetic field, whose poles are close to (but not the same as) the geographic North Pole and South Pole.

Earth has one natural satellite, the Moon, which averages 384,400 kilometres away. The Moon's gravity pulls the water in Earth's oceans to make the tides.

▼ The summit of Mount Everest is the highest point on Earth's surface.

higher, gradually thinning. As well as providing oxygen and water vapour for life, the atmosphere reduces harmful ultraviolet emissions from the Sun, causes small meteors to burn up before they can reach the surface and moderates temperatures.

The seasons

For six months of the year the Northern Hemisphere is slightly closer to the Sun. For the other six months, the Southern Hemisphere

GENERAL INFORMATION

- Earth orbits the Sun at a distance of 147–152 million kilometres.
- Earth's crust is thickest beneath the Himalaya mountains – 75 kilometres. The crust under the oceans is much thinner, usually less than 10 kilometres.

See also:

Natural Forces, Solar System, Water

PLANET EARTH

Q What is inside the Earth?

A The thin outer layer of the Earth (below) is called the crust. Beneath this is the solid mantle that makes up most of the Earth. The mantle is a mixture of rocks and minerals. Right at the centre of the Earth is the core of molten iron and nickel. The inner part of the core is very hot; scientists estimate its temperature reaches 5,430°C.

Q How were the continents formed?

A Scientists believe that the continents (below) were formed from one giant landmass they call Pangaea. This broke in two, then split up into smaller landmasses. These drifted apart until they reached their present places. But they are still moving!

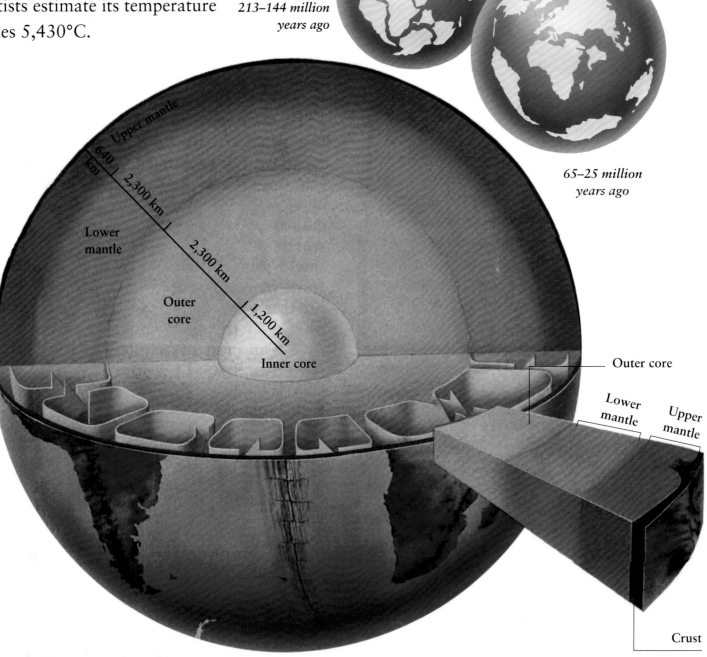

286–248 million years ago

213–144 million years ago

65–25 million years ago

Upper mantle

640 km

2,300 km

Lower mantle

2,300 km

Outer core

1,200 km

Inner core

Outer core

Lower mantle

Upper mantle

Crust

Q Why do we have seasons?

A The Earth takes one year to move around the Sun. But the Earth is tilted on its axis. This means that different parts of Earth receive different amounts of sunlight, and so become warmer or colder as the Earth travels on its journey. When the North Pole is nearest to the Sun, the northern part of the Earth is warmest. Here it is summer. At the same time, the southern part is tilted away from the Sun, and is cooler. Here it is winter.

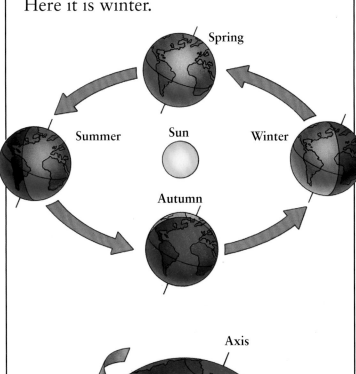

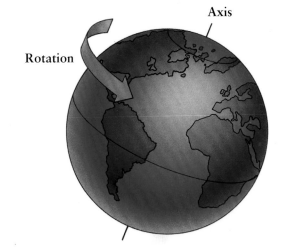

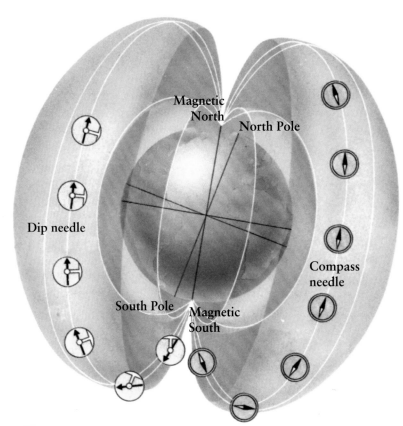

Q Why does a compass needle point north?

A The Earth is like a huge magnet with a force field that covers its whole surface (above). The poles of the magnet are near the North and South Poles. Magnetised objects – such as compass needles – are drawn to these poles. Therefore one end of a compass needle will always point north.

Q What were the ice ages?

A The ice ages (right) were periods in history when the Earth became extremely cold. The last ice age ended about 10,000 years ago. Near the poles, a lot of water froze into ice. This meant that there was less water in the sea and the sea level dropped, leaving large areas of land uncovered.

Earth during ice age

Earth today

NATURAL FORCES

Powerful natural forces are acting on Earth all the time. They come from within the mantle and crust, and from the oceans and atmosphere.

KEY FACTS

Biggest volcanic eruption:
Tambora, 1815
Deadliest tsunami: Indian
Ocean, 2004
Deadliest flood: China, 1931

▼ Molten rock pours out of the caldera of a volcano. It will burn everything in its path.

Movements of tectonic plates and plumes of hot material in the mantle produce volcanoes and earthquakes. Volcanoes happen either where one plate is being pushed under another, causing molten rock (magma) to rise to the surface, or where plumes of hot magma rise up into Earth's crust.

Volcanic eruptions can take several forms, ranging from sheets of magma oozing relatively quietly from the opening (caldera) of the volcano to violent explosions of dust and bombs of red-hot rocks. When a volcano erupts, lots of gases are released, particularly sulphur dioxide. Eruptions often burn crops and buildings, and the explosions drop heavy debris on buildings and people, with disastrous results.

THE TAMBORA ERUPTION

The biggest volcanic eruption in recorded history was Mount Tambora, Indonesia, in 1815. The long-dormant volcano is situated over a zone where one tectonic plate is being pushed under another. The explosion was heard 2,600 kilometres away, and the mountain lost 1,500 metres in height. Tens of thousands of people died, and the cloud of fumes spread around the world. Crops could not grow in North America or Europe in 1816, leading to the worst famine of the 19th century.

Earthquakes

When two of Earth's plates move against each other, pressure builds up along the boundary. Often the plates are locked together, unable to move as the pressure increases. Eventually the stress is so great that the crust tears, and the masses of rock jump past one another. Shock waves quickly spread out, shaking buildings, trees and bridges. This

▲ Floodwater can be immensely powerful – and destructive.

is an earthquake and it can cause great damage. Sometimes many people die as a result.

Storms and floods

Storms are created by movements of the atmosphere. The biggest storms are called hurricanes and cyclones. The winds in some of these storms are strong enough to blow down trees and lift the roofs off buildings. Storms can whip the ocean surface into destructive waves that may damage shipping

and buildings along the coast. Massive electrical charges build up in some storm clouds, producing lightning and thunder.

A tornado, or twister, is like a small hurricane in that strong winds are sucked into a kind of tube of low pressure. A tornado may be only a few metres across, but its winds may reach 400 kilometres per hour.

▼ This tornado looks very dark because of all the dust and debris that is twisting around in it.

▲ In 2005 Hurricane Katrina swirls towards New Orleans in the United States.

GENERAL INFORMATION

- Wind speeds are measured using the Beaufort scale. Force 1 on the scale is a gentle breeze, and force 12 is a destructive hurricane.
- One of the worst months ever for tornadoes was April 2011. More than 300 struck the southern United States, killing 359 people.

See also:

Planet Earth, Water

NATURAL FORCES

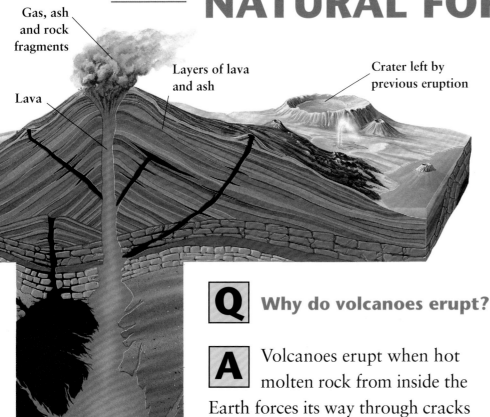

Gas, ash and rock fragments

Lava

Layers of lava and ash

Crater left by previous eruption

Q Why do volcanoes erupt?

A Volcanoes erupt when hot molten rock from inside the Earth forces its way through cracks in the surface (left). This rock – lava – flows from the volcano and cools.

Q What is a seismograph?

Hanging arm

A A seismograph measures earthquakes. When an earthquake occurs, its hanging arm shakes, and the pen marks the paper on the revolving drum.

Q How do we measure wind speed?

A The speed of the wind is measured on the Beaufort scale. This goes from 0 (calm) to 12 (hurricane). The scale describes how things behave at different wind speeds (right). At 1, light air, smoke drifts slowly. At force 6, large trees sway, and at force 10, buildings may be damaged.

Q What is a hurricane?

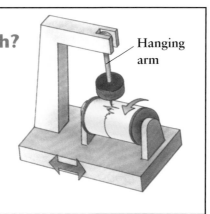

A A hurricane is a very strong whirling storm (right). The winds near the centre can reach 250 km/h. Hurricanes begin over warm tropical seas. The surface water heats up and evaporates to form clouds. This releases the heat and makes the clouds rise. Air is sucked in from the surrounding area, swirling the clouds into a spiral. At the very centre of the hurricane is a calm area called the eye. As hurricanes move, they push the sea into huge waves and may cause floods. When the hurricane reaches land, it slowly grows weaker. But the high winds can still cause great damage to buildings and trees.

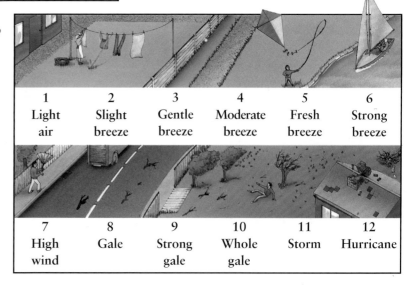

1 Light air	2 Slight breeze	3 Gentle breeze	4 Moderate breeze	5 Fresh breeze	6 Strong breeze
7 High wind	8 Gale	9 Strong gale	10 Whole gale	11 Storm	12 Hurricane

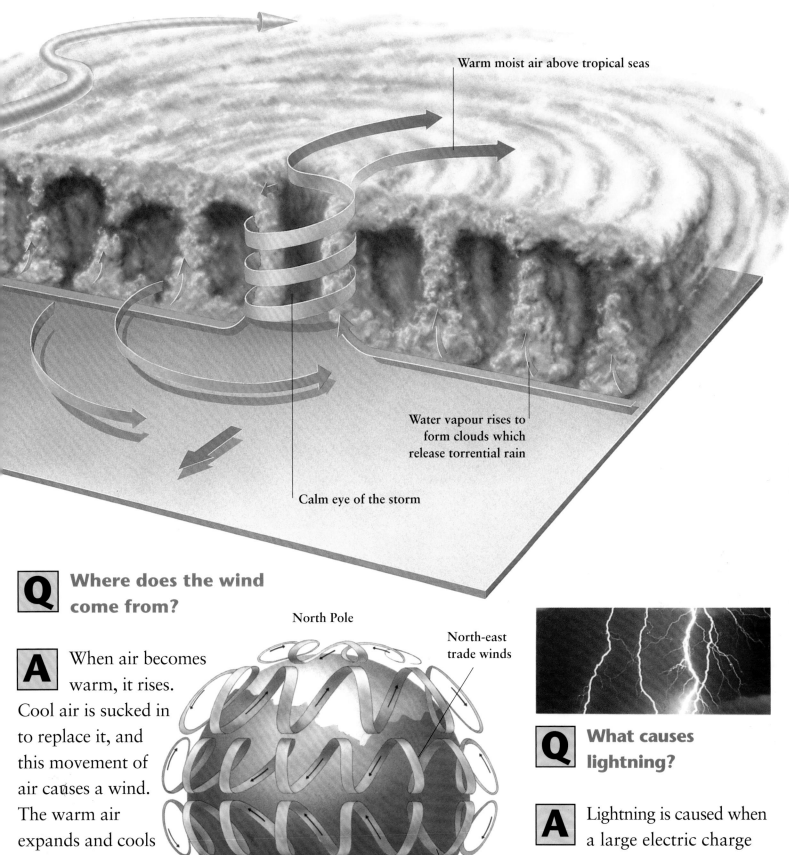

Warm moist air above tropical seas

Water vapour rises to form clouds which release torrential rain

Calm eye of the storm

Q Where does the wind come from?

A When air becomes warm, it rises. Cool air is sucked in to replace it, and this movement of air causes a wind. The warm air expands and cools before falling to the land again. This constant movement of air forms a regular pattern of winds around the world (right).

North Pole

North-east trade winds

South-east trade winds

South Pole

Q What causes lightning?

A Lightning is caused when a large electric charge builds up in a cloud, as a result of ice and water particles rubbing together. The electric charge flashes to Earth, or to another cloud, as lightning (above).

WATER

Water is found in the oceans, freshwater lakes, glaciers and icecaps, and groundwater. There is also water in the atmosphere and in plants and animals. All this water forms the hydrosphere.

Without water, life on Earth could not survive. People and animals need clean water to drink, and so do plants. In some parts of the world this is not always possible, and up to 5 million people die every year because their water is polluted or carries diseases.

Crops need rain or irrigation water. There is hardly a branch of industry that does not depend on a reliable supply of water. Water drives the turbines of hydroelectric power stations and cools the reactors in nuclear power stations that make the electricity we need.

The oceans

Ocean water covers about 71 per cent of Earth's surface. Most of this is in one of five ocean basins (the Pacific, Atlantic, Indian, Southern and Arctic oceans). All are connected parts of the World Ocean. Ocean currents move cold water from high latitudes to tropical regions, and the other way. The combined area of the World Ocean is 361 million square

KEY FACTS

Salt water: 97.5 per cent
Fresh water: 2.5 per cent
Frozen: 1.7 per cent
Liquid: 98.3 per cent

▼ The Dead Sea, between Israel and Jordan, is ten times saltier than the world's major oceans. The saltiness makes it easier to float in the Dead Sea than in other oceans.

THE WATER CYCLE

The water cycle restores freshwater supplies in lakes and rivers and creates much of Earth's weather. When water evaporates from oceans and lakes (and from plants) it goes into the lower levels of the atmosphere as water vapour. This may be carried higher by air currents. When the surrounding air is cool enough, the water vapour forms tiny droplets on particles of dust to form clouds. Many droplets may join together to form bigger drops. These fall as rain or snow on the oceans or land. There, the water runs into rivers and soaks into the topsoil.

kilometres. It has a volume of 1.3 billion cubic kilometres and an average depth of 3,790 metres.

The World Ocean sits largely on oceanic crust made of basalt rock, as do two smaller and separated oceans – the Caspian and Black seas. Other large areas of salt water that do not lie on oceanic crust – for example, the Aral Sea in Kazakhstan and Uzbekistan – are described as salt lakes. Together, saltwater oceans contain 96.5 per cent of the total water on Earth and have an average salinity (saltiness) of about 3.5 per cent, though this figure varies greatly.

Groundwater and ice

About 1.7 per cent of the hydrosphere is made up of groundwater in pores and crevices in rocks beneath the continents and oceans. Some is fresh and some is salty water. The frozen icecaps of Antarctica and Greenland, plus glaciers in many parts of the world, make up another 1.7 per cent of Earth's water. Global warming threatens to melt some of this ice, adding

▲ A blanket of cloud covers low-lying land. Cloud forms when damp air is cooled as it rises over mountains or passes over cold land.

to the liquid water in the oceans – and so raising the sea level. A small fraction of Earth's water is found in the atmosphere and inside animals and plants.

GENERAL INFORMATION

● The combined mass of water in the hydrosphere is estimated to be 1.4×10^{18} tonnes.

● Some of the ice in Antarctica is 1 million years old.

● Frozen water locked up in glaciers flows slowly downhill. The fastest glaciers may travel more than 6 km every year.

▶ When chunks of ice break off the great Antarctic ice sheets, they form floating icebergs.

See also:

Landscape, Natural Forces

WATER

Q What lies under the oceans?

A The sea floor (below) has plains, valleys, mountains and even volcanoes. Near the shore is the shallow continental shelf. This slopes to the plain, about 4,000 metres below. On the plain are deep cracks called ocean trenches, and raised areas called ridges.

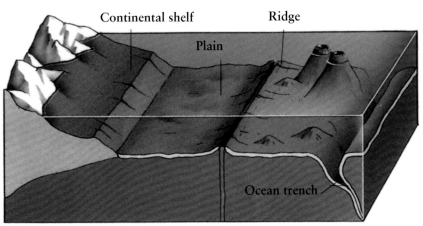

Continental shelf

Ridge

Plain

Ocean trench

Q How much of the Earth is covered by oceans?

A The oceans cover 71 per cent of Earth's surface. The continents are actually huge islands in a continuous stretch of water (below). The water flows around the world in a pattern of warm and cold currents.

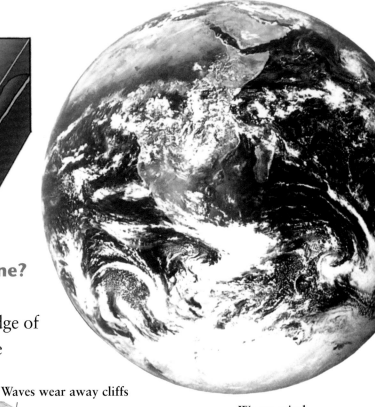

Q How does the sea change the coastline?

A The waves of the sea constantly pound the edge of the land (right). They change the shape of the coastline in two ways. First, the waves smash against the rocks and grind them into pebbles and sand. They hurl the pebbles at the cliffs, slowly wearing them away. But the sea also moves the sand and pebbles to other places. Beaches are formed and the coastline is built up where the sea drops them.

Waves wear away cliffs

Waves grind down pebbles to form sand

Q What is the water cycle?

A Water is always on the move (right), changing from liquid to vapour and back to liquid. The heat of the Sun evaporates water from the oceans, lakes and rivers. Plants also release moisture from their leaves. The moisture rises into the air and cools to form clouds. Winds blow the clouds towards the land. Here the clouds grow cooler, especially over high ground, and it starts to rain. The rain drains into rivers and lakes and then back into the sea.

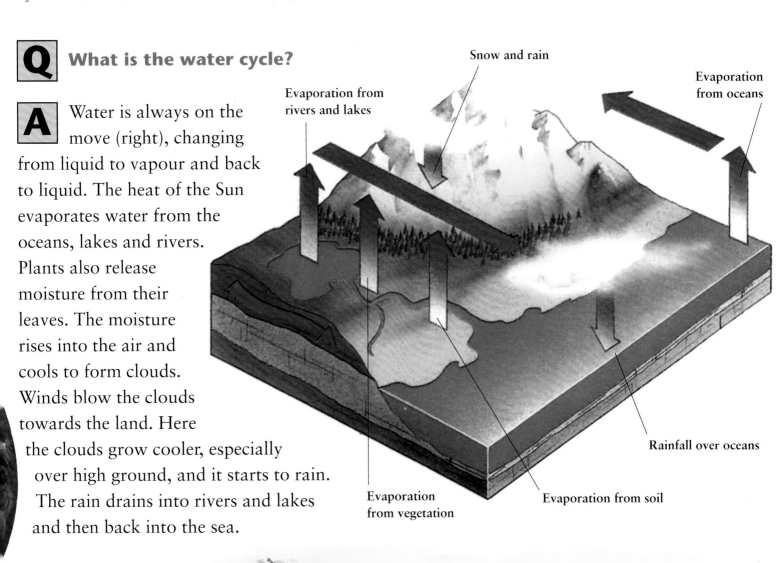

Snow and rain

Evaporation from rivers and lakes

Evaporation from oceans

Rainfall over oceans

Evaporation from vegetation

Evaporation from soil

Q What is a glacier?

A A glacier (right) is a river of ice that forms in cold regions high up in the mountains or near the poles. It slides very slowly downhill, a few metres each year. It carries a mass of rocks that scrape away the valley walls and floor. It later deposits rocks and earth in huge ridges called moraines. If a glacier reaches the sea, large pieces break off and float away as icebergs.

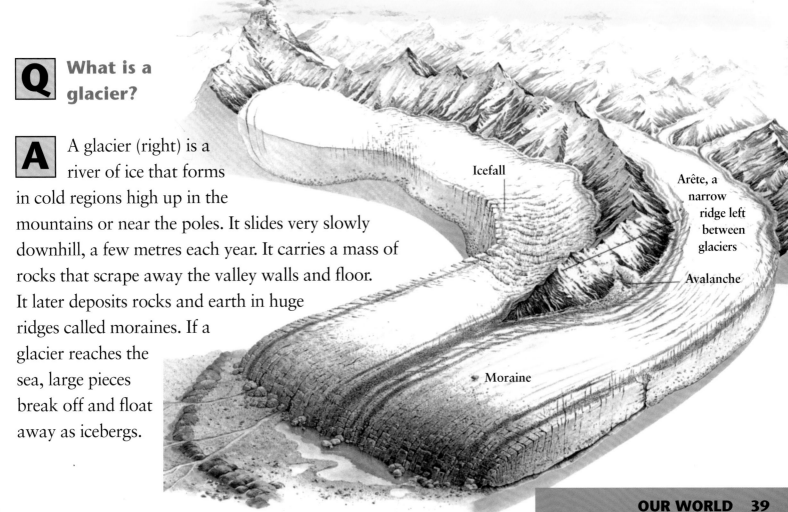

Icefall

Arête, a narrow ridge left between glaciers

Avalanche

Moraine

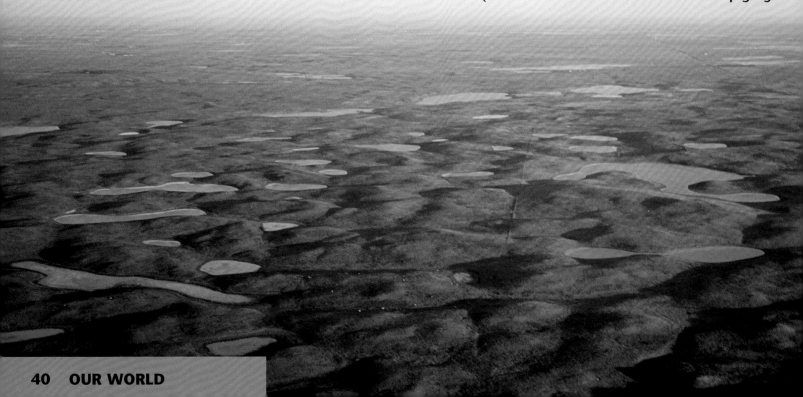

LANDSCAPE

The natural landscape is a combination of landforms and vegetation. Landscape is the product of many different forces, and they are at work all the time.

Some landscapes are relatively new, and others are millions of years old. Many have been altered by the activities of people.

The natural processes that sculpt landscapes are the actions of mountain-building, weather, water, plants and animals. Over millions of years Earth's continental crust has been crumpled into mountain ranges and hills.

Any land that is exposed to the atmosphere experiences weathering. This is the gradual breakdown of rocks by freezing, thawing and chemical processes (for example, the effect of dilute sulphuric acid in raindrops).

Weathering weakens rocks and makes it easier for rivers, glaciers and the wind to erode them (wear them away). Plants sink roots into cracks in the weakened rock. Over time the cracks widen, topsoil is created and more plants – grasses, bushes and trees – grow.

▲ Over millions of years a river has worn its way into these rocky mountains to create a deep gorge.

KEY FACTS

Highest mountain: Mount Everest, 8,848 m
Longest glacier: Lambert Glacier, Antarctica, 400 km long
Longest mountain range: Andes mountains, South America, 7,000 km

▼ Small lakes and small, rounded hills cover this landscape in Canada. It is typical of land that was once covered by an enormous sheet of ice.

▲ Part of this hillside in Thailand has been stripped of its natural forest so people can grow crops.

▲ Ocean waves batter a rocky coastline. Even the hardest rocks are eventually eroded by waves.

FOSSILISED LANDSCAPES

Earth has warmed since the last ice age, so glaciers and ice sheets are much smaller than they once were. Many landscapes in Canada are dotted with hundreds of small lakes. They were formed when blocks of ice melted and left holes that filled with water – kettle lakes. These are called fossilised landscapes because the forces that made them no longer operate.

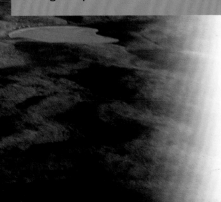

Water and ice

Over millions of years rivers and glaciers have carved valleys and carried huge quantities of rock fragments (sediment) to the sea or to lakes, where the sediment is deposited (dropped). Rivers meander from side to side, widening their valleys and laying down shingle, sand or mud.

At the coast, waves batter and erode shorelines. Rubble from eroded cliffs is carried away by ocean currents, broken into smaller fragments, rounded into pebbles and eventually broken into grains of sand. These are deposited on beaches and sand bars.

Volcanoes and wind

Volcanoes erupt millions of tonnes of lava and dust onto the land around them, changing the landscape. Earthquakes thrust chunks of land higher. In some regions the wind blasts grains of sand at rocks, eroding them into weird shapes.

People change landscapes continuously in many ways: by clearing forests for agriculture, reclaiming parts of lakes, altering the course of rivers, building cities and irrigating deserts.

GENERAL INFORMATION

● Some landscapes have many different types of plants growing on them, while others have few. Much of Siberia is covered by just two species – larch and pine trees.

See also:

Environment, Natural Forces, Water

LANDSCAPE

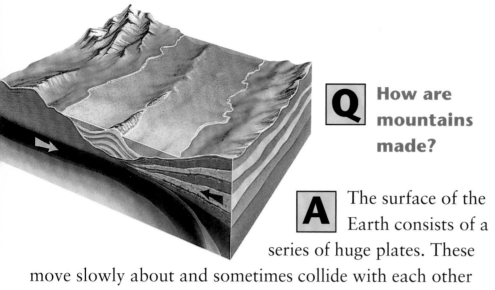

Q How are mountains made?

A The surface of the Earth consists of a series of huge plates. These move slowly about and sometimes collide with each other (above). When this happens, the edges of the plates are pushed up and the layers of rock crumple and fold. Over millions of years, the folds form chains of mountains.

Q How are caves formed?

A Many caves are found in limestone rock (below). They are formed when rainwater soaks down through cracks in the rock. The water dissolves the limestone, making the cracks bigger. Now streams can flow in, under ground. They wear away weak parts of the rock to make caves. Sometimes water drips into the caves. The dissolved limestone forms hanging spikes called stalactites. Pillars called stalagmites form on the floor below.

Q What is soil made from?

A Soil is a mixture of rock particles and humus, which is made from the tissues of dead plants and animals. The humus breaks down and releases minerals that help plants to grow. Below the soil is the rocky subsoil and beneath that the solid rock, known as bedrock.

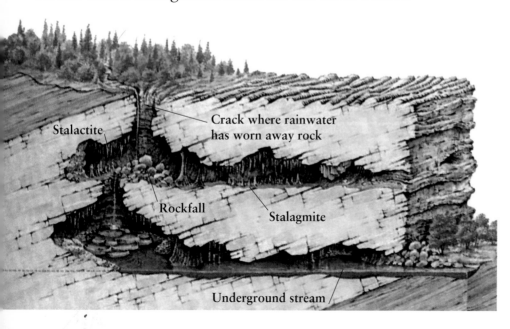

Stalactite

Crack where rainwater has worn away rock

Rockfall

Stalagmite

Underground stream

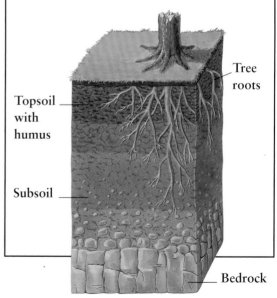

Tree roots

Topsoil with humus

Subsoil

Bedrock

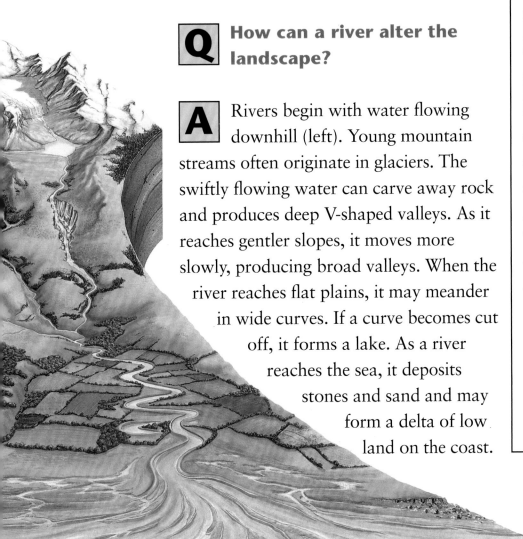

Q How can a river alter the landscape?

A Rivers begin with water flowing downhill (left). Young mountain streams often originate in glaciers. The swiftly flowing water can carve away rock and produces deep V-shaped valleys. As it reaches gentler slopes, it moves more slowly, producing broad valleys. When the river reaches flat plains, it may meander in wide curves. If a curve becomes cut off, it forms a lake. As a river reaches the sea, it deposits stones and sand and may form a delta of low land on the coast.

Q What is an iceberg?

A An iceberg is a piece of ice from a glacier or ice sheet that breaks off at the coastline and then floats in the sea. Only one-eighth of an iceberg shows above the water. This is why they are dangerous to ships. Icebergs may drift for years before they melt.

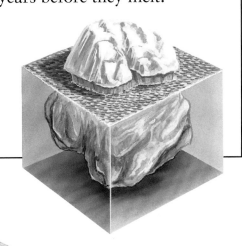

Q How many different minerals are there?

A There are about 3,000 different kinds of minerals on Earth. Each is made from a different set of chemicals. Some minerals, like those forming rocks, may be quite common. Others, such as gold, silver and diamonds, are rare and precious. Minerals are used to make many things, from the lead inside pencils to the mercury inside thermometers.

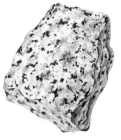

Granite (rock)

Marble (rock)

Limestone (rock)

Slate (rock)

Pyrite (mineral)

Flint (mineral)

Sandstone (rock)

ENVIRONMENT

The environment of a place is all its characteristics, including the chemical make-up of the soil, the climate, and the animals and plants – if any – that live there.

▲ Rainforests are home to more than half of Earth's species of animals and plants.

KEY FACTS

Hottest environments known to support life: hot springs and hydrothermal vents with temperatures of up to 140°C support simple organisms called hyperthermophiles

Coldest environments known to support life: polar ice in the Arctic and Antarctic with temperatures as cold as –15°C supports simple life-forms called cryophiles

▲ Protea flowers in a South African environment called *fynbos*, which has more than 9,000 plant species.

Every place on Earth has its own physical environment. Terrestrial environments are those on land. They include wet tropical rainforests, open grasslands and arid, sun-baked deserts. There are also aquatic, or freshwater (rivers, lakes and swamps), atmospheric and marine environments.

Marine environments are those found in the ocean. They include the intertidal zone, which is the area from which the sea retreats at low tide. The ocean floor thousands of metres below the surface is another type of marine environment.

Biotic or abiotic?

The elements that make one environment different from any other can be divided into biotic and abiotic factors. The biotic factors are the animals and plants that live there.

The abiotic elements include climatic factors. Examples are the amount and strength of sunlight, the range of temperature and humidity, the frequency of strong winds, and the frequency and amount of rainfall and fog.

Abiotic elements also include the chemical composition of the air, soil and water – including pollution. Pollution includes the chemicals released into the air when fossil fuels are burnt and oil that leaks into the ocean from supertankers.

Species richness

Different environments suit different forms of life. Some environments have a very limited range of organisms: the icy Antarctic desert, for example. On the other hand, tropical rainforests, coral reefs and the *fynbos* environment of South Africa have thousands of species. The *fynbos* has varied plant life because its moist, mild winters and hot, dry summers are ideal for different types of plants to flourish.

▲ Organisms that live between the levels of high tide and low tide must be able to live in both salt water and air.

▼ An extreme environment: a jet of steam called a geyser.

GENERAL INFORMATION

- Biodiversity is a measure of how many different species live in an environment. Tropical coral reefs and rainforests are the most biodiverse environments.

- An environment may or may not support life. The red hot lava of a volcano supports no life at all.

See also:

Habitats, Landscape, Planet Earth

HARSH ENVIRONMENTS

Some environments are very extreme. For example, hydrothermal vents on the ocean floor spew out very hot water. These vents support invertebrate animals called Pompeii worms, which live in water as hot as 80°C. The worms have a coating of heat-tolerant bacteria.

ENVIRONMENT

Q What causes the winds?

A Winds are created because of differences in air temperature and air pressure. When air is heated at the equator (below), it rises, cools and then sinks over the tropics. Some moves back again towards the equator, creating the trade winds. The rest is drawn towards the poles as westerly winds.

Water vapour in clouds

Water falls as rain

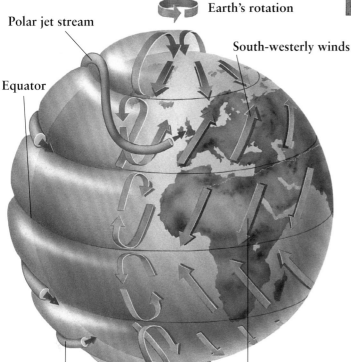

Polar jet stream

Earth's rotation

South-westerly winds

Equator

Trade winds

Subtropical jet streams

Q How are clouds formed?

A Water evaporates from land, lakes and sea (above) and is carried by the air as water vapour. Warm air can hold more water vapour than cold air. As warm air rises and cools – for example, over a mountain – the water vapour condenses to water, forming clouds. Eventually, the water falls from the clouds as rain. The rainwater runs back into the rivers and lakes.

Q What is erosion?

A Erosion is the breaking down of solid rock into smaller particles that are then carried away. Wind, water, gravity, sea and rain are common natural causes of erosion and so is ice (left). The frozen ice in the glacier carves U-shaped valleys as it moves slowly downhill. Most mountain valleys are formed in this way. Today, human activity also causes damaging erosion.

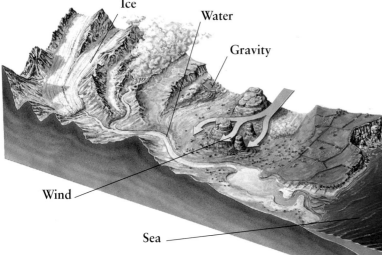

Ice

Water

Gravity

Wind

Sea

Q What is energy conservation?

A We use a lot of energy in our homes. Much of it comes from oil, coal or gas, which are fossil fuels that will one day be used up. If we insulate our houses better, and trap the Sun's heat, we use less fuel. This is called energy conservation. We can also use ever-lasting energy sources, such as wind.

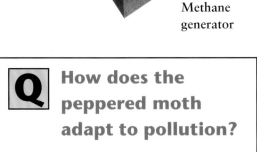

Wind-powered generator

Solar panel

Heat insulation

Water-powered generator

Methane generator

Q Why is pollution harmful?

A Many of the fumes and chemicals produced by cars or industry (below) can damage plants and animals. Even small amounts of some polluting gases or liquids can kill large numbers of living things, and many are poisonous to people as well.

Acid rain

Smog

Q What is deforestation?

A Forests once covered 6 billion hectares of the Earth but now only 4 billion hectares are left (below). The process of cutting down trees is called deforestation and is carried out by people. Trees are important to our survival because, like other green plants, they produce oxygen. Without oxygen, animals, including humans, cannot survive.

Q How does the peppered moth adapt to pollution?

A The peppered moth rests on tree bark where its camouflage hides it from bird predators. The bark in polluted towns may be black and normal camouflage would be useless. In these areas, a black-winged form of the moth is found.

Normal form   Black-winged form

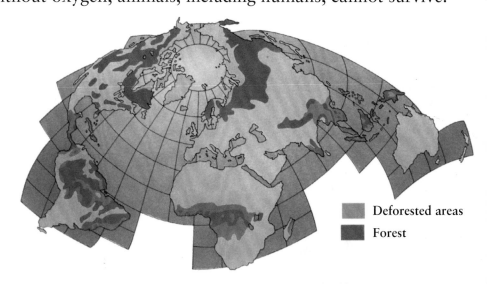

Deforested areas

Forest

HABITATS

A habitat is the set of environmental factors that best suits a species. The best habitat for a wolf is not the same as that for a lion, a shark, a hummingbird or an oak tree.

Every species of plant and animal has slightly different needs from its surroundings. That set of features is called the species' habitat.

Plants

Most plants need a supply of nutrients and water, sufficient sunlight for photosynthesis and support for their roots. However, every plant species has slightly different needs. Some require more moisture, some less. Some can only grow in acidic conditions, others in alkaline soil. Some plants need more sunlight, others less. And many plants depend on certain

▲ This bromeliad plant, growing on a tree, has a specialist habitat.

animals to fertilise them. Therefore, there are thousands of different plant habitats.

Animals

All animals need food and shelter and suitable places to lay eggs or give birth to young. But they all have different habitat requirements. Some graze on grass, others browse canopy leaves and still more hunt other animals.

Some animals need different habitats at different stages of their life. For example, young frogs (tadpoles) and young dragonflies (larvae) have to live in water. Adult frogs can live in water and on land, while adult dragonflies cannot survive in water.

KEY FACTS

Specialist habitat requirements:
koalas, eucalyptus trees; giant pandas, bamboo forest; shoebill storks, papyrus swamps; cacti, deserts and semi-deserts

Generalist habitat requirements:
brown rats, anywhere there are people

▼ Zebras live in tropical grassland habitats. They would not survive in rainforest or dry deserts.

Generalist or specialist

Some animals and plants are not fussy about where they live. Brown rats can thrive anywhere near buildings and human waste, even in the middle of cities. They are called generalist animals.

Other animals have very particular habitat needs. They are called specialists. Giant pandas need lots of bamboo plants, since this is almost the only thing they eat. In the wild, pandas live in a small part of Tibet and south China. There are not man pandas left in the wil

Habitat d

When a hab animals have

NICHES

Sometimes two or more animals share the sam The curlew (the b and the oyster and-white b same pat birds m

the trees the trees will gain after a few change the habitat g a city on it, it will go back to how it once was. is called habitat destruction. Sometimes it means some species of animals or plants become very rare – or die out completely.

GENERAL INFORMATION

● The habitat of an animal or plant is often made up of several different environments. Not all environments support life, though.

See also:

Ecology, Environment, Landscape

HABITATS

Beaver's lodge

Q What is succession?

A Succession is the natural process by which habitats change, and one community of plants and animals is slowly replaced by another. The picture below shows an example of succession at work as a temperate lake silts up, and the dry land eventually becomes oak woodland.

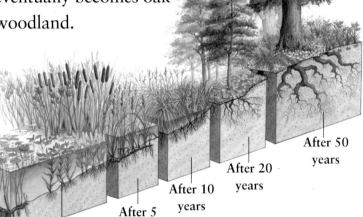

Lake
After 5 years
After 10 years
After 20 years
After 50 years

Q Can animals alter a habitat?

A Some animals can change their habitats. Beavers cut down trees with their strong teeth. Then they use the trees, together with mud and stones, to dam streams. Their homes, called lodges, are large piles of sticks built up from the bottom of the ponds they have created (above). Here, they raise their young, safely away from predators.

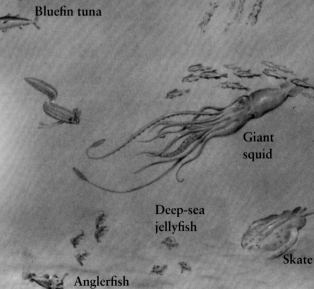

Plankton
Whale
Shark
Dolphin
Bluefin tuna
Giant squid
Deep-sea jellyfish
Skate
Anglerfish

Q What is a habitat?

A A habitat is a place where plants and animals live together as a community. Most creatures live in only one type of habitat and cannot survive elsewhere. Look at the different habitats (right) in an ocean. Most life is found near the surface. A few species of fish and squid live in deeper water. The seabed is the realm of specially adapted marine creatures that cannot survive elsewhere in the ocean.

Q What are the world's main land habitats?

A The world's land habitats range from cold tundra and mountains, through hot deserts and grasslands, to the temperate woods and tropical rainforests, teeming with life. The ten major habitats are shown below. Each has its own type of climate, and plant and animal life.

Q How do wading birds avoid competing for food?

A These wading birds all have specially shaped beaks for catching different creatures on the seashore. So they do not compete for food although they live in the same habitat.

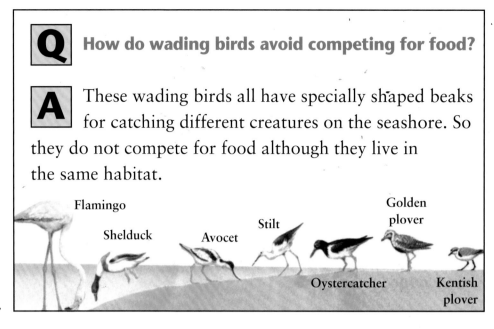

Flamingo
Shelduck
Avocet
Stilt
Golden plover
Oystercatcher
Kentish plover

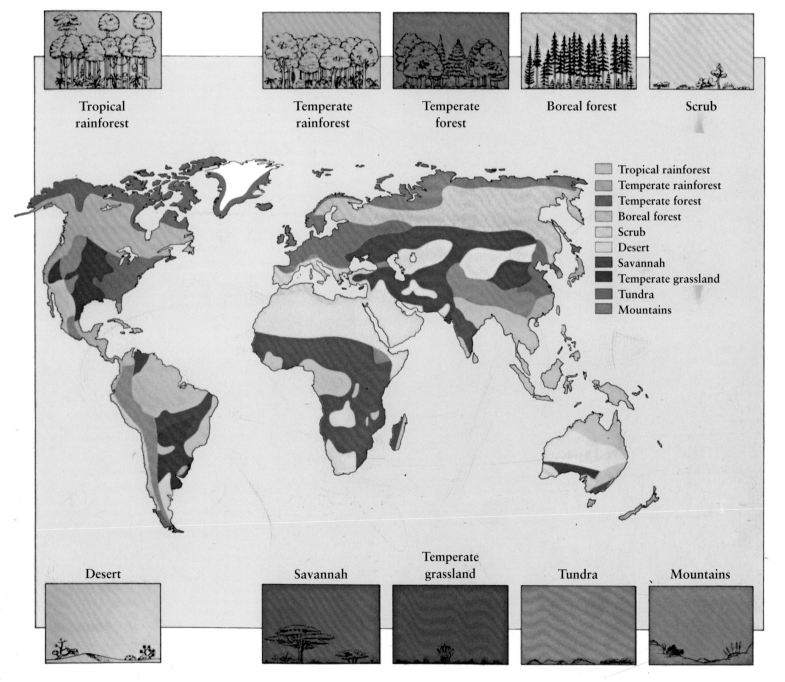

Tropical rainforest

Temperate rainforest

Temperate forest

Boreal forest

Scrub

- Tropical rainforest
- Temperate rainforest
- Temperate forest
- Boreal forest
- Scrub
- Desert
- Savannah
- Temperate grassland
- Tundra
- Mountains

Desert

Savannah

Temperate grassland

Tundra

Mountains

WORLD FACTS

About 71 per cent of Earth's surface is covered by water. The remaining area is land and is divided into seven continents and many oceanic islands.

The continents are Africa, Antarctica, Asia, Australia, Europe, North America and South America. They have all kinds of natural features, including mountain ranges, plains, deserts, rivers and freshwater lakes. Vegetation cloaks these land features, and the beds of lakes and rivers, apart from where cities and roads have replaced them. Every continent is divided into countries, apart from Antarctica, which belongs to no country.

Mountains

The Andes mountains form the longest mountain range. They stretch 7,000 kilometres from the south of Chile along the western side of South America to the north of Colombia and have an average height of 4,000 metres. The Himalayas (of which Mount Everest, Earth's highest mountain, is one peak) form the next longest range. They are 2,400 kilometres long and up to 400 kilometres wide. There are more than 100 peaks of 7,200 metres or more in the Himalayas.

Rivers

Great mountain ranges give rise to great rivers. There are 173 rivers more than 1,000 kilometres long, and many of them start in the Andes, Himalayas or other ranges such as the Rockies (North America), Alps (Europe) or East African Highlands. The longest

▲ Lake Baikal, in Russia, is the world's deepest lake: 1,642 metres at its deepest point.

KEY FACTS

Biggest continent: Asia, about 44.6 million km²

Biggest lakes: by volume, Lake Baikal, Russia, 23,600 km³; by area, Lake Superior, United States/Canada, about 82,350 km²

Longest rivers: Nile, about 6,650 km; Amazon, about 6,400 km

▼ The Bungle Bungle hills in Australia are 350 million years old.

▲ Angel Falls, Venezuela, is the highest waterfall on Earth. Water drops 979 metres from the top.

ever measured was 57.8°C at Aziziya, Libya, in 1922. The Vostok research station in Antarctica had a bitterly cold temperature of −89.2°C in 1983.

The driest part of the world is the Atacama Desert in Chile. It hardly ever rains in some areas of the desert. By contrast Mawsynram, India, has an average of 11.9 metres of rain every year.

river is the Nile, which flows about 6,650 kilometres from Rwanda or Burundi (no one knows exactly) in Central Africa through Egypt to the Mediterranean Sea. The Amazon is the second longest. It flows 6,400 kilometres from the Andes mountains in Peru to the Atlantic Ocean in Brazil.

Lakes

Lake Baikal, Russia, is the biggest freshwater lake by volume (23,600 cubic kilometres). Lake Superior, in the United States and Canada, has the biggest area of 82,350 square kilometres.

Climate

Those regions nearer to the equator tend to be hotter throughout the year than places far to the north and south. The hottest temperature

GENERAL INFORMATION

- Some of the windiest places on Earth are in Antarctica.
- Mountain ranges are often where two or more tectonic plates meet.
- Although surrounded by land, the Caspian Sea is considered to be a small ocean rather than a lake.

See also:

Landscape, Planet Earth, Water

WORLD FACTS

Q Which is the world's largest country?

A Russia has an area of 17,075,400 square kilometres, making it the world's largest country. The second largest country is Canada, with an area of 9,984,670 square kilometres. Close behind it is China, with an area of 9,640,011 square kilometres.

Q Where is the biggest freshwater lake in the world?

A A lake is a large area of water surrounded by land. The biggest freshwater lake by area is Lake Superior in North America, which stretches for 82,350 square kilometres. Some of the largest lakes are actually seas, full of salt water. These include the Caspian Sea and the Aral Sea.

Q Which place has the least rain?

A The world receives an average of 86 centimetres of rain, snow and hail each year. But some places get little or no rain at all. The driest place in the world is Arica in the Atacama Desert, Chile, which receives less than 0.1 millimetre of rain a year. In parts of West Africa and South America, rain falls nearly every day.

Q Which is the biggest island in the world?

A Greenland is by far the world's biggest island, at 2,166,086 square kilometres.

Greenland

Canada

NORTH AMERICA

Lake Superior

USA

ATLANTIC OCEAN

PACIFIC OCEAN

SOUTH AMERICA

Arica

Chile

ANTARCTIC OCEAN

Q Which is the world's smallest country?

A Vatican City is the world's smallest country. It covers only 44 hectares and lies inside another city – Rome, in Italy. Yet it is an independent state, with its own bank, railway station and postage stamps. It is the centre of the Roman Catholic Church.

Q Which is the largest desert in the world?

A A desert is a hot, dry region where there is low rainfall and little can grow. By far the biggest desert region is the Sahara in North Africa. This covers over 9 million square kilometres. About one-seventh of the world's land area is desert.

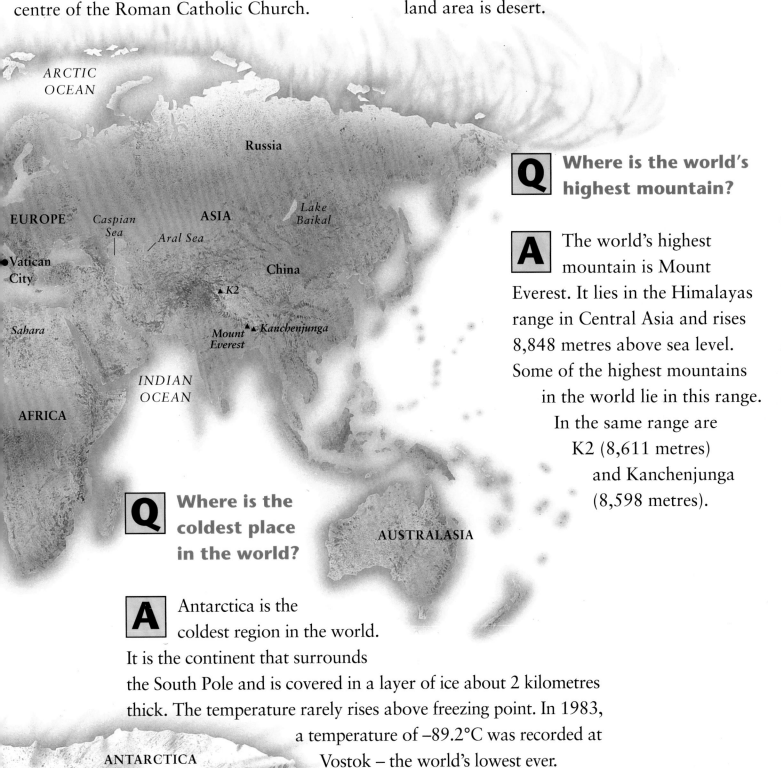

ARCTIC OCEAN

Russia

EUROPE

Caspian Sea

Aral Sea

ASIA

Lake Baikal

Vatican City

China

▲ K2

Sahara

Mount Everest

▲▲ Kanchenjunga

INDIAN OCEAN

AFRICA

AUSTRALASIA

ANTARCTICA

Q Where is the world's highest mountain?

A The world's highest mountain is Mount Everest. It lies in the Himalayas range in Central Asia and rises 8,848 metres above sea level. Some of the highest mountains in the world lie in this range. In the same range are K2 (8,611 metres) and Kanchenjunga (8,598 metres).

Q Where is the coldest place in the world?

A Antarctica is the coldest region in the world. It is the continent that surrounds the South Pole and is covered in a layer of ice about 2 kilometres thick. The temperature rarely rises above freezing point. In 1983, a temperature of –89.2°C was recorded at Vostok – the world's lowest ever.

COUNTRIES AND PEOPLE

A country, or nation, is a territory with a government that oversees trade with other countries and organises the armed forces, planning, transportation and so on.

Each country's government collects taxes from its people to pay for things like education, social welfare and defence. Every country has its own flag and national song, or anthem. Many countries also have a national costume.

A country usually has an official language, and sometimes more than one. India's official languages are Hindi and English, but the United States has no official language. The people who live in a country may be immigrants, who were born elsewhere in the world and speak other languages.

The United Nations organisation recognises 194 countries. Some trace their origins back thousands

▲ People dancing at a festival in Klaipeda, Lithuania, dressed in their national costume. Not all countries have a national costume.

of years. For example, Japan has existed since about 660 B.C. Other countries, particularly in Africa, are relatively new, having gained independence from European empires since the end of World War II. Countries are still being created: South Sudan declared its independence in 2011.

In 2012 the world's total population was just over 7 billion. The country with the most people is China, which had a population of 1.34 billion in 2012 (19 per cent of the world's total). Although many different languages are spoken in China, the country has one government, one flag and one national anthem. The next most populous country is India, with 1.21 billion people in 2012.

Large and small

Russia has a bigger area than any other country – 17,075,400 square kilometres (11.5 per cent of the

KEY FACTS

Most populous country: China, 1.34 billion; India, 1.21 billion (2012 figures)
Biggest country: Russia, 17.1 million km²
Most populous continent: Asia, 3.9 billion (2012 figures)

LANGUAGE

More than 6,000 different languages are spoken around the world. Those spoken by the most people are Mandarin, Spanish, English, Hindi, Arabic and Bengali. More than 845 million people speak Mandarin as their first language. A total of 292 languages are still spoken in China, and more than 100 are spoken in India.

lies between Russia and China, has just 1.7 people per square kilometre. Even within the same country, population densities vary greatly. More and more people live in (or close to) cities, while areas of forest, desert and mountains may have very few people living there.

world's land area). Next biggest are Canada (9,984,670 km^2; 6.7 per cent), China (9,640,011 km^2; 6.5 per cent) and the United States (9,629,091 km^2; 6.5 per cent). The smallest country in the world is Vatican City – just 0.44 km^2.

The population density of countries varies enormously. Monaco, which is bordered on three sides by France and on the fourth by the Mediterranean Sea, has a population density of 16,923 people per square kilometre. In contrast, in China there are only 140 people per square kilometre, on average. And Mongolia, which

▼ A crowded street in Delhi, India's biggest city.

GENERAL INFORMATION

- Some countries cannot agree their borders with their neighbours, and this can lead to territorial disputes or even wars.
- In 2008, for the first time in history, the majority of the world's people lived in cities.

See also:

World Facts

COUNTRIES & PEOPLE

Q **Which continent has most countries?**

A The continent with the most countries is Africa. There are 54 independent countries in Africa. The largest African country is Algeria. It has an area of 2,381,741 square kilometres. The African country with the most people is Nigeria, with a population of over 162 million.

Mediterranean Sea

Algeria

Nigeria

ATLANTIC OCEAN

INDIAN OCEAN

Q **Why do countries have flags?**

A Every country has its own flag. Flags are used as a way of identifying the country, or anything belonging to it, to other nations. The flags above belong to countries that are members of the United Nations.

Q **How many people are there in the world?**

A More than 7 billion people live on the Earth. By the year 2020 the population will probably have reached 7.5 billion. Some places, such as deserts and polar regions, are largely unsuitable for people. Most people live where there is rich farmland or where cities can provide jobs and housing (below). The most populated country is China; it has over 1.3 billion people.

China

Persons per sq km

over 500
201–500
101–200
51–100
11–50
1–10
less than 1

Q What is an ethnic group?

A Over many thousands of years, people in different parts of the world have developed variations in appearance and hair or skin colour. People of similar appearance and colour are said to belong to the same ethnic group. Anthropologists (people who study human development and culture) believe that there may be as many as 5,000 different ethnic groups. Three are shown below.

Q Why do people hold festivals?

A Festivals celebrate special days such as a time of year, like the Chinese New Year (below), or an important event such as the founding of a country, like Australia Day (right).

Q Why do people wear national costume?

A Modern dress is similar in many parts of the world, so many people remember their heritage by wearing a national costume on festival days. The costume usually has a long history. The Breton people of north-west France have a very distinctive costume (right).

EVOLUTION

Evolution is the process of change, usually over long periods of time, by which one species (type) of animal or plant becomes another species.

Animals and plants change so they are better able to thrive in their environment. The English naturalist Charles Darwin (1809–1882) suggested that the variety of life could be explained by a process he called natural selection.

In his book *On the Origin of Species* (1859) he wrote that more individuals are born than survive to become adults. Some animals or plants survive because they have a certain advantage over the others. This advantage could be big cats with sharper teeth, for example, or trees with bigger leaves. The individuals with the advantage live longer, breed more successfully

▲ **Charles Darwin was the first scientist to argue the case for evolution by natural selection.**

and pass on the advantage to their offspring. Over a long period of time there will be more and more individuals that possess the new characteristic. This has been called 'survival of the fittest', but 'natural selection' is a better name. The process of natural selection is the driving force behind the evolution of species.

Darwin's discoveries

In 1831 Darwin set out on a survey ship called HMS *Beagle*. During the voyage he made observations of animals and plants that made him doubt the idea that species never change. While he was visiting the Galápagos Islands, off the coast of South America, he looked closely

KEY FACTS

Fastest evolution: three years in a Canadian population of stickleback fish
Slowest evolution: 550 million years almost unchanged in Pacific Ocean brachiopods called *Lingulata*

▼ **This is one of 13 species of 'Darwin's finches' on the Galápagos Islands. All of them probably evolved from just one species. The variation in beak size and shape caused Charles Darwin to wonder about their origins.**

at the kinds of giant tortoises that lived there. He found that the tortoises on each of the islands in the Galápagos were slightly different. Darwin realised that all the Galápagos giant tortoises had a common ancestor. But each had evolved in a different way so they were best able to thrive in the conditions on their island.

Finches' beaks

Darwin noticed something similar with the finches that lived on the Galápagos Islands. They looked alike in many ways but their beaks were different. Some had long, thin beaks, while others' beaks were shorter and thick. He noticed that the groups of finches fed in different ways. Cactus finches had longish beaks, able to reach into cactus flowers to eat the nectar. Woodpecker finches had long, narrow beaks that they used to pick grubs from holes in trees. Another group (ground finches) used their thick, wide beaks to crush seeds. Darwin said the different finches' beaks had evolved so they could eat different foods.

WHAT IS DNA?

In Charles Darwin's time the way in which characteristics were inherited was not understood. They were sometimes called 'particles of inheritance'. These 'particles' were later understood to be genes. Genes form a code that drives the way cells develop. Genes are made of DNA (deoxyribonucleic acid) and are passed from parents to offspring. Long, coiled-up chains of DNA are called chromosomes.

▼ Part of the DNA strands in a human chromosome.

GENERAL INFORMATION

- In humans there are 23 pairs of chains, called chromosomes, in each cell. The longest of these, if it were stretched out, would be more than 2 metres long.
- If a life form is perfectly suited to its environment it will not evolve. That is why some marine invertebrates have hardly changed for 550 million years.

▲ A fossil of *Archaeopteryx*, the first-known bird. Its ancestors were dinosaurs.

See also:

Environment, Science of Life

EVOLUTION

Q What is evolution?

A The first forms of life appeared on Earth many hundreds of millions of years ago. They were tiny, primitive creatures that lived in water. As millions of years went by, these creatures gradually changed and many different forms of life slowly appeared (above). This process is called evolution and it is still continuing today.

Q How do we know about the past?

A We find out about the past from fossils. If a prehistoric animal died in shallow, muddy water, its body may have been covered with layers of silt that eventually formed solid rock. The animal's soft parts decayed, but the skeleton slowly absorbed minerals and hardened in the rock to become a fossil (left). Millions of years later, if the rock is worn away, we can find the fossil.

Q What does extinction mean?

A Extinction occurs when the last individual of a plant or animal species dies out. In the past, many creatures such as dinosaurs died out naturally – perhaps because of changes in the climate. In the last few centuries, animals such as the dodo (left) and the thylacine (below) have been hunted to extinction by people.

Q What is natural selection?

A Not all animals are as strong as others of the same species. This deer was not fast enough to escape a tiger attack and it will be killed. Other, fitter deer will evade capture and survive to breed. This process of survival of the fittest is called natural selection.

Q How did the horse evolve?

A The horse evolved from a fox-sized forest animal called *Hyracotherium* that lived 50 million years ago. Its descendants such as *Mesohippus* and *Merychippus* grew larger and grazed on open grassland. The number of toes dwindled from four to one and the animals ran on tiptoe. This improved their running speed. Eventually the modern horse evolved.

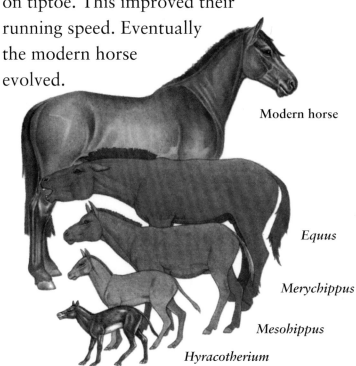

Modern horse

Equus

Merychippus

Mesohippus

Hyracotherium

Q What is adaptation?

A Animals and plants often develop traits that help them survive. Such traits are called adaptations. The long legs and sucker-like toes of this tarsier are adaptations for climbing. Its large eyes help it to see at night.

Q When did our ancestors evolve?

A Our line of evolution split off from ape-like *Ramapithecus* about 12 million years ago. *Australopithecus* (right) was our first ancestor. It lived 4 million years ago. Then came *Homo habilis* 2.3 million years ago and *Homo erectus* 1.8 million years ago. Modern humans (*Homo sapiens*) first appeared up to 400,000 years ago.

PREHISTORIC LIFE

By about 3.9 billion years ago, Earth had an atmosphere that contained the right make-up of hydrogen, oxygen, nitrogen and carbon to allow the creation of life.

KEY DATES

Atmosphere able to support life:
3.9 billion years ago
First vertebrate land mammals:
380 million years ago
Dinosaurs: 230–65 million years ago

▼ A reconstruction of a woolly mammoth. This animal's bones are often preserved in frozen tundra. Woolly mammoths died out about 10,000 years ago.

Energy, possibly from lightning or from radioactive elements, caused the creation of complex chemicals called proteins and nucleic acids. Scientists have found ways in which the genetic molecule RNA (essential for life) could have formed from chemicals present on Earth at that time. They believe simple cells with molecules similar to RNA assembled, reproduced and evolved – giving rise to life.

Single-celled life

The earliest forms of life had just a single cell that lacked a nucleus.

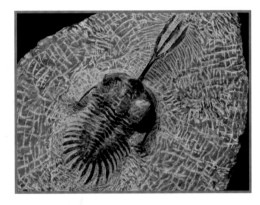

▲ Trilobites roamed the oceans for 270 million years before becoming extinct 250 million years ago.

By about 680 million years ago, some had evolved into forms of life with more than one cell (they were multi-celled). The first multi-celled organisms were simple: they had no bones or other hard body parts so were rarely preserved as fossils. This means our knowledge about them is very sketchy.

Cambrian explosion

The variety of fossils of animals with skeletons grew a lot from about 530 million years ago (in the Cambrian period). This increase in variety is often called the 'Cambrian explosion'. Fossils dating from that time include many of the major groups alive today – and others that have long since become extinct (such as the trilobites).

▶ This diagram can be used to trace the history of life on Earth. Start at the top and work clockwise, finishing at the top again.

Vertebrate animals

The first animals with backbones were jawless fish. They evolved 500 million years ago. Amphibians (370 million years ago) followed, then reptiles (320 million years ago). Some reptiles evolved into dinosaurs (230 million years ago), which ruled the land for 165 million years.

Mammals came later (220 million years ago) and remained small until the dinosaurs were wiped out in the K-T extinction, 65 million years ago. Then the mammals became dominant. Among them were the primates, from which humans eventually evolved.

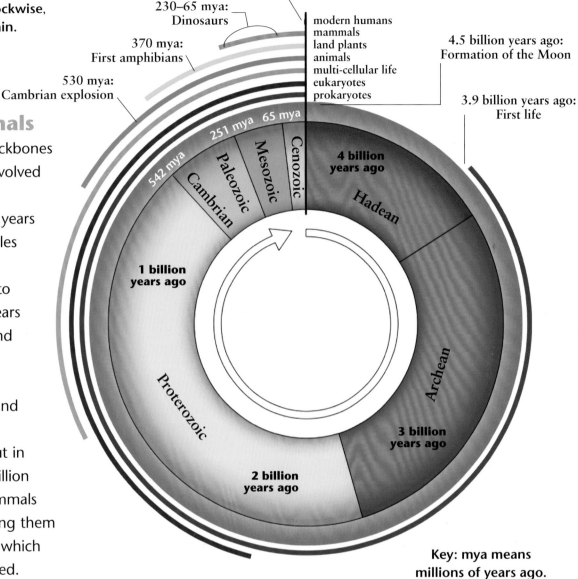

400,000 years: Modern humans

230–65 mya: Dinosaurs

370 mya: First amphibians

530 mya: Cambrian explosion

modern humans
mammals
land plants
animals
multi-cellular life
eukaryotes
prokaryotes

4.5 billion years ago: Formation of the Moon

3.9 billion years ago: First life

542 mya · 251 mya · 65 mya

Cambrian · Paleozoic · Mesozoic · Cenozoic

Hadean

4 billion years ago

3 billion years ago

2 billion years ago

1 billion years ago

Proterozoic

Archean

Key: mya means millions of years ago.

THE FIRST HUMANS

Modern humans (*Homo sapiens*) and chimpanzees probably evolved from the same ancient ancestor. Several other human-like species are now extinct. These include *Homo habilis*, *Homo erectus* and *Homo neanderthalensis* (right), who lived between 400,000 and 30,000 years ago. *Homo sapiens* evolved in East Africa (and possibly elsewhere) 400,000–250,000 years ago.

GENERAL INFORMATION

- Prehistoric animals included dinosaurs, woolly mammoths and human-like species.
- By the time of the K-T extinction, 65 million years ago, all the major groups of animals and plants living on Earth had evolved.

See also:

Dinosaurs, Evolution, Simple Creatures

PREHISTORIC LIFE

Q Which were the first animals to fly?

A Insects have been able to fly for far longer than any other animal. Winged insects probably developed from types of worms that lived in the sea. Some insects were huge, like the giant dragonfly *Meganeura* (right), which lived about 300 million years ago. Its wingspan was more than 70 centimetres.

Q Why did animals begin to live on land?

A The very earliest creatures lived in water. Then plants began to grow on the land. These provided a new source of food and some animals left the water. They developed lungs, instead of gills, for breathing. Their fins developed into legs to help them move on land. The first to come onto land were the amphibians such as *Ichthyostega*. They had fish-like heads and tails, but stronger backbones and stout legs.

Q Which was the earliest known bird?

A The *Archaeopteryx* (below) was a bird that lived about 150 million years ago. It looked like a small dinosaur but was covered with feathers. It also had wings that it spread for gliding through the air. Nobody knows for certain whether it could fly properly. Unlike today's birds, *Archaeopteryx* had three claws on each wing that it used for climbing trees. It also had teeth and a long tail covered with feathers.

Q Why do dinosaurs have such long names?

A The names of dinosaurs look confusing but they each describe something about their owner (right). The names are made up of Greek and Latin terms. The word dinosaur itself means 'terrible lizard'. *Corythosaurus* means 'helmeted lizard'. *Alamosaurus* means 'lizard from Alamo'. *Triceratops* means 'face with three horns'. *Tyrannosaurus* means 'tyrant lizard'. *Ornithomimus* means 'imitator of birds'. *Pachycephalosaurus* means 'lizard with a thick head'.

Corythosaurus

Tyrannosaurus

Alamosaurus

Triceratops

Ornithomimus

Pachycephalosaurus

Q What were early humans like?

A Human-like primates called *Homo habilis* (below) lived about 2 million years ago in East Africa. Their faces were ape-like and their bodies were covered with hair. They walked upright and used sticks, stones and bones as tools.

Q What is a fossil?

A A fossil is the remains of a plant or animal that lived millions of years ago. Some, like this insect (1), have been covered in a hard substance called amber. This is the sap from ancient pine trees. But most, like the plants (2, 3 and 5), have been turned into stone. The shell (4) is of an extinct marine animal called an ammonite.

1
2
3
4
5

DINOSAURS

Dinosaurs were the dominant land-living (terrestrial) animals for about 165 million years. They ranged in size from creatures the size of a domestic cat to giants longer than a bus.

KEY FACTS

Heaviest: *Argentinosaurus*, probably 80 tonnes
Longest: *Amphicoelias*, probably 50 m
Smallest: *Anchiomis*, 35 cm long
Fastest: *Dromiceiomimus*, up to 60 km/h

▼ *Diplodocus* was one of the biggest dinosaurs of all, growing up to almost 50 metres long. Despite its size, this quadruped was not aggressive. It ate leaves from plants.

The first dinosaurs appeared in the Triassic period about 230 million years ago. Most, if not all, terrestrial dinosaurs perished in the K-T extinction at the end of the Cretaceous period, 65 million years ago. Most scientists now believe that some dinosaurs evolved into birds. They call birds 'avian dinosaurs'.

The dinosaurs evolved from reptiles called archosaurs. The fossilised remains of one of the first – *Saturnalia* – was found in Brazil. It was the size of a small dog and ran on two legs (it was bipedal).

Plant- and meat-eaters

Some dinosaurs were herbivores (they ate plants, mostly) and others were carnivores (meat-eaters). Some ran or walked on two legs and others walked on four legs (quadrupeds). Some of the bipedal dinosaurs could run fast.

Scientists generally divide dinosaurs into two groups: theropods and sauropods. Most theropods were carnivores. Some were large but the smallest were less than 1 metre long. Most sauropods ate plants and included the largest dinosaurs of all: some

were 50 metres long, and others weighed 80 tonnes.

The carnivores were built to kill. Many could probably run fast after prey and they had fearsome teeth and strong claws. The plant-eaters tended to be slower, but some had defence mechanisms such as massive body armour (*Saltosaurus*, for example) and horns on their head (*Triceratops*). Some dinosaurs had strange-looking head crests (*Lambeosaurus*).

Bird-like behaviour

Scientists can tell a lot from fossils about how dinosaurs lived. They know that dinosaurs laid eggs. In some species the dinosaurs hatched in nests. Some tucked their head under their arms when they slept, much like many birds do.

◀ This reconstruction of a *Tyrannosaurus rex* skeleton shows what a fearsome predator it was. This bipedal carnivore stood 4 metres tall at the hips and had massive jaws bearing sharp teeth.

Fossilisation does not often preserve feathers but some feathered dinosaurs have been found. The oldest bird-like fossil – *Archaeopteryx* – dates from rocks 150 milllion years old in Germany.

K-T EXTINCTION

So why did most non-avian dinosaurs die out – along with lots of other creatures – 65 million years ago? This time is called the K-T extinction. Scientists believe a huge meteor crashed into Earth where the Yucatan Peninsula now is, in Mexico. After this collision, huge clouds of dust and smoke blocked out the Sun's warming rays. The temperature of the atmosphere chilled, and dinosaurs either did not have the energy to remain active or they starved because most plants died.

GENERAL INFORMATION

● Ancient Chinese people found dinosaur bones more than 2,000 years ago. They thought they were the bones of dragons.

● Western fossil-hunters began to find many different kinds of dinosaurs in the 19th century. New discoveries are made every year, and by 2012 more than 1,000 species had been identified.

See also:

Birds, Prehistoric Life, Reptiles

DINOSAURS

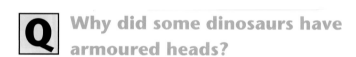

Triceratops

Leptoceratops

Q Which was the tallest dinosaur?

A Many of the huge, plant-eating dinosaurs had long necks. The tallest was *Brachiosaurus* (above), which not only had a long neck but long front legs as well. It could stretch up to 15 metres and probably fed on the tops of trees, much as giraffes do today. It needed legs the size of tree trunks to support its great weight.

Q Why did some dinosaurs have armoured heads?

A Some dinosaurs were meat-eating predators. Not surprisingly, many of the plant-eating dinosaurs developed armoured heads to help defend themselves (above). The head of *Triceratops* was covered with a large plate and carried three forward-pointing horns. *Leptoceratops* was much smaller and lacked *Triceratops'* horns.

Q Which was the most fearsome meat-eater?

A *Tyrannosaurus* (right) was probably the most terrifying carnivorous dinosaur. It was certainly one of the largest. The head was huge and its skull was larger than a man. *Tyrannosaurus* stood upright on massive hind legs and could outrun slower, plant-eating dinosaurs. Its teeth, which were 15 centimetres long, were used to rip and tear the flesh of its prey.

Tyrannosaurus skull

Q How did *Stegosaurus* get warm?

A *Stegosaurus* was a large, 7.5-metre-long dinosaur with a double row of armoured plates on its back. These may have been useful in defence but were probably also used to control body temperature. They would have gathered heat from the Sun's rays to warm *Stegosaurus* up. Breezes passing through the plates would have helped *Stegosaurus* cool off if it was too hot.

Q Were all dinosaurs big?

A Although some dinosaurs were the largest land animals ever to have lived, many were tiny. Among the smallest were species of *Compsognathus* (left). Some were the size of a chicken. Most *Compsognathus* species had long legs and were good runners. This one is trying to catch a dragonfly.

Q How do we know what dinosaurs looked like?

A We can tell what dinosaurs looked like from fossils. These are found in sedimentary rocks from all over the world. Often just a few dinosaur bones are found but sometimes scientists discover complete skeletons.

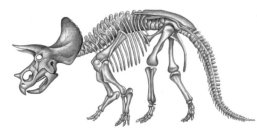

SIMPLE CREATURES

Invertebrates (animals without a backbone) make up 97 per cent of all animal species. The weight of all the earthworms, insects and spiders in the world is many times the weight of its people.

KEY FACTS

Number of species: 1.3–30 million
Largest: colossal squid, more than 12 m long
Smallest: many can be seen only through a microscope

▲ A colourful coral reef grows in shallow water near the coast of Indonesia.

A phylum (plural, phyla) is a large group of animals with some features in common. For example, mammals, birds, reptiles, amphibians and fish all have a backbone. Together they make up the phylum Chordata.

Most creatures do not have a backbone. They are invertebrates. There are 30 phyla of invertebrates. They are sometimes called simple creatures, but many are not simple.

The invertebrates are an incredibly varied group. Some are aquatic – sponges, jellyfish, corals, sea anemones, octopuses, starfish and bivalves. Others live mostly in soil – for example, the annelid worms. Some – like most flatworms – are parasites, living inside other animals. Still more live on plants most of their lives; this is true for most insects and spiders. Some invertebrates swim, and others walk or fly. And some hardly move at all: they are sedentary.

Arthropods

The phylum Arthropoda is the biggest group of simple creatures, with more than 1 million species. They range from crabs and lobsters to insects and spiders. Arthropods have a segmented body covered by an external skeleton (exoskeleton). Each body segment usually has one or more pairs of legs attached to it.

Bivalves, gastropods and octopuses are grouped together in the phylum Mollusca. There are about 85,000 species. They look

SUPER-SIZED SQUID

The largest invertebrates of all are molluscs called colossal squids. They live at great depths in the Southern Ocean and grow to more than 12 metres long. They have the largest eyes of any animal and are the main source of food for sperm whales, which dive to 3,000 metres to catch them.

very different from each other but share certain features. They usually have a head with sensory organs and a muscular foot. And they do not have an internal or external skeleton. A tough, chalky shell often protects them instead.

◀ Squid are cephalopods with eight arms and two tentacles. They are strong swimmers and feed on the seabed as well as in the water column. Squid have three hearts.

Sponges, jellyfish and corals

The sponges (phylum Porifera) live on, and are attached to, the shallow ocean floor. They are perhaps the simplest animals of all. Some of the 5,000 species are very small, but the giant barrel sponge grows to 2.4 metres in height. The jellyfish, corals and sea anemones (phylum Cnidaria) form a varied group of 9,500 species.

While corals and sea anemones are sedentary creatures, jellyfish drift in ocean currents. Individual corals are small, but they form colonies that can be very large. The tentacles of a lion's mane jellyfish grow up to 37 metres long.

Starfish, sea urchins and worms

Most starfish, sea urchins and sea cucumbers (phylum Echinodermata, 7,000 species) have a body arranged into five similar regions around a circular shape. They have lumps of calcium carbonate (called ossicles) embedded in their skin.

GENERAL INFORMATION

● Less well-known groups of invertebrates include the flatworms (phylum Platyhelminthes, 13,000 species), which often live within other animals; round worms (phylum Nematoda, up to 500,000 species); and the segmented worms (phylum Annelida, 9,000 species).

See also:

Insects and Spiders, Prehistoric Life

▲ Lion's mane jellyfish live only in the cold waters of northern oceans.

SIMPLE CREATURES

Q How does a jellyfish sting?

A A jellyfish (right) is a bell-shaped sea animal with its mouth on the underside of its body. Its body is made of two layers of skin with a jelly-like layer in between. Long tentacles hang down from the body. The tentacles have stinging cells that the jellyfish uses to stun its prey or protect itself from enemies. Humans can sometimes be hurt by these stings. Inside each stinging cell is a coiled thread (inset). When something touches the cell, the thread shoots out, sticking into the prey and injecting venom. In this way, jellyfish can catch large fish.

Q How many legs has a centipede?

A A centipede's body is made up of segments. Each segment has one pair of legs attached to it. The centipede in this picture has 18 segments and so it has 36 legs. Some centipedes have only 15 segments and others have as many as 177 segments.

Q How does an octopus catch its food?

A An octopus (right) has eight tentacles and hunts on the seabed for fish or shellfish. It creeps towards its prey and then pounces, grabbing hold with its tentacles. Suckers on the tentacles hold the prey firmly while the octopus drags it to its mouth.

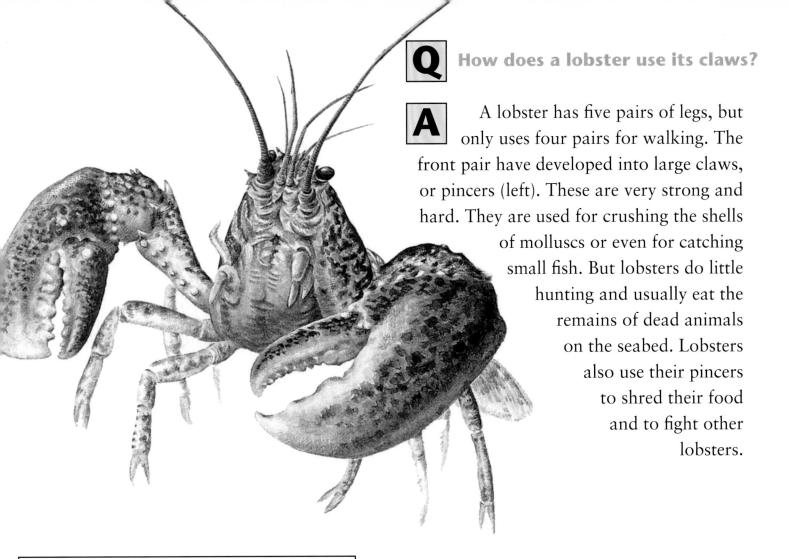

Q How does a lobster use its claws?

A A lobster has five pairs of legs, but only uses four pairs for walking. The front pair have developed into large claws, or pincers (left). These are very strong and hard. They are used for crushing the shells of molluscs or even for catching small fish. But lobsters do little hunting and usually eat the remains of dead animals on the seabed. Lobsters also use their pincers to shred their food and to fight other lobsters.

Q How are hermit crabs different from other crabs?

A Hermit crabs have hard shells on their front parts, like other crabs, but their abdomens are soft. They live inside the empty shells of other sea animals for protection.

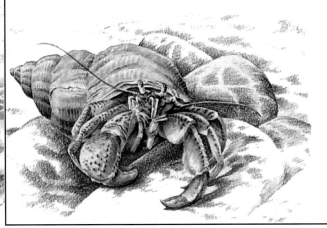

Q Is a starfish really a fish?

A Starfish (below) are not fish but belong to the group of sea animals called echinoderms. The name means 'spiny-skinned'. Starfish have arms but no head, and no front or back. They move slowly by gripping the seabed with water-filled tubes on their arms. The starfish's arms are so strong that they can pull apart the two shells of a mussel to reach the food inside.

INSECTS AND SPIDERS

Insects form the largest group of invertebrates. They include butterflies and moths, dragonflies, bees and wasps, beetles and ants. Spiders are also invertebrates but they are arachnids, not insects.

KEY FACTS

Species of insects: over 1 million
Fastest insects: dragonflies, 55 km/h
Species of spiders: at least 34,000
Most venomous spiders: black widow and Brazilian wandering spider

Adult insects have an external skeleton and a body that is divided into three parts: a head, thorax and abdomen. On the head they have two antennae and eyes made up of many separate sections (called compound eyes). Three pairs of legs are attached to the body. Most adult insects can fly. The oldest-known fossil insect is 400 million years old.

Metamorphosis

Many insects change body form dramatically as they get older. This is called metamorphosis. For example, butterflies and moths start life as eggs, which hatch into flightless, very hungry caterpillars. These grow larger

▲ An adult dragonfly emerges from its dried-out larval case.

before entering an inactive pupal stage. Inside the pupa the insect undergoes a complete change, or metamorphosis, and emerges as a flying adult.

Dragonfly eggs hatch into swimming larvae that live in water. They may live under water for several years before crawling out and emerging as flying adults.

GOLIATH INSECTS

The world's biggest insect is probably one of the goliath beetles, which live in tropical forests in Africa. Adults are up to 12 centimetres long and weigh up to 110 grams. They eat sugary tree sap and fruit. The world's biggest spider is the goliath tarantula, whose legs span 25 centimetres. It sometimes eats small lizards and birds.

Social creatures

Many bees, wasps, ants and termites live in well-organised colonies where different groups perform different tasks. Some build nests, guard eggs and provide food for their young. Some ants protect other insects called aphids so they can feed on a liquid called honeydew that the aphids produce.

Spiders

There are at least 34,000 species of spiders, and they are all carnivores. Spiders have an external skeleton, or cuticle, and two body sections. The prosoma has the brain, eyes and mouthparts. The opisthosoma contains the stomach, reproductive organs and lungs. Four pairs of legs, a pair of fangs with poison glands and a pair of grasping feelers attach to the prosoma.

▲ A tarantula with a tree frog that it has just paralysed.

Spiders often build webs in which to trap insect (or larger) prey. Spiders have special glands to produce the light, strong silk threads needed to make webs and nests. Prey such as flies get trapped in the webs. Other spiders hunt their prey on the ground. Most spiders use venom to kill or paralyse their prey. Only rarely is the venom dangerous to humans.

GENERAL INFORMATION

- Metamorphosis means young and adult insects eat different sources of food. That means there is less competition between the different generations.
- One strand of spider silk long enough to circle Earth would weigh just 500 grams.
- Spiders are arachnids, as are scorpions.

See also:

Prehistoric Life, Simple Creatures

▲ These bees are swarming around the outside of their hive.

INSECTS & SPIDERS

Q How does a spider make a web?

A Spiders make silk in glands near their abdomens. They draw the silk out into threads to build insect traps called webs. The orb spider (right) first fixes threads in a box shape. Then it weaves more threads to the centre. The threads are covered in sticky droplets to catch insects.

Q What is a stick insect?

A Stick insects (right) have long, thin bodies with brown or green colouring, which makes them look just like the twigs or leaves they sit on. Their enemies, such as birds or lizards, often fail to see them. If they are attacked, stick insects fall to the ground and lie still, once again becoming difficult to see.

Q What is inside an insect?

A An insect's body (right) has many of the organs we have, such as a brain and a heart, but they work differently. Insects breathe through holes called spiracles in their hard outer covering. Their gut is a tube running from the mouth to the end of the abdomen. Their blood runs in an open system throughout the body. All the organs are bathed in blood.

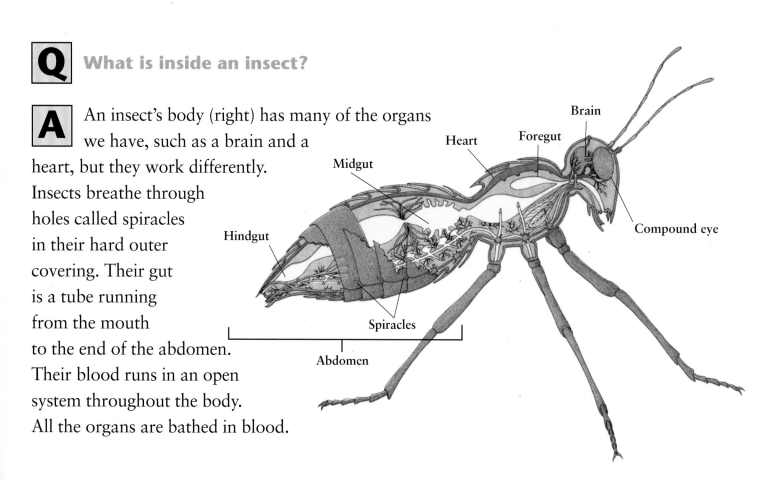

Heart

Midgut

Foregut

Brain

Hindgut

Compound eye

Spiracles

Abdomen

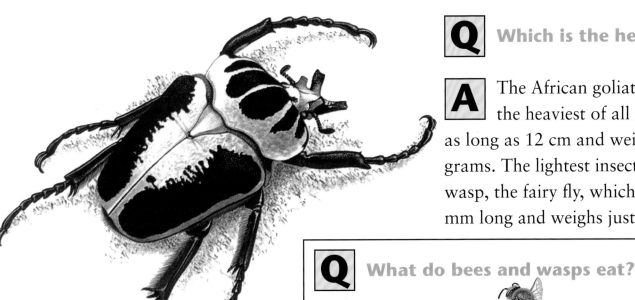

Q Which is the heaviest insect?

A The African goliath beetle (left) is the heaviest of all insects. It grows as long as 12 cm and weighs up to 110 grams. The lightest insect is the parasitic wasp, the fairy fly, which is less than 0.2 mm long and weighs just 0.006 grams.

Q What do bees and wasps eat?

A Bees eat pollen and nectar, which they collect from plants and store in their nests, then turn into honey. Wasps kill other insects as food for their young.

Bee

Wasp

Q How do grasshoppers 'sing'?

A Grasshoppers make sounds by rubbing small pegs on their hind legs against a hard vein on their forewings. Males 'sing' to attract a mate.

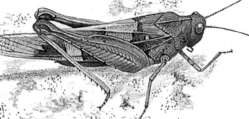

Q How does a butterfly begin its life?

A A butterfly begins life as an egg on a leaf. Out of the egg comes a tiny caterpillar (or larva) which eats the leaf and grows very fast. The caterpillar grows a hard covering and turns into a pupa (or chrysalis). After several days, or even weeks, the pupa case splits open and the butterfly crawls out. As soon as its wings have dried, it can fly away (right).

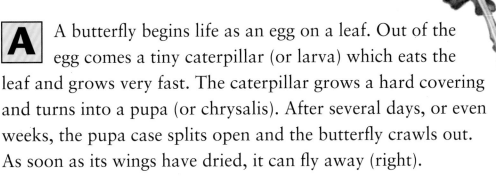

1. Eggs

2. Caterpillar (larva)

3. Pupa (chrysalis)

4. Adult butterflies

FISH

Fish live in water and use gills, rather than lungs, to breathe. They swim in all the world's oceans, freshwater lakes and rivers, apart from those that are too polluted to support life.

Most living fish have jaws, but the earliest fish did not. The first fish also probably had something called a notochord, made of cartilage, rather than a backbone. In all living fish apart from hagfish, the notochord that young fish possess develops into a backbone made of units called vertebrae.

▲ A salmon leaps up a waterfall to reach its spawning grounds.

KEY FACTS

Number of species: 32,000
Largest: whale shark, 16 m long
Smallest: stout infantfish, 8 mm long
Fastest: Atlantic and Indo-Pacific sailfish, 109 km/h

▼ Fish swim around a coral reef in the Red Sea. Some eat algae on the coral while others hunt smaller fish.

What makes a fish?

Fish gain their warmth from the environment around them (they are ectothermic, or cold-blooded). They have a streamlined shape for swimming swiftly and have several fins to help them change direction in the water. Most fish have skin that is covered with scales. Instead of breathing through internal lungs, they have gills on the side of the

head, which extract oxygen from the water.

Fish have good senses. Most have sensitive receptors that form a lateral line system along each side. This system detects the vibrations of other swimming animals.

Types of fish

There are at least 32,000 different kinds of fish, and they range in size from the whale shark, which is 16 metres long, to the stout infantfish, which grows to just 8 millimetres.

Most fish live in the layer of water just below the surface (called the photic zone) but some thrive at great depths and in total darkness. In 2008 scientists investigating the ocean floor near Japan found a shoal of snailfish 7,700 metres below the surface.

Some fish, including most of the sharks, are fearsome predators. The shortfin mako shark is capable of

BIOLUMINESCENCE

Many fish that live in deep, dark ocean waters make their own light. They are bioluminescent. They use the light as a lure to attract prey. The anglerfish (right), for example, has a rod that dangles from its head with a bioluminescent light at the end. The light attracts prey, which the anglerfish then swallows.

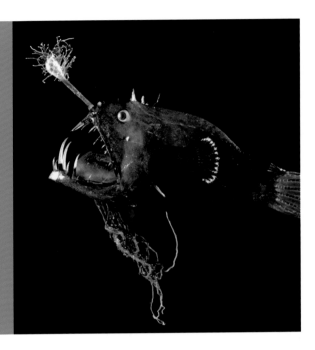

swimming at 50 kilometres an hour in pursuit of smaller fish, and the great white shark can kill prey as large as seals and dolphins.

Most fish lay, or spawn, eggs, from which small fish hatch. Female cod may produce 4 million eggs at once. However, the young develop inside the parent in some species; this is called viviparity.

Commercial fishing

Fish are an important source of food for people. Commercial fishing catches around 93 million tonnes of fish each year. The bulk of this is made up of herring, sardines, anchovies, cod, hake, haddock and tuna. In addition, 48 million tonnes are produced in fish farms.

GENERAL INFORMATION

- The oldest fossil fish was found in China, in rocks of the Cambrian period. The fossil is about 530 million years old.
- A shoal of fish is a loosely organised group, whereas a school is a tightly organised group whose movements are synchronised.

▲ **A whale shark feeds by sucking water and plankton food into its mouth.**

See also:

Prehistoric Life, Science of Life

FISH

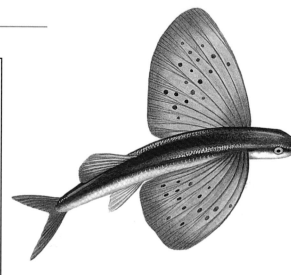

Q What are the main parts of a fish?

A The main parts on the outside of a fish are the gills (for breathing), the fins (for swimming and steering) and the lateral line (for detecting movement nearby).

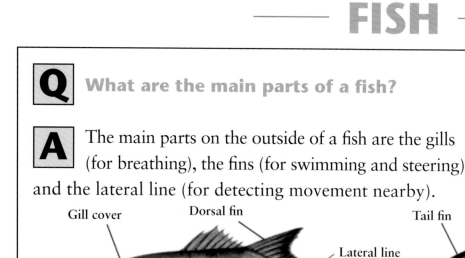

Gill cover

Dorsal fin

Tail fin

Lateral line

Pectoral fin

Ventral fin

Pelvic fin

Q Can fish fly?

A Flying fish (above) have large pectoral fins that act as wings. Their tails propel them out of the water to glide at speeds of 65 km/h.

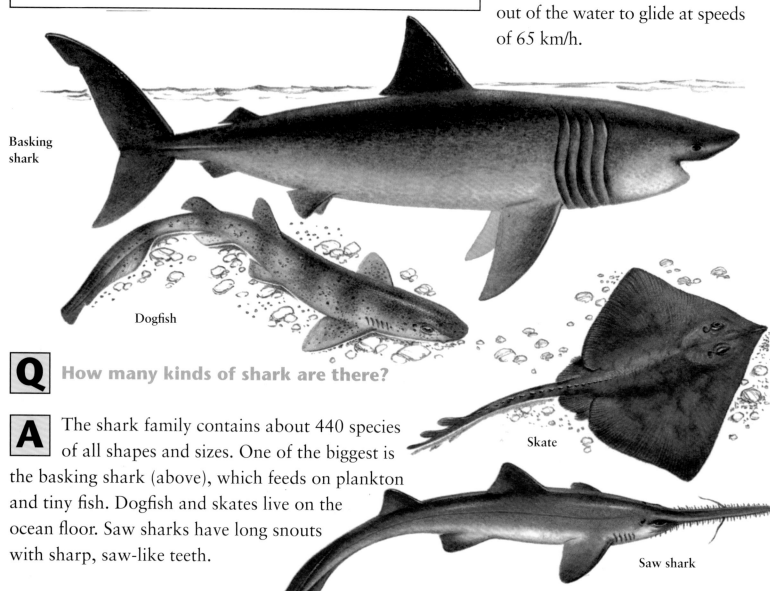

Basking shark

Dogfish

Skate

Saw shark

Q How many kinds of shark are there?

A The shark family contains about 440 species of all shapes and sizes. One of the biggest is the basking shark (above), which feeds on plankton and tiny fish. Dogfish and skates live on the ocean floor. Saw sharks have long snouts with sharp, saw-like teeth.

Q Which fish swims the fastest?

A Sailfish are the fastest swimmers, reaching speeds of up to 109 km/h. The fish's large dorsal fin can lie flat against its body when it is swimming at speed to help streamline it.

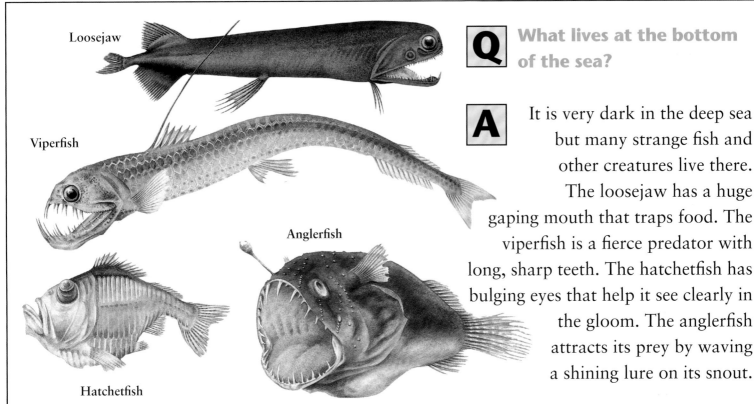

Loosejaw

Viperfish

Anglerfish

Hatchetfish

Q What lives at the bottom of the sea?

A It is very dark in the deep sea but many strange fish and other creatures live there. The loosejaw has a huge gaping mouth that traps food. The viperfish is a fierce predator with long, sharp teeth. The hatchetfish has bulging eyes that help it see clearly in the gloom. The anglerfish attracts its prey by waving a shining lure on its snout.

Q Do all fish lay eggs?

A No. Several species, such as the sailfin molly (below), keep their eggs inside until they hatch. Then they give birth to as many as 140 live young.

Q How do cod find their food?

A Some species of fish, such as the Atlantic cod (below), have a single whisker-like projection on their chins to help them feel for their food. This is called a barbel.

AMPHIBIANS AND REPTILES

Amphibians and reptiles are two groups of ectothermic ('cold-blooded') vertebrate animals. There are lots of similarities between the groups.

KEY FACTS

Number of amphibian species: 6,922 in 2012

Largest amphibian: Chinese giant salamander, up to 1.8 m long

Smallest amphibian: many frogs grow to only 1 cm long

Number of reptile species: 9,547 in 2012

Largest reptile: saltwater crocodile, up to 6.3 m long

Smallest reptile: dwarf gecko, just 1.6 cm long

▲ Tiger salamanders live mostly in burrows, only returning to water to breed.

▲ Jackson's chameleon is a reptile that lives in Africa. Only males have three horns on the head.

Frogs, toads and salamanders are all amphibians. Most have four limbs when they are adults (the exceptions are worm-like creatures called caecilians). Typically, amphibians spend part of their life in water and part on land. Most undergo a dramatic body change from aquatic larvae that breathe with gills to air-breathing adults. This is called metamorphosis.

Frogs and toads start life as eggs, which hatch into limbless tadpoles. Tadpoles grow limbs and lose their tail as they get bigger, eventually changing into froglets

TOADS IN THE DESERT

Amphibians live in all land environments apart from places that are cold throughout the year. Some survive in dry deserts, but they have to make use of any source of water very quickly. In the Mojave Desert in the United States red-spotted toads live under ground for months at a time. They live off water stored in their large bladder. When rain falls, the toads hear the raindrops on the ground above. They dig their way to the surface, drink from a puddle and look for a mate.

or toadlets. Not all amphibians undergo metamorphosis. One example is the Mexican axolotl.

Most amphibians can breathe through their skin as well as through lungs or (in larvae) gills. Some adult salamanders do not have lungs and breathe only through their skin.

Reptiles

Reptiles include crocodiles, snakes, lizards and turtles. They live in a broad range of environments, from deserts to tropical rainforests. Many live in rivers and lakes, and others live in the ocean. Some, like crocodiles, alligators and constrictor snakes, are fearsome predators, capable of tackling and killing large prey. Others, including many snakes, are not large but can subdue their prey with lethal injections of venom. However, most snakes are relatively harmless.

Most reptiles lay eggs, though these can survive out of water, unlike those of amphibians. Some reptiles give birth to live young. Unlike amphibians, reptiles do not have an aquatic larval stage.

▲ Galápagos tortoises live in the wild only on the Galápagos Islands, Ecuador. They can live to over 100 years and weigh 400 kilograms.

GENERAL INFORMATION

- Amphibians evolved from lobe-finned fish in the Devonian period about 360 million years ago.
- Reptiles evolved between 320 and 310 million years ago, in the Carboniferous period; their ancestors were reptile-like amphibians.
- Dinosaurs were a group of reptiles that became extinct 65 million years ago.

▲ The Indian cobra has a distinctive hood on its head and sometimes grows to more than 2 metres long. It paralyses its prey with powerful venom.

See also:

Birds, Dinosaurs, Prehistoric Life

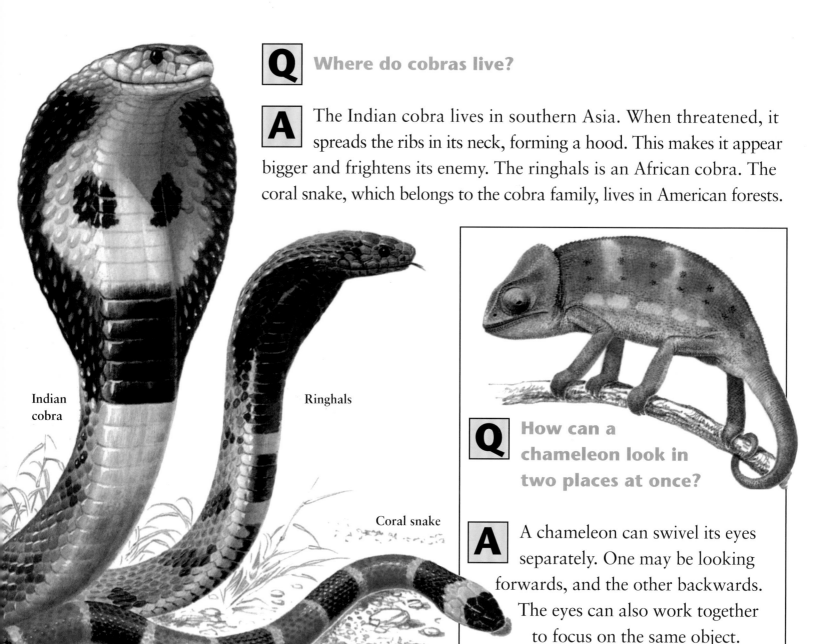

Q Where do cobras live?

A The Indian cobra lives in southern Asia. When threatened, it spreads the ribs in its neck, forming a hood. This makes it appear bigger and frightens its enemy. The ringhals is an African cobra. The coral snake, which belongs to the cobra family, lives in American forests.

Indian cobra

Ringhals

Coral snake

Q How can a chameleon look in two places at once?

A A chameleon can swivel its eyes separately. One may be looking forwards, and the other backwards. The eyes can also work together to focus on the same object.

Alligator

Crocodile

Q How can you tell the difference between an alligator and a crocodile?

A When a crocodile closes its mouth, the fourth tooth in the lower jaw sticks up outside the top jaw. When an alligator does the same thing, this tooth is hidden.

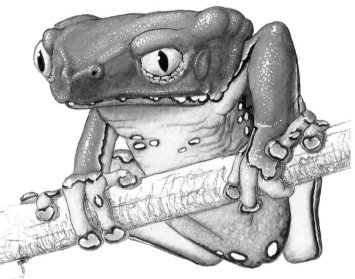

Q How do frogs climb trees?

A The tree frog (left) has round discs at the end of its toes. These act as suckers and help the frog to climb up smooth leaves. The toes are long and can curl around thin twigs. Some tree frogs have sticky webbing between their fingers and toes that enable them to hold on more easily. The frog's belly skin is loose and this also clings to the tree.

Q Why do reptiles flick out their tongues?

A This monitor lizard (right) is flicking out its tongue. Sometimes the tongue touches the ground, and sometimes it waves in the air. The tongue collects tiny chemical traces and takes them back to the mouth where nerve cells work out what the chemicals mean. By doing this, the monitor can pick up signals about food and dangers nearby. Many lizards and snakes use their tongues in the same way.

Q How do frogs jump?

A A frog hops and leaps in just the same way as it swims. It lifts its front legs off the ground and pushes off with its powerful back legs (left). The pressure forces open the large webbed feet, giving the frog a firm base from which to jump. It lands on its front legs and chest and then gathers in its back legs, ready for another leap.

BIRDS

Birds form a large group of vertebrate animals. They live on every continent, including Antarctica, and in every ocean. Most can fly, all have feathers and all lay eggs from which their young hatch.

Birds create their own body heat – they are endothermic (warm-blooded), unlike fish, amphibians and reptiles. Their front limbs have evolved into wings, although not all birds fly.

All birds have a covering of feathers; these are sometimes brightly coloured and used in courtship displays. Birds walk or run on their back limbs. Most birds grasp food with their bill, or beak.

The power of flight

Peregrine falcons are the fastest animals on Earth: they can fly at up to 325 kilometres per hour

▲ In the breeding season many birds moult into bright new plumage. This is a male mandarin duck.

when diving on their prey. And ostriches can run at 70 kilometres per hour. Many birds fly long distances at certain times of year to take advantage of changing food sources. This is called migration. For example, Arctic terns raise their young around the Arctic Ocean but fly south in autumn to spend the next few months in the Southern Ocean. The record distance flown by an Arctic tern is 81,600 kilometres in a single year. Some birds can hover, and hummingbirds can even fly backwards.

Penguins, ducks, gulls and auks are very good swimmers. Gannets plunge into the water from great heights in pursuit of fish, and other species can dive to great depths.

KEY FACTS

Number of species: about 10,000
Largest: ostrich, 2.75 m tall
Smallest: bee hummingbird, 5 cm long
Commonest: domesticated chicken (reared from wild red junglefowl), 24 billion (excluding birds in factory farms)

▼ Ruby-throated hummingbirds weigh just 3 grams. While hovering, their wings beat 55 times per second.

▲ Woodpeckers incubate their eggs and rear their young in a tree hole.

▶ Bald eagles are powerful birds of prey. They eat mostly fish.

Varied diets

Owls, falcons and eagles (birds of prey) eat other birds and mammals. Gannets and ospreys catch fish, and vultures feed on dead animals (carrion). Flycatchers and warblers eat mostly insects, while grouse, finches and buntings have a diet of seeds and shoots. Parrots are particularly fond of fruit, and hummingbirds collect nectar from flowers. Birds' bills are adapted for eating their favourite foods. So, birds of prey have hooked beaks that can tear flesh. Hummingbirds

have long beaks that can probe inside flowers. And finches have stubby bills for crushing seeds.

Eggs and chicks

After mating, adult females lay eggs, from which young birds (chicks) hatch. The number of

INTELLIGENCE

Crows and parrots are some of the most intelligent animals. They can make and use tools. For example, New Caledonian crows make stick probes of different shapes to pull insects from holes in trees. If a crow makes a probe that is particularly good, other crows nearby probably learn to copy that shape.

eggs laid at any one time (a clutch) ranges from one to at least 18. They may be laid on the ground, on a cliff ledge or in a specially constructed nest. The eggs are kept warm (incubated) by one or both parents while the young birds develop inside. Once they have hatched, the chicks are fed by one or both parents until they are able to fend for themselves. This may be before or after they are strong enough to fly.

GENERAL INFORMATION

● **The ancestor of birds was probably similar to *Archaeopteryx*, fossils of which are found in Jurassic rocks in Germany. It has many bird-like features, but scientists are unsure if it was a bird or a dinosaur.**

See also:

Prehistoric Life, Reptiles

BIRDS

Q Which birds sleep in the air?

A Swifts (Alpine swift, below) sleep, feed and even mate in the air. They are perfectly built for flying. Their long, swept-back wings help them fly fast and high in the sky, where they hunt for insects. But their legs and feet are weak. It is hard for swifts to hop or walk. Some swifts spend almost all their lives flying.

Q How do penguins keep their eggs warm?

A King penguins (right) live near the cold South Pole. The females each lay one egg on the ice in midwinter. The male penguin tucks the egg between his feet and his bulging stomach to keep it warm, until it hatches about two months later.

Q How can owls hunt in the dark?

A An owl (below) listens for the sounds of shrews or mice. It swivels its head until the sound is equally loud in both ears. The owl can then pinpoint exactly where the sound is coming from.

Q Why do parrots 'talk'?

A In the wild, parrots are sociable birds, and they call to each other with clicks, squeaks and screams. When they are kept in captivity, they sometimes seem to speak like humans. However, the parrots are not really speaking. They are just copying human voices.

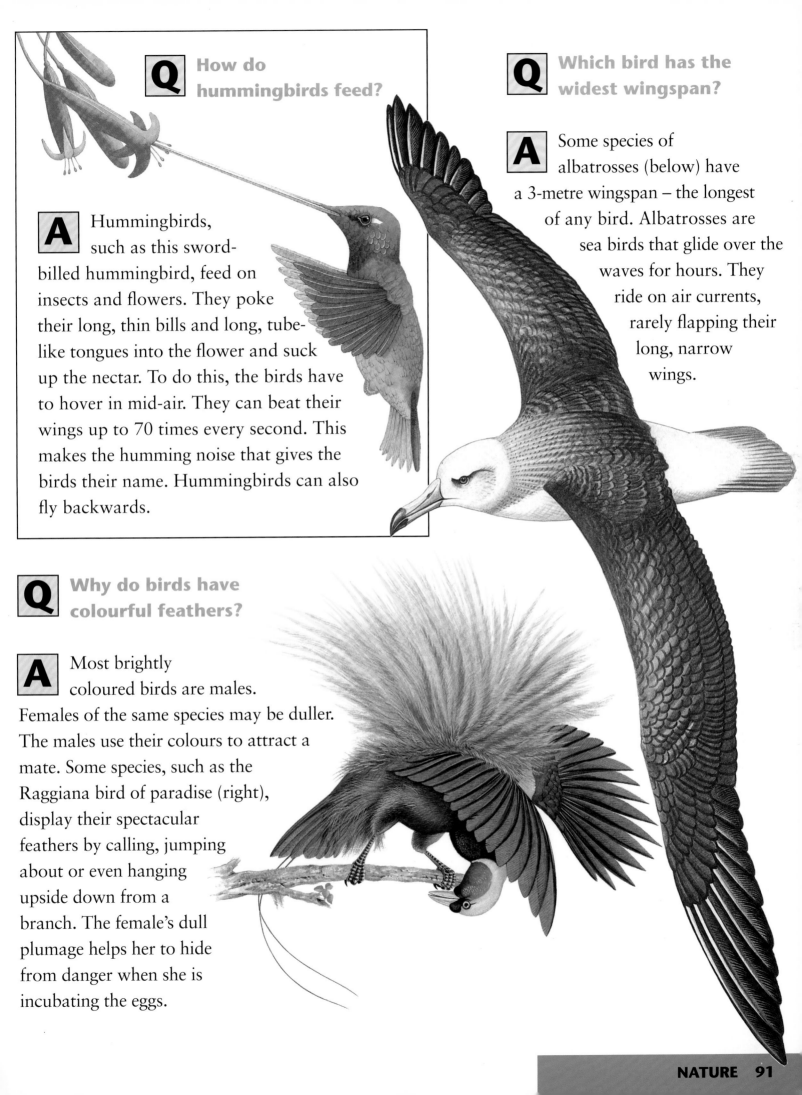

Q How do hummingbirds feed?

A Hummingbirds, such as this sword-billed hummingbird, feed on insects and flowers. They poke their long, thin bills and long, tube-like tongues into the flower and suck up the nectar. To do this, the birds have to hover in mid-air. They can beat their wings up to 70 times every second. This makes the humming noise that gives the birds their name. Hummingbirds can also fly backwards.

Q Which bird has the widest wingspan?

A Some species of albatrosses (below) have a 3-metre wingspan – the longest of any bird. Albatrosses are sea birds that glide over the waves for hours. They ride on air currents, rarely flapping their long, narrow wings.

Q Why do birds have colourful feathers?

A Most brightly coloured birds are males. Females of the same species may be duller. The males use their colours to attract a mate. Some species, such as the Raggiana bird of paradise (right), display their spectacular feathers by calling, jumping about or even hanging upside down from a branch. The female's dull plumage helps her to hide from danger when she is incubating the eggs.

KEY FACTS

Cetaceans: about 86 species live in seas and oceans
Largest: blue whale, 30 m long and 180 tonnes in weight
Deepest diver: sperm whale, 3,000 m
Seals and sea lions: 34 species

SEA MAMMALS

Dolphins, whales, seals and manatees spend their life in water. Seals come ashore to rest and breed, but dolphins and whales never come on to land.

The mammals that are most at home in the sea are dolphins and whales (collectively called cetaceans), manatees and seals. The shape of their bodies helps them move easily through water. Their front limbs have evolved into flippers to help them manoeuvre.

Cetaceans

Cetaceans do not have fur to keep them warm, but they do have a thick layer of blubber beneath their skin to protect them from the cold. Female dolphins and whales give birth to a single calf under water.

Unlike fish, cetaceans have lungs rather than gills so they must come to the surface to breathe air. However, they can go long periods between taking breaths. Some species dive deep in search of food. For example, a sperm whale may dive to 3,000 metres when pursuing squid.

Some cetaceans have teeth and feed on fish and other marine

▼ A humpback whale breaches, or leaps out of the water.

◀ Sea otters eat mostly marine invertebrates, though some populations also eat lots of fish.

OTHER SEA MAMMALS

Some other mammals spend long periods of time in sea water. The herbivorous manatees and dugongs spend their whole life in the tropical waters of the Caribbean, Indian and Pacific oceans. Sea otters live in the cold waters of the northern Pacific Ocean, where they eat shellfish. Polar bears are excellent swimmers and fearsome predators, hunting and eating seals. One was tracked as she swam 687 km of the Beaufort Sea in nine days.

animals. Others filter tiny animals called krill from sea water using baleen plates in their mouths.

'Talking' under water

Whales and dolphins have an excellent sense of hearing. They communicate information with groans, whistles and clicks. Since they can hear very low frequency sounds that have travelled through the water, they are able to keep in touch with other members of their species even when they are far away. They also listen for the echoes of sounds they make when they are searching for food. Even in total darkness they can tell whether an object is large or small and how far away it is; this is called echolocation.

Seals and sea lions

Seals and sea lions (called pinnipeds) are superb swimmers.

▲ Walruses are pinnipeds with distinctive large tusks. They live in the cold Arctic Ocean.

Their limbs are short, flat, wide flippers, ideally suited for swimming. Like cetaceans, seals breathe air at the surface but they can remain under water for up to two hours on hunting expeditions.

They eat fish, shellfish, squid and, in the Southern Ocean, penguins. Some are furry, and all have a layer of insulating blubber. The walrus is a very distinctive pinniped with two long tusks.

Female seals and sea lions give birth to a single calf on land. In some species, males and several females form a family group.

GENERAL INFORMATION

- Cetaceans are believed to have evolved from mammals that lived on land; they probably had the same ancestor as modern hippopotamuses.
- Scientists believe that pinnipeds evolved from a bear-like ancestor about 23 million years ago.

See also:

Environment, Land Mammals

SEA MAMMALS

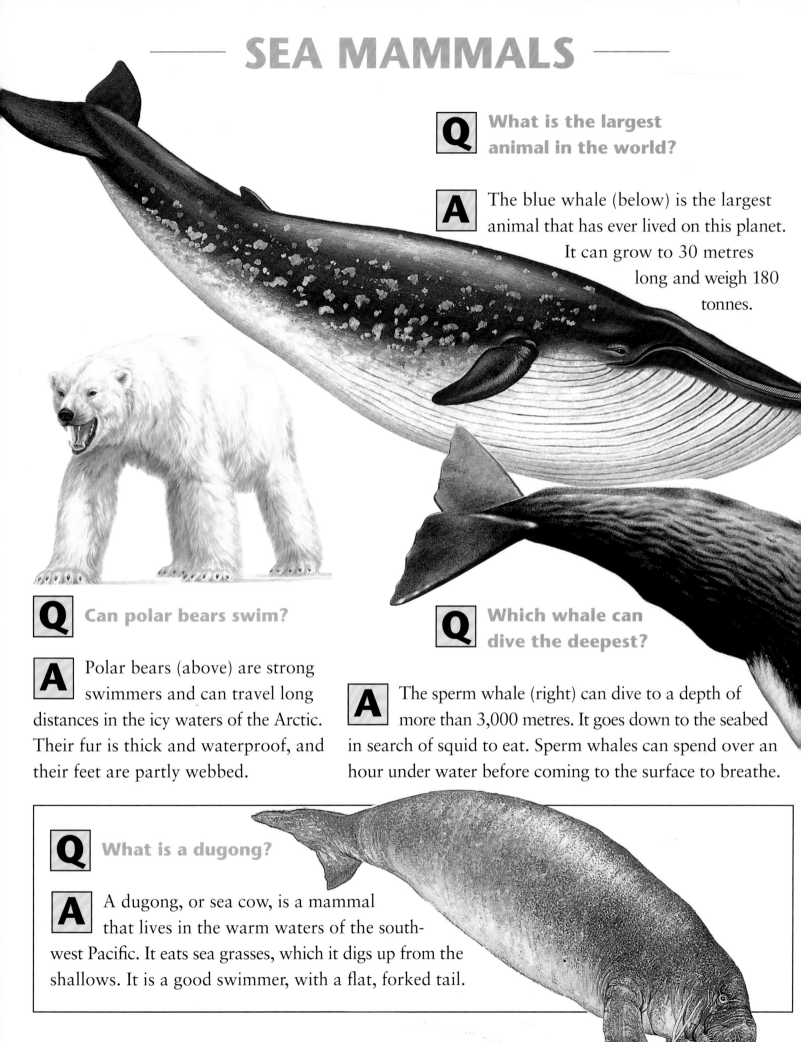

Q What is the largest animal in the world?

A The blue whale (below) is the largest animal that has ever lived on this planet. It can grow to 30 metres long and weigh 180 tonnes.

Q Can polar bears swim?

A Polar bears (above) are strong swimmers and can travel long distances in the icy waters of the Arctic. Their fur is thick and waterproof, and their feet are partly webbed.

Q Which whale can dive the deepest?

A The sperm whale (right) can dive to a depth of more than 3,000 metres. It goes down to the seabed in search of squid to eat. Sperm whales can spend over an hour under water before coming to the surface to breathe.

Q What is a dugong?

A A dugong, or sea cow, is a mammal that lives in the warm waters of the south-west Pacific. It eats sea grasses, which it digs up from the shallows. It is a good swimmer, with a flat, forked tail.

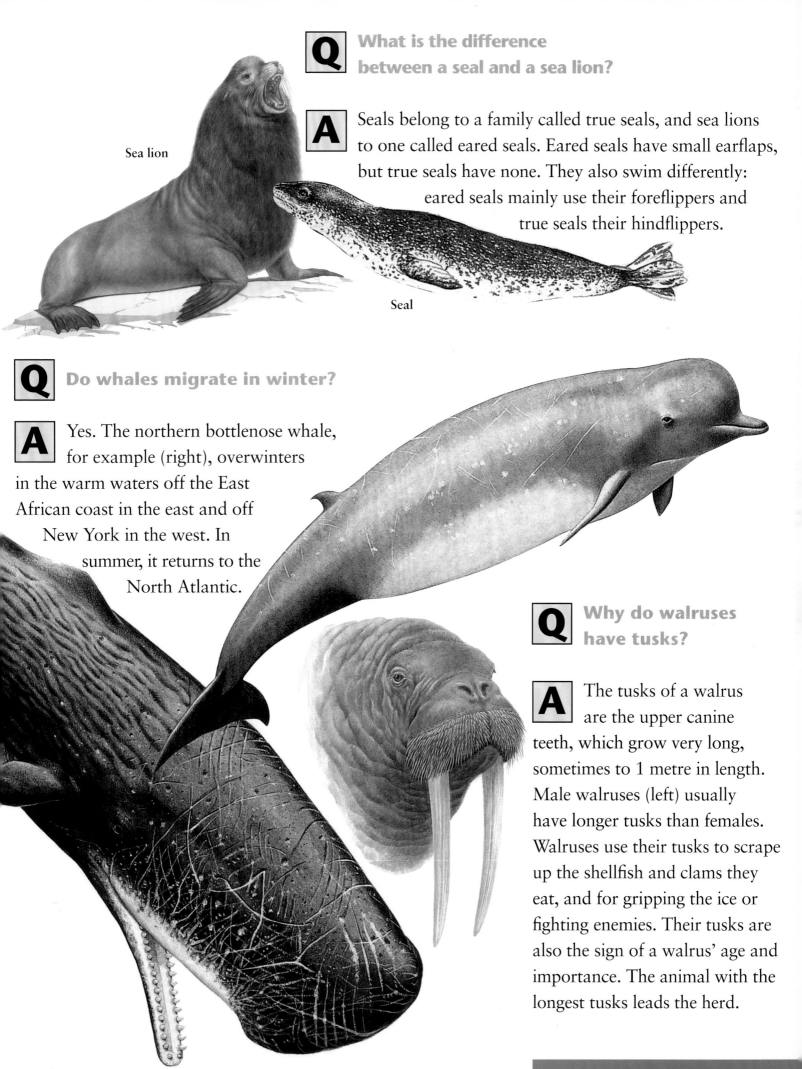

Q What is the difference between a seal and a sea lion?

A Seals belong to a family called true seals, and sea lions to one called eared seals. Eared seals have small earflaps, but true seals have none. They also swim differently: eared seals mainly use their foreflippers and true seals their hindflippers.

Sea lion

Seal

Q Do whales migrate in winter?

A Yes. The northern bottlenose whale, for example (right), overwinters in the warm waters off the East African coast in the east and off New York in the west. In summer, it returns to the North Atlantic.

Q Why do walruses have tusks?

A The tusks of a walrus are the upper canine teeth, which grow very long, sometimes to 1 metre in length. Male walruses (left) usually have longer tusks than females. Walruses use their tusks to scrape up the shellfish and clams they eat, and for gripping the ice or fighting enemies. Their tusks are also the sign of a walrus' age and importance. The animal with the longest tusks leads the herd.

LAND MAMMALS

Mammals are vertebrate animals. All breathe air, make their own body heat (they are warm-blooded, or endothermic) and the females produce milk in mammary glands to feed their young.

KEY FACTS

Number of species: about 5,488
Largest: African elephant, up to 7.3 m long and 12 tonnes in weight
Smallest: White-toothed shrew and bumblebee bat, 3–3.5 cm and 2 g
Fastest: cheetah, sprints at 100 km/h

▼ A young Thomson's gazelle suckles from its mother. This grazing species is very common on the dry grasslands of Kenya and Tanzania in Africa.

Mammals occupy almost every environment on Earth, from the equator to the shores of Antarctica. They live in waterless deserts, lush rainforests, baking-hot African grasslands and icy tundra.

Most animals live on or close to the ground. Some dig burrows in which they sleep and raise their young. Often these animals leave their burrows only at night. Others, including monkeys, squirrels, sloths and some rodents, spend much of their lives high in trees.

Some mammals can fly. The front limbs of bats have evolved over millions of years to form

▲ Microbats have large ears to pick up their echolocation calls.

wings. Those bats that hunt at night have another ability – echolocation. The animals make high-pitched calls that bounce off obstacles and flying insects, enabling them to find their way and hunt in near total darkness.

Food

The variety of food that mammals eat is as varied as the animals themselves. Many graze, browse leaves or pick fruit from trees. Others eat insects and other invertebrates. Some are carnivores, ambushing or pursuing other animals. And a small number of land mammals catch fish from the banks of rivers.

Raising the young

Most kinds of mammals develop for a long time in their mother's womb before they are born. The placenta is the link between the parent and the offspring during this period of gestation, or pregnancy. It ensures nutrients and oxygen travel to the growing embryo and waste products flow the other way. The young are born as miniature versions of the adult. Placental mammals include elephants, cats, bears and rabbits.

Mammals such as kangaroos are marsupials. The young develop inside the mother for a shorter time and are born much sooner. Then, they crawl to one of the mother's nipples to suckle on her milk. The gestation time of a kangaroo is only four or five weeks.

GIANT PANDAS

Giant pandas are very rare mammals that live in China. One reason they are so rare is that they eat only bamboo in the wild, and the bamboo forests are shrinking. Pandas have to eat huge amounts of bamboo – 9 to 14 kilograms a day – because it is not very nutritious. Also, a panda has the digestive system of a meat-eating mammal, so the food is not digested efficiently.

▶ Adult male African elephants are the largest of all the land mammals. Females have the longest gestation period of any mammal – 22 months.

GENERAL INFORMATION

- Land mammals first appeared about 220 million years ago, in the Triassic period, although mammal-like animals appeared long before this time.
- Apart from placental and marsupial mammals there is a third kind, the monotremes, which lay eggs. Echidnas and platypuses are monotremes.

See also:

Habitats, Sea Mammals

LAND MAMMALS

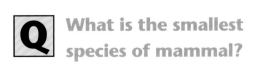

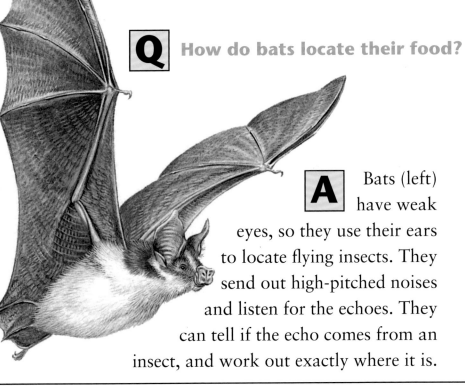

Q How do bats locate their food?

A Bats (left) have weak eyes, so they use their ears to locate flying insects. They send out high-pitched noises and listen for the echoes. They can tell if the echo comes from an insect, and work out exactly where it is.

Q What is the smallest species of mammal?

A The pygmy white-toothed shrew (above) and the bumblebee bat are the smallest mammals. They measure only 3.0–3.5 centimetres and weigh 2 grams. Pygmy white-toothed shrews eat grasshoppers – which may be almost as big as they are.

African elephant

Asian elephant

Q What is the difference between the African and Asian elephant?

A The African elephant is bigger than the Asian, and has larger ears. It also has two lips at the tip of its trunk instead of one.

Q Which is the fastest mammal?

A The cheetah (right) can sprint in short bursts at a speed of nearly 100 km/h, faster than any other land animal. It stalks its prey until it is very close, then breaks cover and runs in long, fast strides.

Q How does a camel survive in the desert?

A Camels (right) can go for weeks without drinking. They lose very little water from their sweat or urine. The camel's fur coat protects it from the heat of the Sun, and it can close its nostrils to keep out sand and dust. Wide feet help it to walk over soft sand without sinking. Despite popular belief, camels do not store water in their humps. The humps are used to store fat, which is used for food.

Q Why does a zebra have stripes?

A Some people believe that a zebra's stripes (above) act as a sort of camouflage, making individual animals hard to spot. But now scientists think there are other reasons for the stripes. They may dazzle lions and other cats that attack the zebra. Or they may help the members of a zebra herd recognise each other.

Q How can you tell a monkey from an ape?

A Monkeys and apes are both primates. Apes, such as the gorilla, have no tail. They have strong arms that are longer than their legs. Most monkeys, like the woolly monkey, have a tail with which they can hang from trees.

Gorilla

Woolly monkey

ECOLOGY

All plants and animals in an area influence each other and their environment, and their environment also influences them. Ecology is the study of these relationships.

Even the smallest area of Earth's surface has many different organisms living on it. All of them affect each other to a greater or lesser degree. Big animals eat small ones. Small animals compete among themselves for food. Even plants compete with each other for valuable light and water.

Food webs

Food webs are one important aspect of ecology. They show how each living thing gets its food.

▲ Road-building projects can block the feeding routes followed by some animals, such as deer. This can harm animal populations.

Plants are called producers. They use light energy from the Sun to produce food from carbon dioxide

KEY FACTS

Producers: plants
Primary consumers: caterpillars, ants, grouse, gazelles, horses
Secondary consumers: thrushes, mice, hedgehogs
Tertiary consumers: hawks, foxes

▼ Killer whales, or orcas, are tertiary consumers. They eat smaller predators such as sea lions. No other animal eats orcas.

and water. This process is called photosynthesis. Animals are called consumers because – unlike plants – they cannot produce their own food. They have to eat plants, other animals or both. Animals that eat only plants are herbivores; they are primary consumers. Animals that eat other animals are called carnivores. There are many more herbivores than carnivores.

AMERICAN BULLFROGS
Introducing an animal to a new place can have a serious affect on its ecology. American bullfrogs were taken to frog farms outside their native North America. They have big appetites. When they escaped they ate large numbers of endangered fish and amphibians in many parts of the world.

Different consumers

Carnivores that eat herbivores are called secondary consumers, and those that eat other carnivores are called tertiary consumers. A killer whale, or orca, is a tertiary consumer and it is at the top of a food chain that starts with tiny plankton in the ocean. Small fish eat plankton and then bigger fish eat the small fish. Seals eat the large fish and orcas eat the seals. Nothing eats orcas so they are at the top of a food chain. Many food chains link up to a form food web.

The environment

The environment is also important. For example, if pollution kills all the plankton in one area, there will be nothing for the small fish to eat. They will die from starvation and then the bigger fish will also starve, unless they can move to an area that has not been affected by the pollution. The effects of the pollution will be felt all the way to the top of the food chain.

Geology is another important environmental factor. Plants will grow only if the soil has the right chemical mix for them. The chemical make-up of soil depends on the underlying rocks (bedrock), so plants will grow only in areas with bedrock that suits them. Insects and other herbivores only eat certain plants – so geology affects the animal life of an area.

▲ Large birds called vultures are carrion eaters – they eat mostly animals that have already been killed and part-eaten by predators.

GENERAL INFORMATION

- Weather and human interference are two important additional elements in an area's ecology.
- Ecologists work out the impact of development on an area's plant and animal life. This is called an environmental impact assessment.

See also:

Environment, Habitats

ECOLOGY

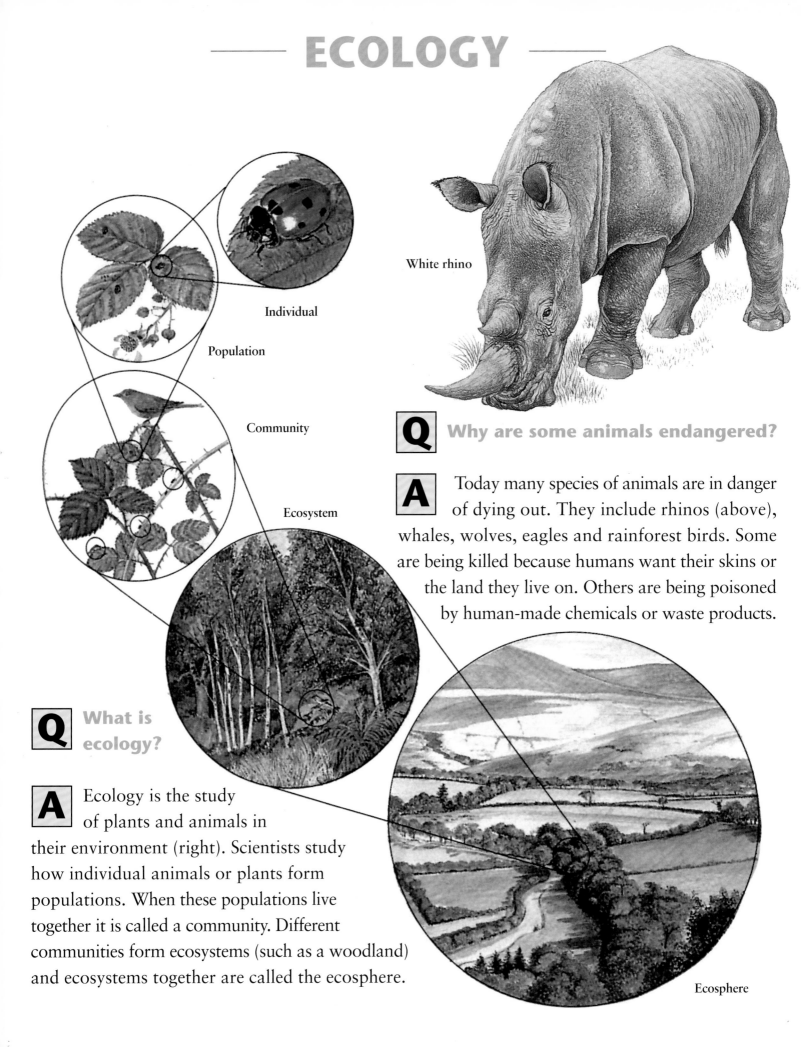

Individual

Population

Community

Ecosystem

White rhino

Q **Why are some animals endangered?**

A Today many species of animals are in danger of dying out. They include rhinos (above), whales, wolves, eagles and rainforest birds. Some are being killed because humans want their skins or the land they live on. Others are being poisoned by human-made chemicals or waste products.

Q **What is ecology?**

A Ecology is the study of plants and animals in their environment (right). Scientists study how individual animals or plants form populations. When these populations live together it is called a community. Different communities form ecosystems (such as a woodland) and ecosystems together are called the ecosphere.

Ecosphere

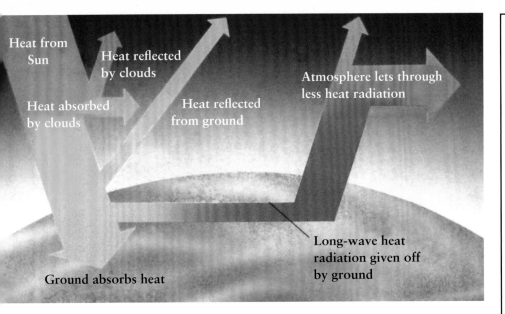

Heat from Sun

Heat reflected by clouds

Heat absorbed by clouds

Heat reflected from ground

Atmosphere lets through less heat radiation

Long-wave heat radiation given off by ground

Ground absorbs heat

Q What is the greenhouse effect?

A Heat comes to the Earth from the Sun. Most of it is then reflected back into space. But some gases trap the heat inside the Earth's atmosphere, which grows warmer like a greenhouse. This is what is known as the greenhouse effect (above).

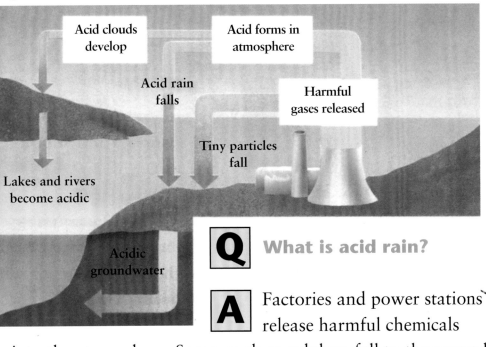

Acid clouds develop

Acid forms in atmosphere

Acid rain falls

Harmful gases released

Tiny particles fall

Lakes and rivers become acidic

Acidic groundwater

Q What is acid rain?

A Factories and power stations release harmful chemicals into the atmosphere. Some, such as sulphur, fall to the ground as tiny particles. The rest are dissolved by the moisture in the atmosphere. When it rains, these chemicals come down, too. This is called acid rain (above). It damages trees and other plants, and poisons the soil. Eventually acid rain drains into rivers and lakes, where it kills many fish.

Q Why are some insects called pests?

A Some insects harm people or crops. The Colorado beetle and the mint-leaf beetle damage food crops. The death-watch beetle destroys timber in buildings. The mosquito carries diseases.

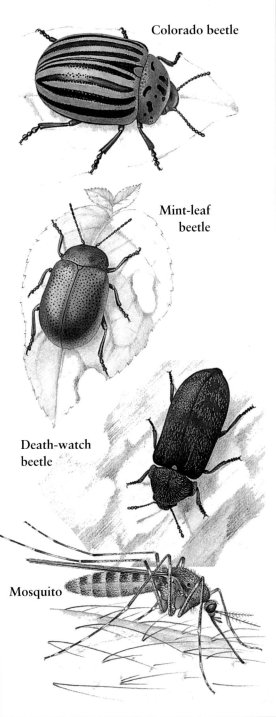

Colorado beetle

Mint-leaf beetle

Death-watch beetle

Mosquito

ANIMAL BEHAVIOUR

Animals' behaviour is adapted to suit their surroundings. A polar bear needs to hunt seals to live, for instance, so it would not thrive in a forest.

KEY FACTS

Largest territory: mountain lions in North America have home ranges as large as 2,000 km²

Loudest: baleen whales' low-frequency calls and songs travel many kilometres through ocean water

Longest pregnancy: African elephant, 660 days

Fastest aerial predator: peregrine, up to 325 km/h

A hummingbird would soon perish in the frozen wastes of Greenland, where there is no nectar for it to eat. How animals feed, find shelter, breed and communicate are life-and-death aspects of their behaviour. No two species behave in exactly the same way.

Feeding

Animals' bodies are adapted for life in certain environments. So is their behaviour. Body form (anatomy) and behaviour are closely linked. Animals' bodies are suited to digesting certain types of food. An animal that eats only one type of food – for example, bamboo for a giant panda – is called a specialist.

▲ Red deer stags (adult males) grapple with their antlers for the right to mate with a female.

If it is deprived of this food, it will starve. Likewise, plant-eating gazelles or giraffes will not become meat eaters if the grass and leaves disappear. They will simply starve. Similarly, meat-eating lions or wolves will die if they can no longer hunt animals. Since feeding takes up such a lot of wild animals' time, their food requirements dictate much of their behaviour.

The main types of hunting are grazing and browsing vegetation, feeding on carrion, and hunting live animals (from invertebrates to large mammals). Each requires different skills. A cheetah sprints after gazelles at great speed, hoping to outrun them. An osprey dives into a lake to catch a fish.

COMMUNICATION

Animals communicate to warn of danger, share information about food, scare away rivals or tell prospective partners that they want to mate. They do this by sound – from the roar of a lion to the quiet whistles of a small bird – or by visual signals. A chimpanzee's facial expression (left), for example, shows other members of its group if it is happy or anxious.

And a leopard drops from a tree onto squirrels below.

To avoid being eaten, many animals are active only at night (they are nocturnal), but there are also nocturnal predators, such as cats and owls.

The absence of food also affects animal behaviour. Some birds and mammals migrate (move long distances) in search of food at certain times of the year when their usual food becomes scarce. For some birds, these journeys may be thousands of kilometres.

Mating

Some animals are territorial. That means adults that are ready to breed (usually the males) defend areas large enough to provide

▶ **Male ruffs spread their bright head feathers to impress the females, or reeves.**

▲ **The giraffe's very long neck allows it to eat leaves that other mammals cannot reach.**

food for them, their partner or partners and their offspring. A lion will require, and defend, a much larger territory (or home range) than, say, a small bird. Birds sing

and frogs croak to proclaim their territories and indicate that they are looking for a partner. Many male mammals, and some birds and reptiles, fight over a territorial boundary or for the right to mate with a female. Male birds of many species moult into brighter feathers at the start

GENERAL INFORMATION

- Some animals live in dense colonies. This gives them an advantage. If a predator approaches a meerkat or gull colony, lookouts sound a warning. All members of the colony benefit.
- The males of some bird species perform elaborate courtship displays in the breeding season.

See also:

Birds, Land Mammals, Reptiles

ANIMAL BEHAVIOUR

Q How do musk ox
protect their young?

A When threatened by enemies,
such as wolves, a herd of musk ox
(right) form a line facing them, or form a circle
with the calves in the middle (below). Big males
may dash out and jab the attackers with their
huge, powerful,
curved horns.

Q Why do some animals
come out only at night?

A Animals that come out only at night
are called nocturnal. They may be
nocturnal in order to catch other nocturnal
animals or to avoid daytime
predators, or both.
Nocturnal animals
often have large
eyes and good
eyesight. They also
need a keen sense
of smell and
good hearing
to listen out
for danger.

Q How do chimps
show their moods?

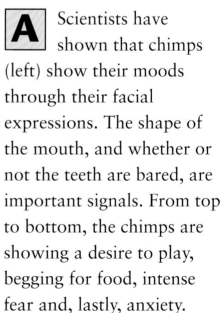

A Scientists have
shown that chimps
(left) show their moods
through their facial
expressions. The shape of
the mouth, and whether or
not the teeth are bared, are
important signals. From top
to bottom, the chimps are
showing a desire to play,
begging for food, intense
fear and, lastly, anxiety.

Q How does the honeyguide get its name?

A Honeyguides (below) live in Africa and India and are so called because they lead honey badgers and people to the nests of wild bees using a series of calls. After the nest has been raided for honey, the bird gets the chance to feed on bee grubs from the open nest.

Q How are young cuckoos reared?

A A female cuckoo (below) lays an egg in the nest of another bird and takes away one of the host's eggs to make room for it. The host bird has the task of feeding and rearing the young cuckoo. As it grows up, the young cuckoo tips the host bird's eggs and young from the nest. By the time it is ready to leave the nest, the young cuckoo may be several times the size of its long-suffering foster parent.

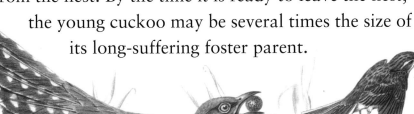

Q Why do animals defend their territory?

A Not all animals have territories but many do. If food is limited, the animal may defend a territory to guard its food supply. With other species, such as these cassowaries (right), the males fight over a territory in which to nest and rear their young. Territorial animals know exactly where the boundaries of their own territory lie.

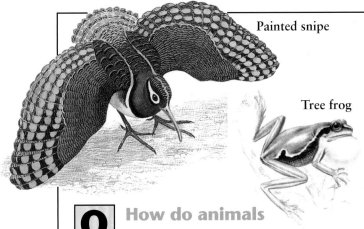

Painted snipe

Tree frog

Q How do animals communicate?

A Animals signal to each other mainly by using visual signals, such as shape or colour, and by sound. Birds such as the painted snipe have showy wings that they fan out to make an impression. Many birds sing to mark their territories or attract a mate. Most frogs produce a croaking song to mark their territories or attract a mate.

PETS

A pet is any domesticated or tamed animal that is kept as a companion and cared for affectionately. Cats and dogs are the most common pets.

KEY FACTS

Most common pets: cats and dogs
Oldest pet cat: Crème Puff, United States, lived to 38 years
Oldest pet dog: Bluey, Australia, lived to 29 years
Oldest pet rabbit: Hazel, United Kingdom, lived to 16 years

O ther very popular pets are birds, freshwater fish, rabbits and other small mammals, reptiles and horses. Some pets bond easily with their owners. Examples include dogs, cats, guinea pigs, rabbits, horses and birds. Others are kept as companions but do not easily bond – for example, fish.

▲ Lorikeets and parrots can learn to copy simple phrases.

The first pets

People first tamed animals to do work or provide food. Then they adopted some as pets. Dogs were one of the first animals

◀ Horses require space for exercise and stabling, but they make good companions.

to be domesticated. They were originally used to help hunt and herd animals, and to provide an alarm. The first-known example of dogs being kept by people was 14,000 years ago in Germany. The ancient Egyptians probably kept dogs for hunting and as pets as long as 5,000 years ago. Killing a greyhound was considered a very serious offence in ancient Egypt. Later, the Egyptians also captured wild cats, tamed them and kept them as pets.

In the 19th century the range of pets grew much bigger, including

▲ Cats need to be groomed (left) and dogs exercised (above) if they are to stay healthy.

bears and monkeys. People now understand that animals such as these cannot be cared for humanely in captivity. However, people care for many smaller exotic pets, including snakes and lizards, amphibians, rats and insects.

The pet trade caused problems when animals were taken from the wild, reducing their populations. It is now considered bad practice to take animals from the wild: pets should be bred from captive stock.

The pet industry

Pets need food, shelter and health care. A whole industry has grown up around pet care. Seed became available for birds in the 19th century, and the first dog food was sold in England in the 1860s. It is now possible to buy food for every imaginable type of pet. Bedding and toys are available, and veterinarians are trained to provide health care for sick animals. Pets even have microchips fitted so they can be identified if they get lost.

PETS AND HEALTH

People's health may be improved by having a pet and they may lead happier, more relaxed lives. Some doctors believe that keeping a pet may help reduce blood pressure and the chance of having a heart attack. Care homes for elderly people often have pet dogs and cats for this reason.

GENERAL INFORMATION

● In 2007 there were 82 million cats, 72 million dogs, 11 million birds, 7 million horses and millions of other pets in the United States alone.

● People in 14th-century China kept goldfish in bowls. Later, the English queen Elizabeth I (1533–1603) had a pet guinea pig.

See also:

Animal Behaviour, Farm Animals

Q Who were the first people to keep cats as pets?

A The first people to keep cats (right) were probably the ancient Egyptians, over 3,000 years ago. Cats caught the mice, rats and other vermin that raided the grain stores. The cats were well looked after and became pets. In the end, they were worshipped as part of the Egyptian religion. Anyone who killed a cat would be sentenced to death.

Q Why do some rabbits have lop ears?

A This brown and grey lop rabbit has very long, drooping ears. Lops have been specially bred over several centuries by mating does (female rabbits) and bucks (male rabbits) with long ears. Other rabbits (such as chinchillas) are bred to have long fur.

Q Which is the biggest scent hound in the world?

A The biggest of the scent hounds is the bloodhound (right). It has an extremely good sense of smell, more than a million times better than a human's, and is used to track criminals. Hounds are often bred with particular characteristics to help them hunt their prey. Otterhounds, for example, are excellent swimmers, and beagles are bred for stamina, enabling them to run long distances.

Otterhound

Beagle

Bloodhound

Q How quickly do mice breed?

A A female mouse is ready to have babies when she is seven weeks old. Three weeks after this, she could give birth to as many as 10 young. She may go on producing new litters of babies every 20 to 30 days. In one year, a single mouse could have more than 100 babies!

Shubunkin   Common goldfish

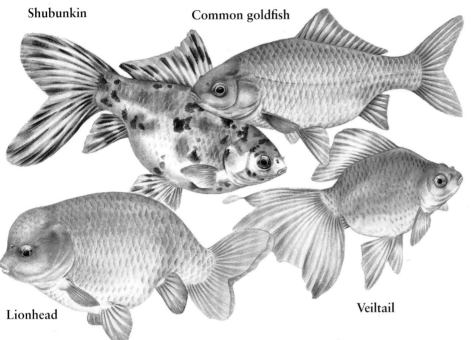

Lionhead   Veiltail

Q How did budgerigars get their name?

A Budgerigars (below) got their name from the Australian Aborigines. The Aborigines liked to catch and eat this wild bird so they called it 'betcherrygah', which means 'good cockatoo'. Budgerigars are popular as cage birds. They are brightly coloured and can be taught to mimic the human voice.

Q How many kinds of goldfish are there?

A Goldfish (above) are related to wild carp. The Chinese have bred carp in ponds for more than 2,000 years. They probably picked out the red- and gold-coloured fish and kept them as pets. There are now more than 150 different varieties of goldfish and its close relative, the koi carp. The shubunkin is covered with grey, gold, red or blue patches, with black markings. The common goldfish is very hardy and can live through very cold winters, even if the water ices over. Some goldfish have been bred to have special features. The lionhead has a swelling on top of its head. The veiltail has a long double tail that hangs down like a veil. Other varieties have bubbles on either side of the head, or scales that are almost invisible.

FARM ANIMALS

The domestication of animals probably began around the time people first started living in settled communities, about 11,000 years ago.

▼ Piglets feed from their mother. Pigs are reared for their meat.

Early farmers started to domesticate sheep, goats and pigs for their wool, milk and meat. Then cattle and chickens were reared for their meat, milk and eggs. Later, oxen and horses were harnessed and put to work to plough fields. More recently, other animals have been kept by farmers, including ostriches and llamas.

Pigs, goats and sheep

Pigs, descended from wild boars, may have been the first animals to be domesticated, 11,000 years ago. Pigs are easy to keep. They do not require large areas to graze and are not fussy eaters. Pork, sausage

▲ Some cows are bred especially for their milk. Others are reared for their meat.

meat, bacon, gammon and ham are all forms of pig's meat.

Domestic goats are descended from wild goats. They are kept for their milk – which tastes very different from cow's milk – meat, fur and skin.

Sheep are probably descended from wild mouflon. There are more than 200 breeds of sheep, and possibly 1,000. They are bred for their woollen fleeces, meat (lamb and mutton) and milk. Sheep need large areas of grass to graze.

Cattle and horses

Cattle are reared for their dairy products (milk, butter and cheese), meat (beef and veal), leather and dung (an important fuel source in parts of India and Africa). Cattle are also valuable draught animals –

they are able to pull heavy weights, especially ploughs.

Horses were harder to domesticate than some other animals. However, they became very versatile farm animals, able to pull ploughs, carry heavy loads and provide transport. The first domestication of horses was around 6,000 years ago and there are now more than 300 breeds. In some parts of the world, horses are no longer used as farm animals but are kept mostly for people to ride.

▲ Oxen are bulls or cows that have been trained to do farmwork. Here a water buffalo pulls a plough in a rice field, or paddy.

GENERAL INFORMATION

- In high-intensity factory farms, chickens are forced to grow quickly and are slaughtered for their meat when they are only six weeks' old.
- Free-range, or organic, chickens are allowed to grow at a natural rate. They also have space to wander around, more like their wild ancestors did.

CHICKENS

The most numerous farmyard animal is the chicken, whose ancestor, the red junglefowl, still lives wild in South and South-east Asia. Chickens are kept for their meat or for their eggs. There are more than 50 billion intensively farmed chickens, and the United States has the biggest population.

See also:

Animal Behaviour, Pets

FARM ANIMALS

Q What is the most popular cart-horse?

A The Percheron (left) is the most popular cart-horse breed in the world. It is named after Perche, the region of France where it was first developed and used. Standing more than 16.1 hands (1.6 m) high, this gentle giant can pull immense loads without much effort. It was originally used for pulling heavy loads but today is just as popular as a show horse.

Q How are beef and dairy cattle different?

A Dairy cattle, such as this Friesian (left) and dairy shorthorn (right), are lighter in build than beef cattle. The udders are big so they can hold large volumes of milk. Before a dairy cow can produce milk, she has to give birth to a calf. After the birth, she continues to produce milk for up to 10 months or so. Dairy cows are usually milked twice a day.

Duroc   Berkshire

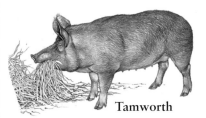

Tamworth

Saddleback

Q What meats do pigs provide?

A Pigs are reared for their meat, which is either eaten fresh as pork, or in cured form (dried, salted or smoked) as bacon and ham. Different pig breeds serve different needs. The Duroc, Berkshire and Saddleback are primarily pork breeds while the Tamworth is a bacon breed.

Q Why are there different cattle breeds?

A Different breeds of cattle are suited to different climates around the world. The most successful breed of beef cattle is the Hereford. It is ideal for cool climates. For hot climates, breeds such as the Kankrej are ideal. It is popular in India. The Santa Gertrudis also thrives in hot places and is widely farmed in Texas, USA.

Santa Gertrudis

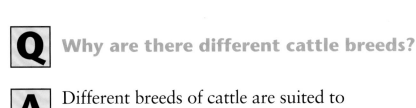

Kankrej

Hereford

Q Why do people raise chickens?

A People keep chickens (right) for three main reasons: for their meat, for their eggs and lastly for show. There are many different breeds. The Leghorn is the best egg-laying breed while the Barnvelder is kept for meat.

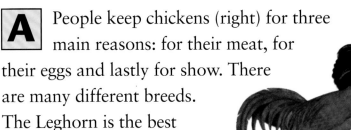

Leghorn   Barnvelder

Q How long have people kept goats?

A Goats (right) have been kept as herd animals for at least 9,000 years. They are bred for their meat, milk and skins. In some countries, goats are used to carry loads and to pull small carts. In many countries, goat numbers are very high and they damage wild plant life by overgrazing.

Q What is sheep wool used for?

A The quality of sheep wool varies from breed to breed and can be used for a range of purposes. The wool from the German blackface is fine and makes excellent cloth. That from the Corriedale is coarse and springy and is used for tweeds and carpets.

Corriedale

German blackface

KEY FACTS

Smallest flowering plant:
duckweeds in the genus *Wolffia* are only
1–2 mm across

Largest flowering plant: a quaking
aspen grove in Utah, USA, covers 43
hectares, has 47,000 trunks and is one
genetically identical organism

Tallest plant: a redwood in California
is 116 m tall

PLANT LIFE

Plants make up the kingdom Plantae, which
includes flowering plants, conifers, ferns, mosses
and green algae, but not seaweeds and fungi.
Animals could not survive without plants.

Most plants are called
vascular plants. They
live on land, have a
system of leaves, stems and roots,
and have cell walls made of a
substance called cellulose. Most get
their energy from photosynthesis.
That means their leaves use the
energy of sunlight to make food.

The root systems of most
vascular plants grow in the ground,
but some – epiphytes, for example
– grow on other plants. Other
vascular plants are parasites: they
get their nutrition from the
plants that they grow on.

Flowering plants

About 90 per cent of all plants are
called angiosperms, or flowering
plants. They include daisies, orchids
and broad-leaved trees. A flowering
plant usually has roots to anchor it
in the soil. These take up water and
nutrients. Above ground, a stem
carries these to the leaves. The
flowers are the reproductive parts
of the plant. They produce fruits
and seeds when they have been
fertilised.

◀ A bee feeds on a pitcher plant.
If the bee falls into the cup, or
pitcher, of digestive juices, the
plant will digest it.

Seeds

Flower

Leaf

Stem

Roots

▲ The parts of a flowering plant.

Non-vascular plants

Not all plants are vascular.
Bryophytes, including mosses
and liverworts, for example, can
only survive where moisture is
always available. Most remain
small throughout their lifetime.
Bryophytes do not produce flowers
or seeds but instead reproduce by
releasing spores.

Plants and animals

Almost every aspect of animal life depends on plants. Oxygen, which is vital for animals' respiration, is a waste product of plants' photosynthesis. And plants take up carbon dioxide, the build-up of which would be harmful to animals. Plant-eating animals (herbivores) need plants for their food, especially grasses, leaves and fruits. Meat-eating (carnivorous) animals also depend on plants since they eat the herbivores.

▲ A grove of aspen trees in North America. Since the root systems of all these trees are connected, this is actually one enormous tree, not many individual ones.

TOXIC PLANTS

Some plants contain toxins (chemicals) that hurt, or even kill, any animals that eat them. Western water hemlock (right) contains the toxin cicutoxin, which attacks animals' central nervous system, causing fits and, eventually, death.

GENERAL INFORMATION

- At least 300,000 species of plants are known, most of them seed plants and most of them gaining their energy from photosynthesis.
- The first land-living plants that practised photosynthesis probably evolved around 1,000 million years ago, in the Proterozoic period.

See also:

Animal Behaviour, Ecology

PLANT LIFE

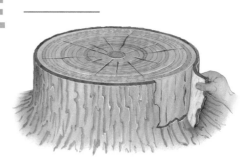

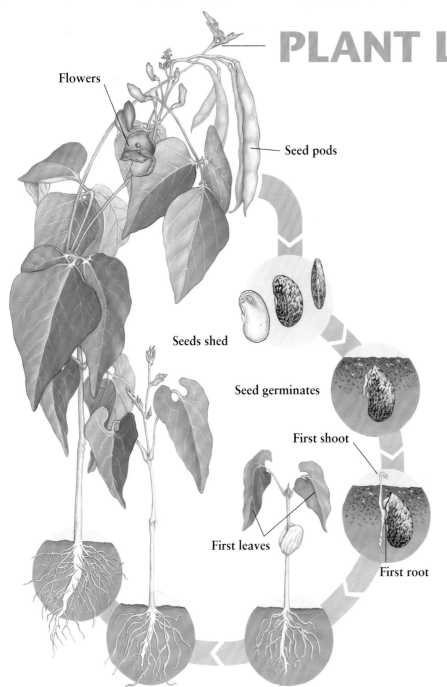

Flowers

Seed pods

Seeds shed

Seed germinates

First shoot

First leaves

First root

Q How does a plant complete its life cycle?

A Every year, plants (above) produce large numbers of seeds, which fall to the ground. Many die but some will germinate. Tiny roots and shoots grow from the seed and soon the plant increases in size. As the plant grows larger, more and more leaves are produced and eventually flowers appear. Pollen from male flowers fertilises female flowers and the base of the flower begins to swell. It is here that this year's seeds are being made, completing the plant's life cycle.

Q How can you tell a tree's age?

A Every year a tree grows a new layer of wood just beneath the bark. If a tree is cut down, the layers can be seen as rings in the cross-section through the stump (above). By counting the rings you can tell its age.

Q Why do plants need sunlight?

A Plants make their own food by combining a gas called carbon dioxide, which they get from the air, with water from the soil. This process is called photosynthesis (below). To power the process, the plant uses the energy of sunlight. A green pigment in the leaves called chlorophyll traps the Sun's energy.

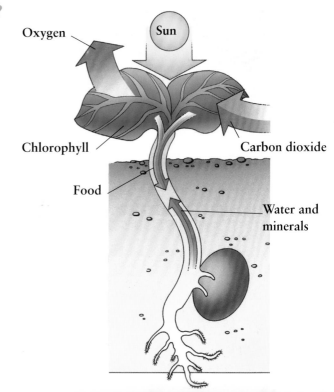

Oxygen

Sun

Chlorophyll

Carbon dioxide

Food

Water and minerals

Q Which plants eat animals?

A Venus fly traps and pitcher plants (right) can absorb nutrients from animals. Venus fly traps have leaves that trap insects and digest them. Pitcher plants have flask-shaped leaves in which water collects. Insects fall in, drown and decay.

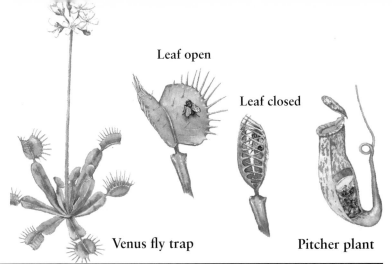

Leaf open

Leaf closed

Venus fly trap

Pitcher plant

Q What are fruit 'pips'?

A Fruit pips are the seeds of the plant that produced the fruit. There are many types of fruit and most are juicy and nutritious. Many animals eat them. The seed may be swallowed whole and passed out in the animal's droppings later on. In this way, the plant has its seeds scattered, or dispersed.

Q Why do plants produce flowers?

A Plants produce flowers (below) to reproduce and create a new generation. Flowers bear the male and female parts. Many flowers have colours and scents that attract insects. The insects take male pollen to the female parts of other flowers. The pollen of some flowers is carried by the wind.

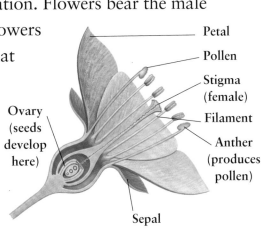

Petal

Pollen

Stigma (female)

Filament

Anther (produces pollen)

Ovary (seeds develop here)

Sepal

Q How do daffodils survive the winter?

A Daffodils have leaves and flowers above ground only for a few months each spring. During the winter they live as onion-like bulbs in the ground. The bulbs are full of food and are protected from winter frosts by the soil above them.

Bulb cross-section

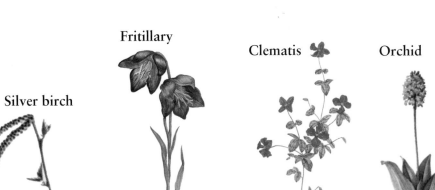

Fritillary

Clematis

Orchid

Silver birch

EARLY CIVILISATIONS

As the world became warmer following the end of the Ice Age, between 10,000 and 5000 B.C., farming communities grew up in several regions.

KEY DATES

Jericho: established by 9400 B.C.

Mesopotamian civilisations: from 4500 B.C.

Minoan civilisation, Crete: 3500–1200 B.C.

Egypt's Old Kingdom: from 2650 B.C.

Indus Valley civilisation, South Asia: 2600–1900 B.C.

Assyrian civilisation: 2000–612 B.C.

Shang Dynasty, China: 1766–1100 B.C.

▼ An artist's impression of a ziggurat being built. The first of these amazing towering structures was built in Mesopotamia about 2500 B.C.

Previously, hunter-gatherer communities had grown crops on land for short periods of time before moving on again. After 10,000 B.C. people began to build permanent settlements. One of the first was Jericho (now in the Palestinian West Bank). In 9400 B.C. it had around 1,000 residents, with strong walls surrounding it.

Mesopotamia

People began to domesticate dogs, sheep, goats, cattle and pigs. Farming communities spread to North Africa and to southern Europe. From about 4500 B.C., a civilisation developed in Mesopotamia (part of

▲ An example of Sumerian cuneiform script.

modern Iraq) between the Tigris and Euphrates rivers. The Sumerian people began to develop an organised society with cities, laws and a shared culture and religion. Sumerian writing (called cuneiform script) is the oldest known. Moist

NINEVEH

In 612 B.C. the city of Nineveh, situated on the Tigris River, was capital of the Assyrian Empire. Covering an area of 7 square kilometres and with a population of at least 120,000, it was probably the biggest city in the world. One Assyrian ruler, Sennacherib, built a magnificent palace. Strong walls surrounded the city, which had 15 gates.

wax tablets were marked with reed ends to form different shapes. These spelt out words. Thousands of these tablets still exist.

Building and trade

The Sumerians worshipped several gods and they built temples on top of layered platforms called ziggurats. These, and dwellings, were built with mud bricks. Mud was an easy raw material to acquire since plenty became available each time the Tigris or Euphrates flooded. Irrigation canals from the rivers ensured crops were kept watered throughout the year.

The Sumerians traded with people as far away as the Indus Valley (now part of Pakistan and India) and Anatolia (Turkey). The

▼ **The army of Sennacherib, an Assyrian king, attacks the rival city of Jerusalem in c.700 B.C.**

Sumerian city-states were often at war with each other.

Assyria

Between 2400 and 612 B.C., the Assyrian civilisation grew up in the Fertile Crescent, also centred on the floodplains of the Tigris and Euphrates. Year-round agriculture, the potter's wheel and

▲ **The excavated ruins of the massive stone walls that surrounded Jericho.**

the cartwheel originate from this time and region. Small cities grew up all across the area, including Uruk and Ur. The first code of law was developed as well as early mathematics and astronomy.

GENERAL INFORMATION

- The Indus Valley civilisation (2600–1900 B.C.) covered a large area of what is now Pakistan and India. It had cities with brick houses.
- The Minoan civilisation (3500–1200 B.C.) on the island of Crete was based around some grand palaces, including Knossos.

See also:

Ancient Egypt, Biblical Times

EARLY CIVILISATIONS

Q How can we find out about ancient cities?

A Archaeologists dig up the ruins of ancient cities (below). They divide the site where the city once stood into squares. Each square is given a number. The archaeologists remember the original position of anything they discover by noting the number of the square they find it in. In this way, they can build up a picture of what the city once looked like.

Q Why was Babylon important?

A Babylon (below) stood on the River Euphrates in Mesopotamia (now part of Iraq). At first it was one of a series of small cities. Then Babylon grew in power. By 1700 B.C., it controlled an empire, known as Babylonia, which covered the southern part of Mesopotamia. Much of the wealth Babylon gained from the empire was used for building. The Hanging Gardens were a series of irrigated gardens probably built high up on the terraces of ziggurats.

Q What was a ziggurat?

A A ziggurat was an artificial hill built in a series of layers, or platforms. At the top was a temple. To build a ziggurat (below), huge mounds of clay were strengthened with reeds and covered with bricks. Ziggurats were built in the cities of Mesopotamia from about 2500 B.C. to 500 B.C. and in ancient New World civilisations.

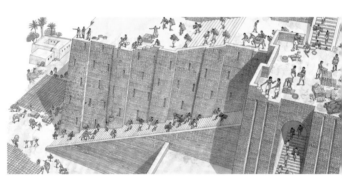

Q What was the Neolithic?

A This was a period in pre-history (a period where we have no written documents) during which agriculture became a way of life (above). People grew crops of wheat and barley and kept domestic cattle and sheep. Villages were scattered, and people rarely travelled more than a few days' walk from home. The Neolithic period lasted from about 9000 B.C. to 3000 B.C.

Q What were cylinder seals?

A These were cylinders, generally of stone, that were used to roll clay over such things as jars, or locks to storehouses, to seal them (right). The cylinders were generally carved with a design. This meant that a pattern was produced when the clay was rolled out. Writing was often carved on to cylinders so that it could be transferred to clay tablets.

Q Who was Solomon?

A Solomon was King of Israel from approximately 970 B.C. to 922 B.C. He was well known for his immense wealth and wisdom. He encouraged trade and Israel became rich. Solomon extended Israel's empire and started many building schemes, including the building of the first temple at Jerusalem (left), and a palace for himself and his queen.

ANCIENT EGYPT

The Nile Valley was settled as early as 6000 B.C. Later, the kingdoms of Upper and Lower Egypt were unified, with a new capital at Memphis.

KEY DATES

Upper and Lower Egypt as separate lands: c.5500–3100 B.C.

Early Dynastic Period: 3100–2650 B.C.

Old Kingdom: 2650–2150 B.C.

Middle Kingdom: 2040–1640 B.C.

New Kingdom: 1532–1070 B.C.

Conquered by Alexander the Great: 332 B.C.

King Narner was the first ruler of the unified kingdom in around 3000 B.C. Life in the fertile valley depended entirely on the Nile River, which flooded every autumn, laying rich silt (mud) over the surrounding plain. The nutrient-rich silt gave the valley the best farmland in the ancient world. Crops grew during the warm winters and were harvested in spring, providing food for the people and a surplus that could be stored away or traded.

Culture flourishes

Since vast deserts surrounded the Nile Valley, the Egyptians did not have aggressive neighbours nearby. And although Egypt was invaded several times, it also had long periods of

◀ Masons shape blocks of stone for a pyramid.

▲ A wall painting in the tomb of Sennedjem, a workman who lived during the reign of Ramesses II.

peace. This meant that all aspects of culture could thrive undisturbed. A form of writing with characters called hieroglyphs was developed around 3000 B.C., and literature – including poetry and storytelling – flourished. Music, dance and other leisure activities, including ball games, were very popular. Courts gave rulings on the rights and wrongs of disputes.

Most people lived in mud-brick houses, with wooden furniture and floors covered with reed mats.

▶ Cats were much admired and, after death, they were often mummified.

Men and women milled flour, baked and ate bread, vegetables, figs and dates, and – less often – fish and meat. People also worked in the fields or tended animals, especially cattle.

Craftsmen

Some people had other skills and were employed as craftsmen or writers (scribes). Craftsmen were valued more highly than farmers, and scribes were more important than craftsmen. In most respects, men and women were considered to be equals. Two

women even went on to become rulers (pharaohs). Life expectancy was about 35 years for men and a little less for women. Many children died at a young age from diseases.

The pyramids

The ancient Egyptians developed technology, working with glass, metals, stone and dyes. Architects and stonemasons were skilled and some of their constructions survive. The first pyramid was built at Saqqara in 2630 B.C. Later monuments included the great pyramids of Giza and the temples at Thebes. Sculptors carved images of the

gods they worshipped, their pharaohs and everyday scenes.

An army carrying bows and arrows, spears and shields defended Egypt. Later, horse-drawn chariots were also used.

GENERAL INFORMATION

- The pharaoh Ramesses II (1303–1213 B.C.) ruled over Egypt at its most powerful. He led an army against the Hittites in 1274 B.C.
- The Egyptian army was not strong enough to prevent Alexander the Great (356–323 B.C.) from conquering Egypt in 332 B.C.

See also:

Ancient Greece, Early Civilisations

THE PHARAOHS

For a period of over 3,000 years, Egypt had more than 170 rulers in at least 30 families, or dynasties. Rulers were called pharaohs and they were considered to be gods. From around 2630 B.C., dead pharaohs were mummified and buried inside huge pyramids. The most famous pharaoh, Tutankhamun (c.1341–1323 B.C.), ruled from the age of nine to his early death at 18. He was buried with a fantastic gold mask.

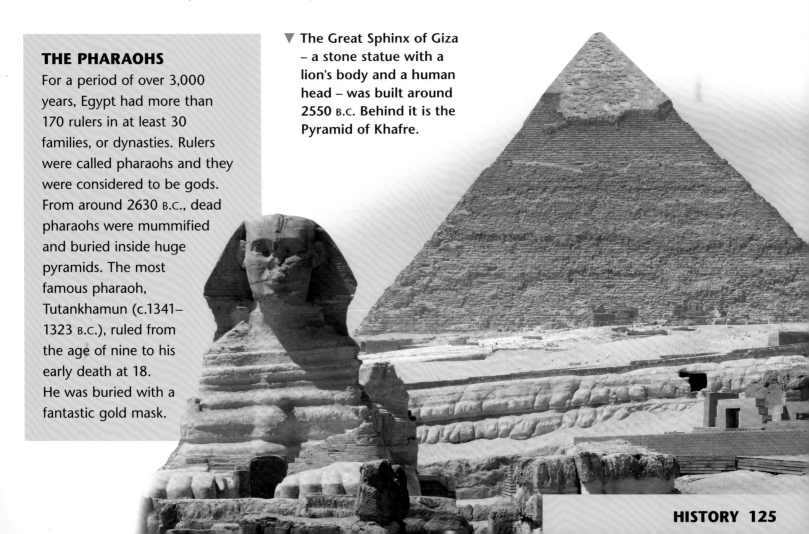

▼ The Great Sphinx of Giza – a stone statue with a lion's body and a human head – was built around 2550 B.C. Behind it is the Pyramid of Khafre.

ANCIENT EGYPT

Q How did the Egyptians use chariots in battle?

A The Egyptian army began to use chariots after 1500 B.C. The chariots were made from wood and leather, and were drawn by two horses. They carried two men. While a charioteer drove, a soldier behind would fire arrows at the enemy.

Q What was life like in the Egyptian army?

A The picture below shows the army of Ramesses II, ruler of Egypt from 1279 B.C. to 1213 B.C., in camp. The chariot horses are tethered, and one chariot is being repaired. A band of foot soldiers is being trained. The soldiers are carrying spears and axes with bronze heads, and bows made from two antelope horns tied together. Egyptian soldiers also fought with scimitars, which are curved swords.

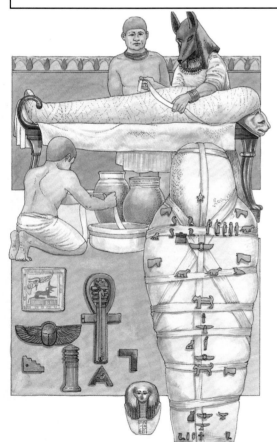

Q What is a mummy?

A The Egyptians believed that people's spirits lived on after death. Because the spirits were attached to the dead body, the body had to be preserved so that it could enjoy the afterlife (left). First, the brain was taken out through the nose, and the heart and other organs were cut out. The body was dried, stuffed with linen and spices, and treated with resin and perfumed oils. Then it was wrapped in long linen bandages. At this stage, it is known to us as a mummy. The chief embalmer wore the mask of Anubis, the jackal god who protected the dead. Small charms (amulets) were placed inside the layers of wrappings to protect the body. Finally, the mummies of important people were sealed in grand tombs.

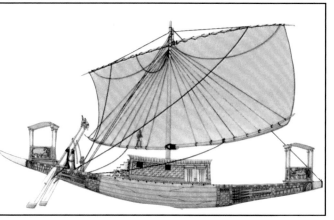

This boat carried cargoes up and down the River Nile. It had a huge sail, which was wider than it was tall. One man stood in the stern, directing the boat by moving the double steering oars. There were lookout posts at each end of the boat.

Q **What was life like in an Egyptian town?**

 Egyptian houses were made of dried mud and built close together (left). Wet mats were spread across the floors to cool the air. Most of the housework, such as cooking and washing, was done outside. People often kept goats and geese in their backyards, as well as pet animals such as dogs, cats and monkeys.

Q **How were the pyramids built?**

A Between 2630 B.C. and 1640 B.C., Egyptian kings were buried in tombs inside huge pyramids. Stonemasons quarried, shaped and smoothed blocks of stone. The blocks were then lashed to sledges. These were dragged over wooden rollers, which were kept damp to prevent friction. Mud-brick ramps were used to bring the stones up to where they were needed (below).

ANCIENT GREECE

The thinkers of ancient Greece laid the basis of Western science and culture. Greece was made up of several independent communities, or city-states.

KEY DATES

Archaic Period: 800–480 B.C.
Battle of Marathon: 490 B.C., Persian attack on Greece is defeated
Classical Period: 480–323 B.C.
Hellenistic Period: 323–146 B.C.
Roman invasion: 148–146 B.C.

▲ Ancient Greeks such as Hippocrates (460–377 B.C.) strongly believed in the benefits of washing.

In around 800 B.C. the Greeks began to form city-states, each of which governed itself. Some were very large. For example, Athens had a population of about 250,000. Others were much smaller. There were city-states as far away from Athens as Syracuse (Sicily) and Miletos (Turkey).

Some were ruled by one person with absolute power. Others were governed by groups of wealthy individuals. And there were some city-states in which ordinary men took part in making political decisions, but women and slaves were excluded from debates.

▲ The Greek mathematician Pythagoras (c.570–495 B.C.) explains his ideas to students.

Ancient Greece laid the foundations of modern philosophy and science. Socrates, Aristotle and Plato wrote about questions of morality, natural history and the purpose of life. Poetry, plays and other literature flowered in ancient Greece. The most famous playwrights were Aristophanes, Sophocles and Euripides.

The Greeks believed in many gods, who supposedly lived on Mount Olympus, in northern

Greece, and performed ceremonies and sacrifices in their honour. They dedicated an athletic competition, the Olympic Games, to Zeus (the king of the gods) every four years.

Athens and Sparta

A Greek's first loyalty was to his or her city, and wars between city-states were frequent. From about 500 B.C., the two most influential Greek city-states were Athens and Sparta. Athens was the centre for literature and philosophical thought. There, public life was based around the agora, or marketplace, where most political debates took place. Athens was an important military power with a very strong navy.

However, Sparta, to the south, had the strongest army. Boys joined military school at the age of six and did not return to their families until they were 30. Fearing that Athens was becoming too powerful, Sparta attacked it in 431 B.C. After the Spartans cut off supplies of food to their enemy, the Athenians were forced to accept defeat in 404 B.C. Sparta became the strongest Greek state for a while, but Macedon, further north – under Alexander the Great (356–323 B.C.) – unified the rest of Greece and made it stronger. Sparta eventually lost its independence in 146 B.C. when the Romans invaded.

ALEXANDER THE GREAT

The last great Greek leader was Alexander the Great (356–323 B.C.). He conquered lands as far from Greece as India. At that time Greek culture dominated large parts of Europe, Asia and North Africa. It continued to be important even after political control of Athens and Sparta passed to the expanding Roman Empire in 146 B.C. The last of the Greek states to fall to Rome was Egypt in 30 B.C.

▲ The ruins of the Temple of Apollo at Delphi, which date from the 4th century B.C.

GENERAL INFORMATION

● One of the biggest events in ancient Greek history was the Battle of Marathon in 490 B.C. A massive Persian attack on Greece was defeated by a much smaller – but better equipped – force of Greeks from the cities of Athens and Plataea.

See also:

Ancient Rome, Early Civilisations

▼ The Parthenon in Athens was built as a temple dedicated to the goddess Athena.

ANCIENT GREECE

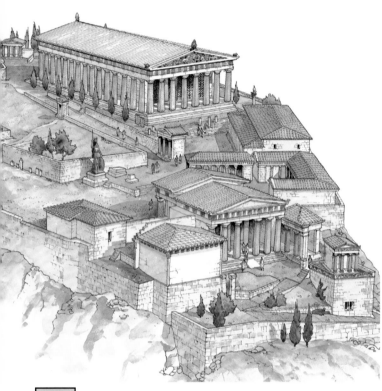

Q What was the Parthenon?

A The Parthenon (above) was a temple in Athens which honoured the Greek goddess Athena. It was built between 447 B.C. and 432 B.C. on a hill called the Acropolis, above the city. The temple had 46 pillars and was made of white marble. Its ruins still stand today.

Q What did a Greek soldier wear in battle?

A A Greek foot soldier (right) was called a hoplite. He wore a linen shirt with metal armour plates on the shoulders. A bronze breastplate covered his chest and stomach, and greaves (shin guards) covered his legs. He wore a bronze helmet with a tall crest on his head. The hoplite carried a shield and a spear. Round his waist was a belt with a short sword. Hoplites fought in close formation.

Q What was a trireme?

A A trireme was a Greek warship (right). It was powered by 170 oarsmen who sat on three levels. Each level had oars of different lengths. The trireme sank enemy ships with a long ram built into its bow.

Q Why was the marketplace important?

A Each city in Ancient Greece had its own government. In the 5th century B.C., Athens was the most powerful of these cities and controlled an empire. Its empire brought Athens trade

and prosperity, and the marketplace became an important part of city life. It was the city's public business area. Here, people would buy the food they needed. It was here, too, that politics might be discussed. Athens was the first ever democracy. This meant that each citizen could participate in how the city was governed. However, only free men who had been born in Athens were counted as citizens.

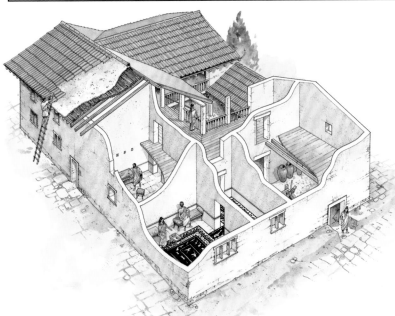

Q How was Greek pottery made?

A One person would shape the pot by hand (below), while another would paint it. The pots, which were made of clay, were decorated with scenes from daily life, or might show the deeds of gods, goddesses and heroes.

Q What were Greek houses like?

A In the 5th century B.C., wealthy Greeks had grand houses made of clay bricks, with stone or tile floors (above). There were separate rooms for eating, cooking, washing and sleeping, built around an open courtyard. The poorer people lived in houses with only one or two rooms.

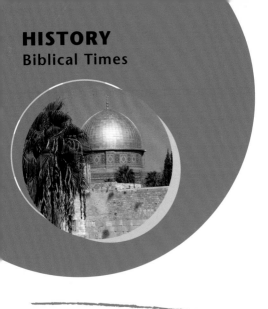

BIBLICAL TIMES

The Holy Land is the area between the Jordan River, the Mediterranean Sea and the Red Sea. It was the birthplace of Judaism in around 1800 B.C. and was regularly fought over by warring empires.

KEY FACTS

922 B.C: kingdoms of Israel and Judah founded

586 B.C: Babylonian Captivity

332 B.C: Alexander the Great invades

63 B.C: taken into Roman Empire

4 B.C: King Herod dies

c. A.D. 32: crucifixion of Jesus Christ

A.D. 70: First Jewish Revolt crushed

▼ **The Church of the Holy Sepulchre, Jerusalem, was built on the probable site of the crucifixion of Jesus.**

In the 8th century B.C., the lands between the Jordan River and the Mediterranean Sea were divided between Israel in the north and Judah in the south. This was the region where Judaism, the first religion to worship a single god (monotheism), had been practised since around 2000 B.C. Samaria was the capital of Israel and Jerusalem was the capital of Judah.

Babylonian Captivity

After an invasion by the Assyrians in 722 B.C., many Jews were forced out of their homeland. And in 586 B.C., Babylonians invaded Judah,

taking many Jews to work in Mesopotamia (the land between the Tigris and Euphrates rivers, now Iraq). This event was called the Babylonian Captivity and it is referred to in the Old Testament of the Bible. More than two centuries later, in 332 B.C., the Greek general

JERUSALEM

A city has existed on the site of Jerusalem for 5,000 years. It became capital of Judah and the spiritual home of the Jewish religion. It remained the capital after the Romans appointed Herod as king of what they called Judea in 37 B.C. Under Herod's rule the city prospered, and many lavish buildings were begun. At that time Jerusalem's population rose to more than 120,000.

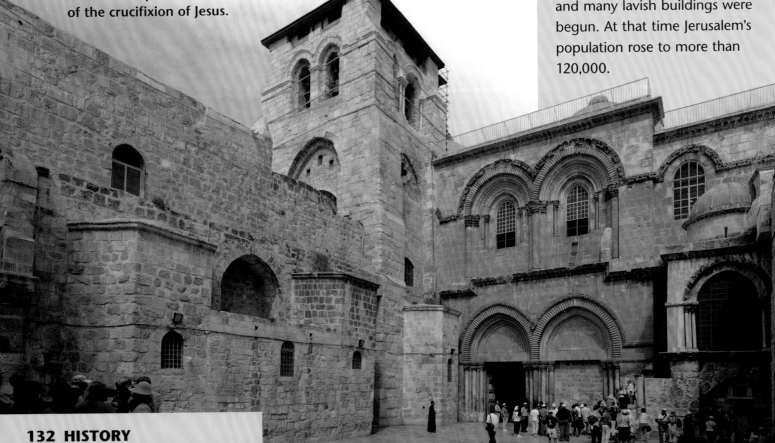

▲ The Dead Sea Scrolls contain ancient religious texts, including sections of the Old Testament.

Alexander the Great conquered the Holy Land as part of his assault on the Persian Empire. The Jewish people were encouraged to embrace Greek culture.

Rule by Rome

Antiochos IV, who ruled the Holy Land in the 2nd century B.C., banned the Jewish religion and tried to force the Jews to worship the Greek gods. Judas Maccabeus led an uprising against his policies in 167 B.C. and managed to win back the Temple in Jerusalem. A few years later an independent Jewish state was set up.

However, in 63 B.C., the Roman general Pompey declared Rome's authority over the region. In 37 B.C.

▶ Roman soldiers patrolled Jerusalem in the 1st century A.D.

▲ The Masada ruins, where Jews were besieged by Roman troops.

King Herod was made ruler of the area called Judea. Herod died just before Jesus was born.

From A.D. 44 Rome ruled Judea directly. There were several uprisings against Roman rule. After the First Jewish Revolt, in A.D. 70, the Roman emperor Titus ordered the destruction of the Temple at Jerusalem. Many Jews were killed or forced into exile. Others committed mass suicide at the clifftop fortress of Masada in A.D. 73.

GENERAL INFORMATION

- In the period of Roman rule, real power in Jerusalem lay in the hands of the governor appointed by the Romans. Pontius Pilate held the position when Jesus Christ was crucified around A.D. 32.

See also:

Ancient Greece, Ancient Rome

BIBLICAL TIMES

 Q Where was Canaan?

 A Canaan was the land we now know as Israel. In about 1250 B.C., the Israelites, led by Joshua, invaded Canaan. The Canaanites were better armed and fought from horses and chariots (above), but the Israelites were able to defeat many Canaanite cities.

Q How did Greek culture spread?

A Alexander the Great was king of Greece from 336 B.C. to 323 B.C. He conquered many lands (below), including the Bible lands of Syria and Egypt. The Hebrews who lived there began to translate their holy scriptures into Greek.

Q Who were the Assyrians?

 A These were a people who built up a powerful empire from their homeland in Mesopotamia (now part of Iraq). They were enemies of the Hebrews from about 860 B.C. to 612 B.C. The Assyrians were skilled in many areas of warfare. They used machines such as those shown above to capture fortified cities. The machines protected the soldiers while they knocked down the walls with battering rams. Other soldiers distracted the defenders by scaling the walls with long ladders.

Q Who was Herod the Great?

A Herod was king of Judea (a part of Israel) from about 37 B.C to 4 B.C. He had a number of palaces built for himself. The largest of these was the Upper Palace in Jerusalem (left), from which Herod governed.

Q Why was the Sea of Galilee important?

A The Sea of Galilee (in Israel) was rich in fish. Fishermen sailed in boats about 6 metres long. The fish were sold throughout the Roman Empire, bringing wealth to the region.

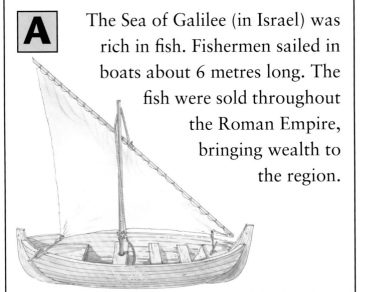

Q Why were carpenters important in biblical times?

A Wood was the main material for making tools such as ploughs and yokes (above). Furniture was also made from wood. Jesus and his father, Joseph, are described as carpenters in the Bible.

Q What did Jerusalem look like in Old Testament times?

A Jerusalem (left) was founded some time before 2000 B.C. King David made it the Israelite capital in about 1000 B.C. Jerusalem was surrounded by strong walls and contained fine palaces, but it remained comparatively small with narrow alleyways and poor housing. King David's son, Solomon, later built a temple and palace in the city.

ANCIENT ROME

The ancient city of Rome was the heart of one of the longest-lasting empires in history. At its height, the Roman Empire extended from Asia to Spain.

KEY DATES

753 B.C.: city of Rome founded

509 B.C.: Roman Republic established

44 B.C.: Julius Caesar declares himself dictator – the end of the republic

A.D. 96–180: empire at its strongest

A.D. 395: empire splits into West and East

A.D. 476: Western Empire falls

A.D. 1453: Eastern, or Byzantine, Empire finally falls

▼ For Romans, feasting was an opportunity to catch up on the latest gossip.

▲ At its height, the Roman Empire stretched as far as north-west Europe. This mosaic of the snake goddess Medusa is in a Roman villa in England.

According to legend, the city of Rome was founded in 753 B.C. by Romulus, who became its first king. The last king was overthrown in 509 B.C., when a republic was declared. The republic was ruled by popular assemblies of male citizens, the Senate (made up of wealthy nobles) and two chief magistrates, called consuls.

The republic had an efficient and well-trained army, which by the end of the 3rd century B.C. had conquered much of Italy, although it did suffer some defeats, notably to Hannibal's Carthaginians at the Battle of Cannae in 216 B.C. Roman army generals enjoyed great political and military power and one, Julius Caesar, declared himself dictator for life in February 44 B.C. This marked the end of the republic. However, Caesar was assassinated on 15 March 44 B.C. Then a struggle for power developed between his son Octavian and Mark Antony. Octavian became the first emperor of Rome in 27 B.C., taking the name Augustus.

The empire grows

Over the next few hundred years the power of Rome continued to grow. In creating their empire, the Romans were often ruthless. They destroyed entire cities and enslaved whole populations. However, they also brought peace, an advanced culture and the rule of law. In A.D. 212 the many different peoples in the empire were united by and system of money. Aqueducts carried water to the cities. Wealthy citizens built luxurious homes with central heating, while slaves worked their households and farms. Poorer people lived crowded together in apartment houses.

Decline and fall

In the 3rd century, Germanic peoples attacked Roman provinces in the north of the empire. In A.D. 330 the emperor Constantine moved his capital to the old Greek city of Byzantium (modern Istanbul), which was renamed Constantinople. Then in A.D. 395 the Roman Empire was divided:

the Western Empire had its capital in Rome, and the Eastern Empire became known as the Byzantine Empire. German tribes attacked the Western Empire and in A.D. 476 Rome's last emperor, Romulus Augustulus, gave up the throne.

▲ Street trading was an important part of life in Roman cities.

common citizenship. By this time the empire's road system had been finished, allowing free trade and travel over long distances. The umbrella of the empire offered a high level of public services and a standard code of law, government

▼ The Colosseum arena in Rome was a triumph of Roman design and building technique.

GENERAL INFORMATION

- At the end of the 5th century A.D., the Roman Empire covered an area of about 5.8 million km² and had a population of some 166 million.
- At this time, life expectancy averaged 38 years: 41 years for women and 35 years for men.

See also:

Ancient Greece, Biblical Times

CHRISTIANITY

As the Roman Empire grew, the old gods of Greece and early Rome no longer seemed relevant. People began to worship the emperors and to become interested in religions from the eastern part of the empire. Christianity began in the Roman province of Palestine. Early Christians were unpopular with the authorities and were persecuted. However, their religion spread throughout the empire and was eventually made legal in A.D. 313 by the emperor Constantine.

ANCIENT ROME

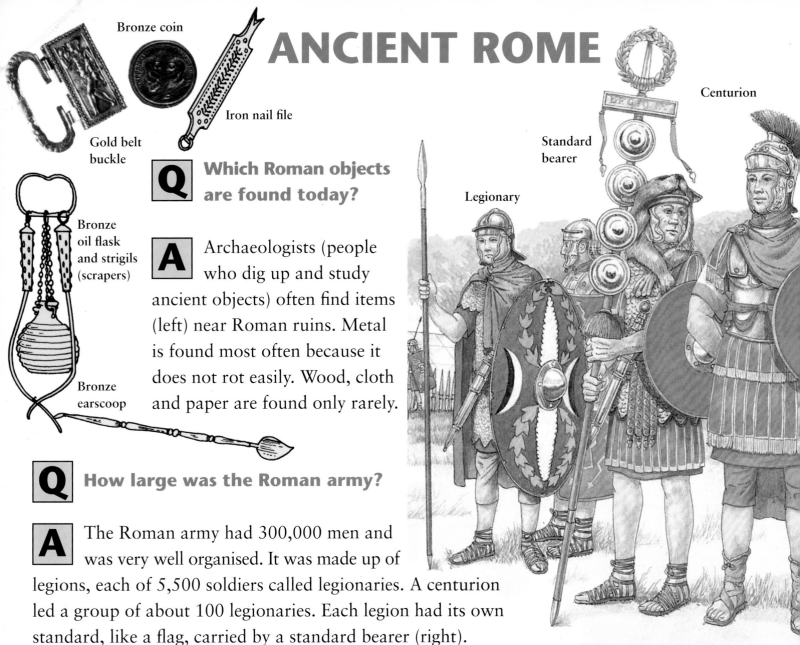

Bronze coin

Gold belt buckle

Iron nail file

Bronze oil flask and strigils (scrapers)

Bronze earscoop

Legionary

Standard bearer

Centurion

Q Which Roman objects are found today?

A Archaeologists (people who dig up and study ancient objects) often find items (left) near Roman ruins. Metal is found most often because it does not rot easily. Wood, cloth and paper are found only rarely.

Q How large was the Roman army?

A The Roman army had 300,000 men and was very well organised. It was made up of legions, each of 5,500 soldiers called legionaries. A centurion led a group of about 100 legionaries. Each legion had its own standard, like a flag, carried by a standard bearer (right).

Q How large was the Roman Empire?

A In A.D. 211, the Roman Empire covered the land shown on this map (right). About 100 million people lived in the Roman Empire. The lands were divided into areas called provinces. Each province had a governor who collected the taxes and kept law and order.

- • town
- — road
- ▨ Roman Empire A.D. 211

0 ——— 800 km
0 ——— 600 mi

ATLANTIC OCEAN

Eburacum

Londinium

Colonia Agrippina

Augusta Treverorum

Moguntiacum

Augusta Vindelicorum

Burdigala

Lugdunum

Poetovio

Apulum

Troesmis

Narbo

Genua

Bononia

Oescus

Black Sea

Segovia

Tarraco

Salonae

Byzantium

Sinope

Emerita Augusta

Rome

Thessalonica

Nicomedia

Corduba

Caesarea

Tingi

Iol Caesarea

Athens

Ephesus

Tarsus

Carthage

Syracuse

Antiochia

Mediterranean Sea

Bostra

Leptis Magna

Caesarea

Cyrene

Alexandria

Q How did the Romans protect themselves in battle?

A To protect themselves from enemy spears and arrows, Roman legionaries would form a tortoise (below). A group of soldiers would crowd together and lock their shields to form four walls and a roof. It was called a tortoise because it looked like a tortoise's shell.

Roman tortoise

Q What did the Romans build?

Temple

A The Romans were skilful engineers and architects. They built many fine buildings as well as temples to worship their gods. This cross-section through an amphitheatre shows how the arches were designed to carry the enormous weight of the building. The Romans were also famous for their road-building.

Amphitheatre

Road

Q What ships did the Romans build?

A The Romans built merchant ships, to carry food and other goods, and warships. The merchant ship was broad and deep so that it could carry thousands of containers of goods. The war galley was long and narrow so that it could travel fast and also turn quickly. It was powered by oarsmen as well as sails, so it could move quickly even when there was no wind.

A small warship

A medium-sized merchant ship

MIDDLE AGES

The Middle Ages was the period of European history that started in A.D. 476, when the Western Roman Empire fell. It ended in 1453 when the Ottoman Turks captured Constantinople.

KEY DATES

A.D. 476: Western Roman Empire falls

A.D. 768: Charlemagne crowned

1088: University of Bologna, Italy – one of the first great medieval centres of learning – is founded

1095–1291: Crusades are fought

1348–1350: Black Death kills millions

1453: Ottoman Turks capture Constantinople

▲ **Magnificent 12th-century stained glass in Chartres Cathedral, France. At this time, the power of the Catholic Church was immense.**

▲ **Charlemagne's kingdom covered roughly what is now France in A.D. 768, and expanded across Europe under his rule.**

For about 300 years after Germanic tribes removed the last Western Roman emperor, Europe was made up of a collection of small states and kingdoms. Then Charlemagne (c. A.D. 742–814), the king of the Franks, began to build a new empire – the Holy Roman Empire – across much of Europe. This period marked the start of the Middle Ages.

Feudalism

In the early Middle Ages, kings struggled to control their nobles, who were sometimes more powerful than they were. In many parts of Europe between the 9th and 14th centuries, kings and lords gave gifts of land to their nobles. In return, the nobles gave the lords their loyalty and fought for them in times of war. Similarly, the nobles granted land to peasants (farmers of small plots of land) – on condition that the peasants worked for them. This system of loyalties and services was called feudalism. It was not until the end of the 14th century that the idea of rulers whose authority came from the people took shape.

The church

Under feudalism, the Catholic Church grew more and more powerful. Monasteries became centres of learning, monks hand-copied books and bishops established cathedral schools, some of which became universities.

Late Middle Ages

Great changes swept across Europe during the 14th and 15th centuries. Between 1315 and 1317 a great famine wiped out 10 per cent of Europe's population, then in 1337

▲ Jousting knights on horseback. This was a popular form of entertainment in the Middle Ages

THE CRUSADES

After Muhammad founded the Islamic religion in A.D. 610, Muslim armies conquered many regions. Islam was usually tolerant of other religions, but Christianity and Islam clashed between 1095 and 1291 in a series of wars called the Crusades. The Crusaders wanted to protect Christian holy sites in Palestine (modern Israel, Lebanon and Syria). The Crusaders built castles like Krak des Chevaliers (below) in Syria.

the Hundred Years' War began between England and France. The biggest disaster was a plague called the Black Death, which killed one-third of Europe's population between 1346 and 1350.

The power of the church began to fade in the 15th century. Its control over knowledge and learning weakened, allowing greater freedom of thought. This was the beginning of the Renaissance. In 1453 Constantinople fell to the Muslim Ottoman Turks. The Middle Ages was drawing to a close.

GENERAL INFORMATION

- Early centres of learning grew from cathedral schools and included Bologna in Italy, Paris in France and Oxford in England.
- The Hundred Years' War (1337–1453) was a series of conflicts between England and France.

See also:

Ancient Rome

MIDDLE AGES

Q Who was buried at Sutton Hoo?

A In A.D. 625, the Saxon King Raedwald died.
He was buried at Sutton Hoo, in Suffolk,
England. The king was laid out in a wooden ship,
27 metres long (below), which people believed
would take him to the next world. Spears, dishes,
coins, armour and a stringed instrument called a lyre
were found inside the ship when it was discovered in
1938. Also found were silver and gold ornaments,
such as these gold clasps (right). The ship
and the king were buried under a huge
mound of earth.

Q What was the Domesday Book?

A William of Normandy conquered England in 1066.
In 1086, he ordered a survey of all his English
lands to check that he was receiving the rent and taxes
to which he was entitled. His officers travelled about
the kingdom asking a series of questions, such as the
name of each estate and who owned it (right). The
answers were written in the Domesday Book. It gives us
a detailed picture of what life was like in the Middle Ages.

Q How were cathedrals built in the 12th century?

A During the 12th century, a new style of church architecture was introduced, which allowed buildings to be much larger and more elaborate than before. This style was known as Gothic architecture (left). The inside of the cathedral was enlarged by building aisles of columns on each side. Arches were built on the outside of the main structure to support the enormous weight of the roof. Each wall was pierced with windows, which let in light and made the walls lighter.

Q What were the Crusades?

A The Crusades were religious wars fought between the 11th and 13th centuries. They were fought to win back the Holy Lands from non-Christians. The First Crusade began in 1095, after Palestine had been captured by Turkish Muslims. The crusading armies were usually led by knights on horseback. Foot soldiers fought with spears and crossbows.

Q What was Paris like in the 14th century?

A The centre of the city of Paris (above) was an island in the River Seine, joined to the rest of the city by bridges. Barges brought goods down the river from all over France. Most houses were made from wood, but the grander buildings were built from stone. Grandest of all was the great Gothic cathedral of Notre-Dame.

EARLY AFRICA

The most famous ancient civilisation in Africa was in Egypt. Later, there were several other, less well-known kingdoms south of the Sahara Desert.

KEY DATES

2650 B.C: Old Kingdom of Egypt founded

c.400 B.C: Kingdom of Axum established in Ethiopia

A.D. 1137: Ethiopian Empire founded

1220–1450: Kingdom of Zimbabwe

1230–c.1600: Kingdom of Mali

1440: Benin Empire (now Nigeria) founded

1468–1591: Kingdom of Songhai

Several great empires developed in different parts of Africa during the 13th and 14th centuries. These included the empires of Ethiopia, Zimbabwe, Mali, Benin and Songhai.

Mali and Songhai

The Kingdom of Mali was founded in the early 13th century. It grew rapidly and by the early 14th century covered 1.3 million square kilometres, including much of what is now Senegal, Mali, Burkina Faso and Niger. At its peak the population was 40–50 million.

The secret of ancient Mali's success was trade. It exported huge amounts of gold, salt, ivory and slaves, which were carried to all parts of North Africa and beyond on camel caravans. Cities such as Taghaza, Niani and Timbuktu were important trading posts. These cities had large mosques and were centres of learning as well as trade.

At one time, the Kingdom of Mali produced half the Old World's gold. The main currency was gold dust. The imperial army had up to 100,000 troops, including a large cavalry section. Before it started to

GREAT ZIMBABWE

The ancient walled city of Great Zimbabwe (above), in the modern state of Zimbabwe, was built between 1200 and 1450. It was the capital of the ancient Kingdom of Zimbabwe. Within its stone walls, which enclose an area of 24 hectares, up to 20,000 people lived in thatched huts with walls of clay and granite gravel.

decline in the 15th century, Mali was the second-largest empire in the world – after the Mongul Empire of Asia.

Between the early 15th century and the late 16th century, the Kindgom of Songhai grew out of part of Mali, with its capital at Gao on the Niger River.

▼ A ceremonial mask dating from the time of the Benin Empire.

Colonial rule

Africa's wealth had long interested European traders. The Portuguese began mapping the African coastline in the 15th century, then they set up colonies and began exporting slaves from West Africa. The trade in slaves continued until the 19th century.

The British, French, Germans, Belgians and Italians were all desperate for the raw materials found in Africa. These included copper, bauxite, gold and diamonds. These countries established colonies and took large parts of Africa for their empires. By the late 19th century most of Africa was ruled by European nations. Only Abyssinia (now Ethiopia) and tiny Liberia remained independent.

▼ The Great Mosque at Djenné was originally built in the 13th century in the Kingdom of Mali.

▲ Debre Damo church in Ethiopia was built for Christian worship in the 6th century. At that time it was in the Kingdom of Axum, later part of the Ethiopian Empire.

GENERAL INFORMATION

● The Zagwe Dynasty was founded by Mara Takla Haymanot in 1137 and marks the beginning of the Ethiopian Empire. This survived until it was overthrown in 1270 by the Solomonid Dynasty, which continued in power until 1974.

See also:

Ancient Egypt, Great Explorers

EARLY AFRICA

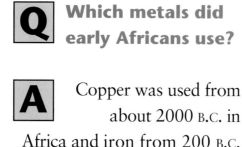

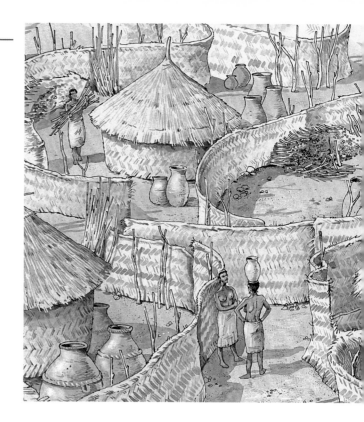

Q Which metals did early Africans use?

A Copper was used from about 2000 B.C. in Africa and iron from 200 B.C. Statues cast in bronze or brass were a special art form in the Benin Empire (A.D. 1200–1700) in West Africa. This one (left) shows a hunter returning home. He has an antelope slung over his shoulders with its legs tied.

Q What was the Great Trek?

A In 1806 the British captured the Dutch Cape Colony in southern Africa. Many Dutch farmers, called Boers, did not like British rule. In 1836 the Boers set off with their families on a Great Trek. They settled north of the Orange and Vaal rivers. The republics they founded are now part of South Africa.

Q What was Great Zimbabwe?

A The modern state of Zimbabwe (in southern Africa) is named after the ruins of some huge stone-walled enclosures that were found in the hills of south-central Zimbabwe. Great Zimbabwe (above) was where the ruler of the city lived and was the centre of religious life for his people. This is how it would have looked in the 15th century.

Q What were early African villages like?

A South of the Sahara, Africa was populated by hundreds of different tribes, each with its own culture. Whatever their way of life, the villages, such as this one in Chad (left), shared much in common. Houses were built from wood, clay or grass. Round huts were very common, each being used for a single purpose such as cooking or sleeping. Individual huts were usually grouped together around a courtyard in which the family lived. Many Africans still live in traditional villages and huts.

Q What was the East Coast Trade?

A The east coast of Africa was for a long time an important source of trade in gold, ivory, slaves and other goods. First to exploit it were the Arabs who sailed as far south as Madagascar from about A.D. 700 onwards. In 1498 Portuguese ships (right) began to take part in the rich East Coast Trade. Wars were fought between the Arabs and Portuguese for control of ports and sea routes. Other European nations including the Spanish, Dutch and English also exploited the trade.

EARLY AMERICA

North and South America were colonised later than other continents (apart from Antarctica). Archaeological evidence suggests that the first Americans arrived from Asia.

KEY DATES

A.D. 250–900: Mayan civilisation (Classic Period)
Early 13th century–1533: Inca civilisation
1428–1521: Aztec civilisation
1519–1521: Spanish conquest of Mexico
1835–42: Seminole War between Seminole people and US Army
1876: Battle of Little Bighorn

▼ An artist's impression of the Battle of Little Bighorn. A combined force of Lakota Sioux, Northern Cheyenne and Arapaho Native Americans defeated Custer's famous 7th Cavalry.

The first people to arrive in America probably crossed from Siberia to Alaska about 40,000 years ago. Some settled in the far north and others moved south-east along the Pacific coast. Still more moved inland. Groups settling in different areas adopted their own cultures and traditions.

Other people probably arrived in South America after crossing the Pacific Ocean from South-east Asia (and possibly Australia).

North Americans

Different cultural traditions developed in the Pacific north-west (including the Chinook and Tlingit tribes); the south-west (Apache and Navajo tribes); the Great Plains (Apache, Cheyenne and Sioux); and the east (Cherokee, Seminole and Shawnee). Most tribes were nomadic (they moved from place to place) or partly nomadic hunter-gatherers. Many depended on buffalo for meat, fur and skins. Others cultivated crops, and some lived in permanent dwellings. When European settlers began to move west across the Great Plains, their interests clashed with those of the Native North Americans.

LAST STAND

The last Native American victory over European settlers was at the Battle of Little Bighorn in 1876. Native Americans tried to stop the settlers looking for gold on their land. Lieutenant Colonel George Custer led an attack on a Lakota Sioux camp. He and many of his men were killed.

▲ Hernán Cortés (left) meets the Aztec emperor Moctezuma II.

◄ Machu Picchu in Peru was probably built for the Inca emperor Pachacuti (1438–1472).

Aztecs and Incas

Several civilisations in Central and South America pre-date the arrival of European settlers. The Aztec Empire was based on the city of Tenochtitlan, near present-day Mexico City. The Mexican people founded the city in 1325. In 1428 an alliance with other local tribes formed the basis for a large empire. The Aztecs, as the people of the alliance were known, grew crops and traded for other goods. They worshipped many gods, who they tried to please by making sacrifices in spectacular temples. The Spanish explorer Hernán Cortés (1485–1547) conquered the empire in 1521 and claimed it for Spain.

The Incas built a vast, powerful empire centred on Cuzco (now in Peru) in the Andes mountains. At its peak in the early 1500s the empire stretched from Ecuador to northern Chile. Roads connected different regions. The Incas lived in villages and ate corn, potatoes, beans, peppers and guinea pigs. Spanish conquerors broke up the empire in the 1530s.

◄ Tikal was one of the most important cities of the Mayan civilisation. The city was at its largest around A.D. 830.

GENERAL INFORMATION

● The Mayan civilisation of Central America started to develop as early as 2600 B.C. It was at its peak from A.D. 250–900.

● Inca buildings were built from expertly cut and perfectly fitting stones. All Inca men had to serve as soldiers at some time during their lives.

See also:

Great Explorers

EARLY AMERICA

Q Who were the first people to live in America?

A About 40,000 years ago there was a bridge of land between America and Asia. This was the time of the last ice age. Hunters (below) crossed over from Asia in small bands, following animals such as reindeer and bison. Slowly, these settlers spread southwards into the heart of the continent.

Q When did Inuits first live in America?

A The Inuit people began to move into America from Asia around 3000 B.C. They then spread eastwards across the far north of Alaska and Canada. Some Inuits build temporary structures of snow called igloos (below).

Q What kind of houses did the Plains Native Americans live in?

A In the 1400s, many Native Americans of the Great Plains were farmers. They built large, dome-shaped houses called lodges (right). A lodge had a wooden frame, covered with soil, turf and skins. Entry was through a covered passage. Inside, there was a fireplace in the centre of the lodge. A hole in the roof above let out the smoke. Around the walls were wooden platforms that were used as beds. Before the Spanish introduced horses, the Plains Native Americans used dogs for hunting.

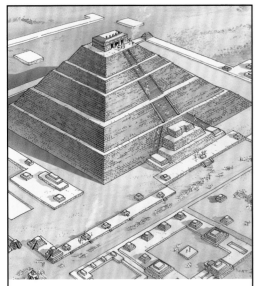

A The Aztecs ruled a huge empire in Mexico from A.D. 1428 to A.D. 1521. Their capital city was Tenochtitlan, built on swampy islands in Lake Texcoco. Over 300,000 people lived there. Goods were brought to the great markets by a system of canals, and each day vast crowds came to trade. This picture (below) shows the ceremonial centre of the city, with Aztec nobles and warriors. The temple of Quetzalcoatl is before them and, beyond it, the double temple pyramid dedicated to the gods of war and rain.

Q What was the Pyramid of the Sun?

A The Pyramid of the Sun was the largest and oldest building in the Mexican city of Teotihuacan, which was built in A.D. 150. Standing over 70 metres high, the pyramid had a flat roof on which there was probably a temple dedicated to the sun god.

Q How did the Incas travel about their empire?

A The Inca Empire stretched for nearly 4,000 kilometres along the west coast of South America. The Incas built a network of roads across their empire to transport goods, move troops and send messages. The roads were made as straight as possible, but zigzagged up steep slopes. Bridges, hung from cables of twisted plant stems, were fixed across ravines and rivers. There were no wheeled vehicles, so most people walked. However, important officers were carried in litters (a type of chair carried on poles, left).

GREAT EXPLORERS

Since the beginning of human history, people have had the urge to set out on journeys in search of new lands or to trade with people far away.

KEY DATES

1492: Christopher Columbus lands on the islands of the Bahamas

1498: Vasco da Gama reaches India via the Cape of Good Hope

1639: Ivan Moskvitin crosses Siberia to the Pacific coast

1768–1779: James Cook explores the Pacific Ocean

1911: Amundsen reaches the South Pole

▲ **A postage stamp commemorating the great explorer Magellan.**

Often, explorers have discovered previously unknown places simply to find out more about Earth. Ancient civilisations around the Mediterranean Sea sent expeditions in search of new lands thousands of years ago. Ancient Egyptian explorers travelled by ship to a place they called Punt on the east coast of Africa in around 2500 B.C. The Vikings (from Scandinavia) visited Iceland and Greenland around A.D. 1000. Between 1271 and 1295 the adventurer Marco Polo (1254–1324) journeyed from Venice, in Italy, across Asia to China – and back again.

The golden age

Improved navigation techniques allowed sailors to make more daring voyages in the 15th century. Portuguese explorers and traders explored the west coast of Africa. In 1488 Bartolomeu Dias (c.1450–1500) was the first European to sail around the southern tip of Africa. A few years later Vasco da Gama (c.1460–1524) followed his route but continued all the way to India, opening up an important trade route. Then, in 1492, Christopher Columbus (1451–1506) set out across the Atlantic Ocean, unsure

▲ **Christopher Columbus and the crew of *Santa Maria* land on the Bahamas in 1492.**

of what he would find. He finally made landfall on the islands of the Bahamas, just off the coast of North America. Many Spaniards followed Columbus, eventually conquering the Aztec and Inca empires of Central and South America. These conquests brought great wealth to some Europeans.

In 1519 another Portuguese explorer, Ferdinand Magellan (1480–1521), sailed south and found his way around the southern tip of South America and across the Pacific Ocean to the Philippines. Although Magellan did not survive to see his home country again, one of his ships did. This was the first vessel to sail all around the world.

RACE TO THE SOUTH POLE
It was widely expected that a British expedition led by Robert F. Scott (1868–1912) would be first to the South Pole. However, the Norwegian Roald Amundsen (1872–1928) led a rival team that used dogs to pull its sledges. This plan worked, and Amundsen reached the South Pole in December 1911. Scott's party (left) pulled their sledges themselves. By the time they reached the pole, 33 days after Amundsen, they were exhausted. They died before they could make it back to their ship.

Later discoveries

Captain James Cook (1728–1779), from England, explored the Pacific Ocean. He was the first European to see the Hawaiian islands and Antarctica, and he also explored the coasts of Australia and New Zealand. Other adventurers visited the Pacific coast of North America, the Saint Lawrence River in Canada and the coast of Brazil. Although the African coastline was known, non-Africans had never visited most of the continent's interior. Mungo Park (1771–1806) and David Livingstone (1813–1873) were tireless individuals who followed

▼ Livingstone showed that the Zambezi River in Africa was not navigable along its whole course.

and mapped the courses of Africa's Niger and Zambezi rivers, respectively.

The Northeast Passage, the seaway that connects northern Norway, Siberia and the Bering Strait, was first navigated in 1878–1879. In 1909 the American Robert Peary (1856–1920) was the first person to reach the North Pole.

GENERAL INFORMATION

● The Age of Discovery is the period from around 1420 to 1660 when Europeans opened up many new (mostly maritime) trade routes. It was a bridge between the Middle Ages and the modern era.

See also:

Early Africa, Early America

GREAT EXPLORERS

Q Where did Christopher Columbus land when he discovered America in 1492?

A Columbus sailed from Spain across the Atlantic in his ship the *Santa Maria* (below). He was trying to reach China. Instead, in 1492, he landed on the island of San Salvador in the Bahamas.

Q Who was Marco Polo?

A Marco Polo was a Venetian who travelled from Venice, in Italy, to China with his father and uncle. He arrived in China in 1275 and stayed for 17 years. He worked for the Chinese ruler, Kublai Khan (above). He described his travels in a famous book.

Q Why was Ferdinand Magellan famous?

A In 1519, Ferdinand Magellan, a Portuguese navigator, sailed round the tip of South America, into the Pacific Ocean (right). Magellan himself was killed in 1521, but one of his ships completed the first round-the-world voyage.

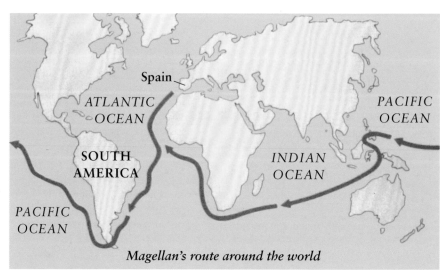

Magellan's route around the world

Q Who was the first European to cross Africa from east to west?

A In 1874, H. M. Stanley (above) set out with 350 others from Bagamoyo on Africa's east coast. After exploring Lake Victoria, the expedition reached the Congo River. Despite attacks from hostile tribes, they followed the river all the way to the sea on the west coast. The great journey took 999 days. Of those who set out, only 114 people survived.

Q Who led the first expedition to the South Pole?

A Roald Amundsen of Norway landed his party on Antarctica in 1911. Amundsen and four men started for the South Pole on sledges drawn by dogs. They reached the pole in less than two months (right). The journey back was even quicker and everyone returned safely. Soon afterwards, Robert Falcon Scott's British expedition also reached the pole. But none of the five men survived the return trip.

INDUSTRIAL REVOLUTION

The Industrial Revolution began in Britain in the 1760s. Until that time, craftsmen had made everything, from clothes to cartwheels, by hand.

KEY DATES

1712: Thomas Newcomen invents simple steam engine

1764: spinning jenny invented by James Hargreaves

1775: powerful steam engine patented by James Watt

1783: puddling process invented by Henry Cort; this revolutionises the production of iron

The revolution started from small beginnings. In 1721 a water-powered silk mill began working in Derby, England. This was one of the first factories, but it was only small.

Everything changed after an Englishman called James Hargreaves (1720–1778) invented the spinning jenny in 1764. This machine span eight threads of yarn at once (and became even faster in later years), so doing the work of eight people. There were 20,000 spinning jennies in use by the time of Hargreaves' death.

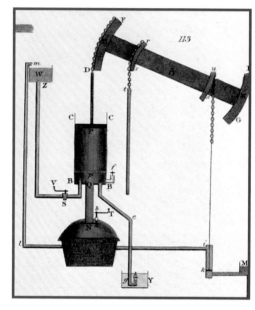

▲ Thomas Newcomen invented this steam engine in 1712 to pump water from mines. The steam engine was a vital source of power later, in the Industrial Revolution.

The need for power

In 1769, Richard Arkwright harnessed the new spinning jenny to a waterwheel to draw power from the energy of a river's flow. He built textile factories, called mills, beside rivers. These were the first big factories. Many were built in Manchester, which became the world's first industrial city. Barges moved goods along canals, but this was slow transport. The newly invented steam engine, and the laying of thousands of kilometres of rail tracks, was to speed things up.

▲ The Iron Bridge, raised in Shropshire, England, in 1779, was the first arched bridge made from cast iron.

The Industrial Revolution spread to the United States late in the 18th century. In 1789 the Englishman Samuel Slater (1768–1835) arrived in New York and set up textile factories there. Four years later Eli Whitney (1765–1825) invented the cotton gin, a machine that could rapidly comb cotton fibres. This dramatically changed the American cotton industry and set the country on the road to industrialisation.

▲ **Labour in the Industrial Revolution was often provided by children like this girl in a textile mill.**

In the early years of the 19th century, steam engines that burnt coal proved to be far better sources of energy than waterwheels.

Without the need for water power, factories no longer had to be close to rivers. They could be anywhere within reach of coal supplies. People flooded into big manufacturing centres such as Manchester, Leeds, Bradford and Glasgow in Scotland.

Canals and railways

The Industrial Revolution affected many other kinds of manufacturing. Ironworks and steel mills were built to make tools, machines and engines for other factories. Railway networks connected coal mines with factories and factories with ports, from

◄ **Mines like this early 19th-century tin mine provided the raw materials for rapidly growing manufacturing industries.**

where ships then took products all over the world.

England, where it all began, became the world's most powerful nation. The industrialisation of Belgium, France, Germany, the United States and other countries followed later in the 19th century.

GENERAL INFORMATION

● **Some cities grew rapidly during the Industrial Revolution as large numbers of people left the countryside to work in factories. Manchester, England, grew from 22,000 people in 1771 to 100,000 in 1810 and 400,000 in 1860.**

See also:

Industry, Machines

INDUSTRIAL REVOLUTION

STEAM ENGINE

Q Why were early steam engines important?

A Steam engines allowed industry to develop. The first steam engines were built in the early 1700s. They were used to pump water out of mines. In the 1770s, James Watt produced a steam engine that was much more powerful. This was used to power many machines including spinning and weaving looms, and farm ploughs and threshers.

Q Where was the first steam railway in Britain?

A The very first railway carried goods between Stockton and Darlington in the north of England. It was opened in 1825, and was followed in 1830 by a line between Manchester and Liverpool (right). This carried both goods and passengers.

A Jethro Tull made the first seed drill in 1701. Before this, seed had been scattered by hand. The drill sowed the seed in straight lines, so there was less waste and the crop was easier to weed and cut.

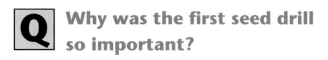

Q What was the Industrial Revolution?

A The Industrial Revolution is the name given to a time of great change in Britain. Before the 1700s, people made goods in small quantities, by hand. During the 1700s, machines were invented that made goods much more quickly. Manufacturing industry had begun, and it soon spread around the world. Factories were built (above), and people moved from the countryside to the towns to work in them.

Q Which new goods were made in the Industrial Revolution?

A New spinning and weaving machines enabled the textile industry to develop, and cheaper clothes could be made. Basic products such as iron and steel were used, and the steel industry developed. New methods were found to make many important products, such as rails, pans and muskets. At the same time, machine tools, such as the lathe, were invented.

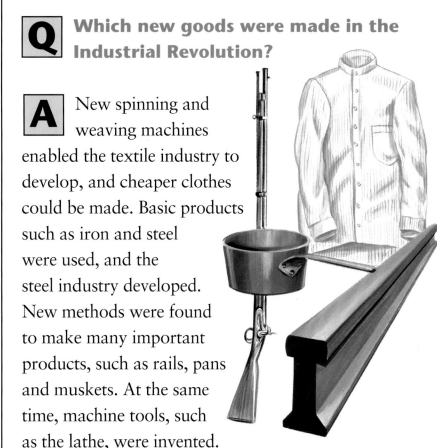

THE WORLD WARS

The 20th century witnessed two long and bloody wars that changed the world and the lives of millions of people for ever.

KEY DATES

World War I: 28 July 1914 to 11 November 1918

Battle of the Somme: 1 July to 18 November 1916

World War II: 1 September 1939 to 8 May 1945 (Europe) or 15 August (Japan)

Attack on Pearl Harbor: 7 December 1941

Atom bombs dropped: Hiroshima, 6 August 1945; Nagasaki, 9 August 1945

▼ Much of the fighting in World War I was done from flooded, muddy trenches.

World War I started after a Serbian terrorist shot the heir to the throne of the Austro-Hungarian Empire in 1914. Austria declared war on Serbia and was joined by Germany and the Ottoman Turks. Britain, Russia, France, Belgium and Japan sided against them. World War I had begun.

The German plan was to sweep through Belgium and into France, but by Christmas 1914 the opposing armies in north-east France had reached a stalemate. In the east there was fierce fighting between Russia on one side, and Germany and the Turks on the other. After the Russian Revolution in November 1917, Vladimir Lenin (1870–1924) withdrew Russia from the war. The United States declared war on Germany in 1917 in protest against German submarine attacks on its shipping in the Atlantic Ocean. American involvement helped tip the balance and the German Kaiser signed a ceasefire in the autumn of 1918. More than 14 million people had died in the war.

World War II

In 1933 Adolf Hitler (1889–1945), head of the Nazi Party, came to power in Germany. He blamed Germany's defeat in World War I on a Jewish plot. He ruled Germany as a dictator and was determined to build a great German empire. His armies invaded Poland in 1939, using the new fighting technique of *blitzkrieg* ('lightning war'). The Germans swept through much of western Europe but failed to invade

▲ A war cemetery in Belgium, where tens of thousands of soldiers who died in World War I are buried.

▲ Russian soldiers raise the Soviet flag over Berlin just before the German surrender in 1945.

◀ Troop carriers land Allied forces on a beach in Normandy, France, during the D-Day invasion.

Britain. After first siding with Hitler, Russia's leader Joseph Stalin (1878–1953) had to switch sides when Germany invaded Russia in 1941.

Hitler's allies included the Italian dictator Benito Mussolini (1883–1945) and the military leaders of Japan. By May 1942 the Japanese had seized much of South-east Asia, but their devastating attack on the American naval base at Pearl Harbor, Hawaii, in 1941 brought the United States into the war.

The tide turns

By 1943 the tide of war had turned against Germany in Europe. Russian troops eventually destroyed the powerful German Sixth Army at Stalingrad and began to regain lost territory. On D-Day (6 June 1944) Allied troops (American, British and Canadian) landed on the north coast of France. They rapidly fought their way east and finally joined up with the Russians in Germany. Hitler committed suicide in April 1945. More than 48 million soldiers and civilians died in the most destructive conflict ever.

THE PACIFIC THEATRE

The war in the Far East (sometimes called the Pacific Theatre) ended shortly after the end of the war in Europe. It was brought to a dramatic conclusion when American planes dropped two atomic bombs on the Japanese cities of Hiroshima and Nagasaki.

GENERAL INFORMATION

- In World War I, Russia suffered the most deaths (3.3 million), followed by the Ottoman Turks (2.9 million).
- In World War II, Russia (23.4 million) and China (over 10 million) suffered the most deaths.

See also:

Countries and People

THE WORLD WARS

Q When were aircraft first used in battle?

A Aircraft were used in battle for the first time during World War I (1914–1918). At first they were used to spy on enemy troops, but later guns and bombs were fitted. The triplane (above) was preferred to the biplane as it was easier to manoeuvre.

Q What caused the outbreak of World War I?

A The murder of the heir to the Austrian throne, Archduke Franz Ferdinand, on 28 June 1914, started World War I (1914–1918). He was killed by a Serb, causing Austria to declare war on Serbia.

Q What was trench warfare?

A During World War I, soldiers dug trenches (below) as protection against weapons such as machine guns and heavy artillery. Soldiers would live in the trenches for weeks on end. Attacks were often made from the trenches.

Q Who led the Germans during World War II?

A Adolf Hitler (left) led the Germans during World War II (1939–1945). His aim was to build a German empire. In 1938 he forced Austria to merge with Germany, and Czechoslovakia to hand over territory. In 1939 he declared war on Poland. This caused Britain and France to declare war against Germany, but by the end of 1940 France was defeated and Britain isolated. The US declared war on Germany in 1941, after an attack on Pearl Harbor by Japan (which was allied to Germany). Germany was defeated in 1945.

Q What sort of weapons were used in World War II?

A Aircraft played a decisive role in many battles, while armoured tanks made land warfare highly mobile. Aircraft carriers enabled aircraft to attack from the sea.

Tank

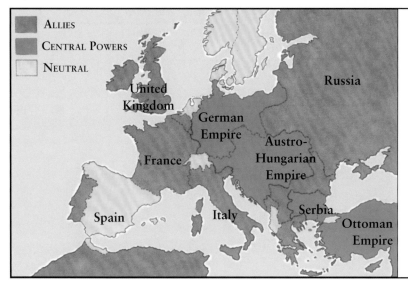

Allies
Central Powers
Neutral

United Kingdom
Russia
German Empire
France
Austro-Hungarian Empire
Spain
Italy
Serbia
Ottoman Empire

Q **What were the main alliances during World War I?**

A The two main alliances during World War I were those who fought with the German Empire (known as the Central Powers), and those who fought against the German Empire (known as the Allies). Neutral countries did not fight on either side.

Q **What was D-Day?**

A D-Day was a code name used in World War II. It was given to the date when 130,000 British, American (right) and Canadian troops were due to land in France and free it from the Germans. The date was changed several times due to bad weather. D-Day eventually took place on 6 June 1944.

Spitfire

Stuka

Aircraft carrier

HUMAN BODY

The human body is an amazing living machine. It is made up of bones, muscles, organs, water and lots of chemicals, all working in perfect harmony.

KEY FACTS

Skeleton: a baby has more than 270 bones, but an adult has only 206

Blood: a blood cell takes, on average, just 60 seconds to circulate the body

Nerves: information travels at different speeds along different nerve neurons

Diet: a person in Europe or North America will eat about 50 tonnes of food in their lifetime

▼ Babies grow quickly if fed nutritional food. Mother's breast milk is recommended for the first six months of a baby's life. It is easy for the baby to digest and has the right quantities of nutrients. Breast milk also helps build the baby's immune system.

The cell is the basic unit of the human body – as it is with all other living things. Most cells join with other cells to make tissue. There are four main types of tissue: epithelial tissue covers the body's surface; connective tissue helps join parts of the body; muscle tissue makes movement possible; and nervous tissue carries nerve signals.

Skeleton

Different kinds of tissues are combined in the body. The skeleton forms a bony structure

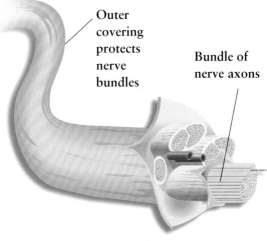

Outer covering protects nerve bundles

Bundle of nerve axons

▲ **Axons, or nerve fibres, carry electrical impulses from one part of the body to another.**

that supports the body, provides attachments for muscles and protects delicate organs. There are 206 bones in an adult human's body. Of these, 29 are in the skull, which surrounds and protects the brain. The rib bones protect the two lungs.

The spinal cord, one of the key parts of the nervous system, is protected by the backbone, or spine, which is actually a series of 26 small bones called vertebrae.

Each arm has a humerus, a radius and an ulna bone, to which muscles are attached. Each leg has a femur, or thigh bone, a tibia and a fibula. There are 27 bones in each hand and 26 to 28 bones in each foot.

GENERAL INFORMATION

- A healthy body needs the right kind of carbohydrates to produce energy and for the vitamins and minerals they contain. These are called complex carbohydrates and are found in vegetables and whole-grain bread.

- The human body also needs proteins to build, maintain and replace tissues such as muscles and organs, and red blood cells. Lean red meat, chicken, fish, dairy products, eggs, nuts and lentils are good sources of protein.

See also:

Science of Life, Senses and Organs

Muscles

The body has more than 600 muscles, which move different parts of the body. There are three main types of muscles. Skeletal

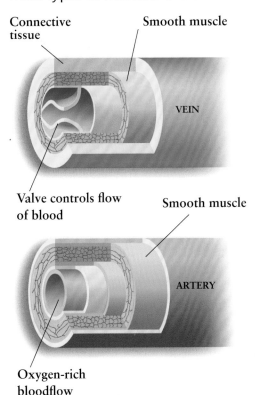

Connective tissue

Smooth muscle

VEIN

Valve controls flow of blood

Smooth muscle

ARTERY

Oxygen-rich bloodflow

▲ There are more than 600 muscles in the human body. Athletes use many of them when hurdling.

muscles are joined directly to bones and move arms, legs and other body parts. They are attached to the bones by hard, rope-like tissues called tendons.

The walls of the heart are made of cardiac muscle. This is called involuntary muscle because it works without us thinking about it. The third type is smooth muscle, which is not attached to bones and does things such as move food through the digestive system.

◄ Veins carry oxygen-poor blood to the lungs, while arteries carry oxygen-rich blood from the lungs.

GLANDS

Glands are tissues that secrete a variety of important substances. There are two kinds: exocrine glands and endocrine glands. The salivary glands (which produce saliva to begin the digestion of food) are exocrine glands. So is the liver, the second largest organ, after the skin. The pancreas is also an exocrine gland. It controls the level of sugar in the blood. Endocrine glands release chemical messages, or hormones, into the bloodstream. One example is the pituitary gland, which controls the water balance inside the body.

HUMAN BODY

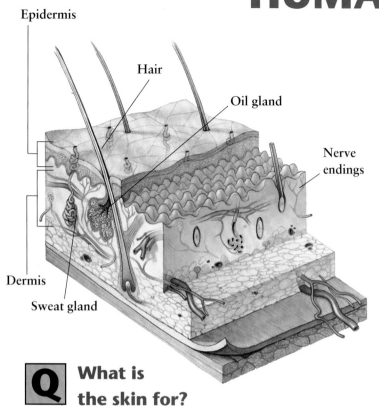

Epidermis

Hair

Oil gland

Nerve endings

Dermis

Sweat gland

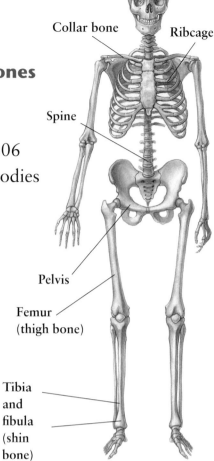

Skull

Collar bone

Ribcage

Spine

Pelvis

Femur (thigh bone)

Tibia and fibula (shin bone)

Q How many bones do we have?

A Humans have 206 bones in their bodies (right). There are 29 in the skull, 26 in the spine, 32 in each arm and 31 in each leg. Other bones form the ribcage.

Q What is the skin for?

A The skin (above) is the protective outer covering of our body. It contains nerve endings, which detect pain; sweat glands, which keep the body cool; and hair. It also prevents the body from losing too much water.

Q How do muscles work?

A There are more than 600 muscles in the body (right). Most of them move parts of the body or help it to stay upright. Muscles cannot push, they can only pull. Many of them work in pairs, attached to bones by tendons. One muscle tightens and becomes shorter, pulling the bone after it. If it relaxes, and the other muscle tightens, the bone moves back.

Neck muscles turn head

Upper arm muscles bend and straighten elbow

Chest muscles used in breathing

Q What is inside a bone?

A Bones are not solid. They have a strong outer layer of compact bone, with lightweight, spongy bone inside. In the centre is the soft marrow, which makes new red cells for the blood.

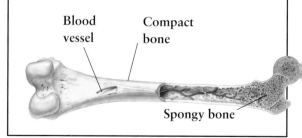

Blood vessel

Compact bone

Spongy bone

Q What are veins and arteries?

A When blood leaves the lungs, it carries oxygen. This blood travels along vessels called arteries. The body absorbs the oxygen, and the blood travels back to the heart through veins (below).

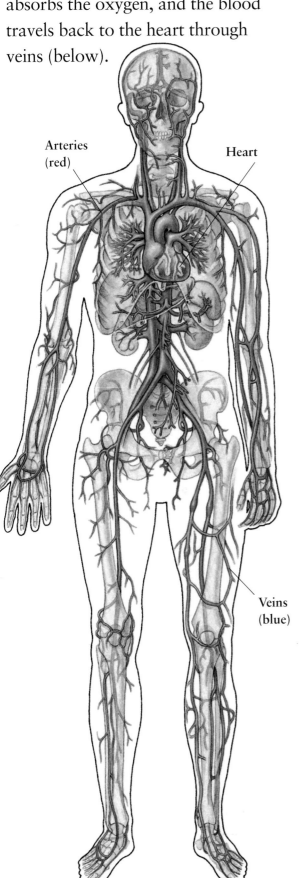

Arteries (red)

Heart

Veins (blue)

Q How does the heart work?

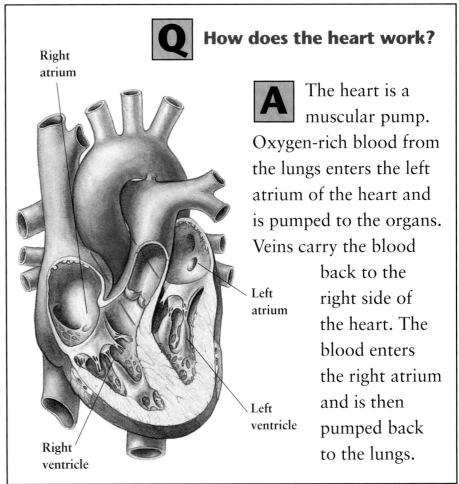

Right atrium

Left atrium

Left ventricle

Right ventricle

A The heart is a muscular pump. Oxygen-rich blood from the lungs enters the left atrium of the heart and is pumped to the organs. Veins carry the blood back to the right side of the heart. The blood enters the right atrium and is then pumped back to the lungs.

Q How do our joints work?

A Joints are the places where bones move against each other. Shoulders and hips have ball and socket joints. These allow movement in any direction. Elbows have hinge joints, which allow them to move backwards and forwards. A pivot joint allows the head to turn sideways.

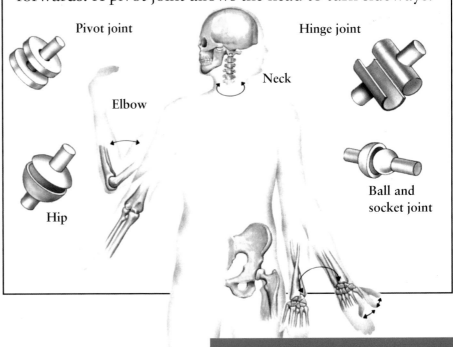

Pivot joint

Hinge joint

Neck

Elbow

Hip

Ball and socket joint

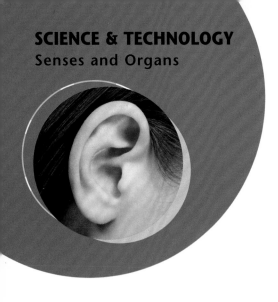

SENSES AND ORGANS

The human body has lots of different organs, each of which has a special job. Without any one of them, the body would not work properly.

Without some organs, the body would not be able to function at all. The body's organs include the heart, lungs, brain, liver, stomach and small intestine. The skin is the largest organ. It protects the body from air, water, dirt and bacteria. Organs such as the eyes and ears give us our senses.

Lungs and heart

Air passes from the nose and mouth and through the windpipe, or trachea, which branches into the two lungs. Thousands of tiny tubes called branchioles carry air to

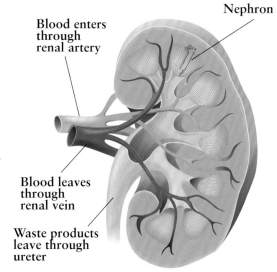

Blood enters through renal artery

Nephron

Blood leaves through renal vein

Waste products leave through ureter

▲ A cross-section through a human kidney. There are at least one million nephrons, which filter waste from the blood.

alveoli, where oxygen passes into tiny blood vessels called capillaries. This oxygen is vital for the body to function. Waste carbon dioxide passes the other way, from the capillaries to the alveoli and then out of the body. This whole process is called the respiratory system. It works in harmony with the blood circulatory system.

The heart is a muscular pump at the centre of the circulatory system, which carries blood to all parts of the body. The heart pushes oxygen-rich blood from the lungs around the body in arteries.

KEY FACTS

Brain: although it weighs only 2 per cent of the body, it uses 20 per cent of the body's oxygen intake

Blood vessels: if joined up, the lungs' blood vessels would stretch 2,400 km

Sense of smell: the human nose can recognise about 50,000 different scents

Skin: the outer layer of skin cells is shed and regrown every 27 days on average

◄ Our senses are important for for seeing, hearing, smelling, tasting and touching.

It pumps blood that lacks oxygen through veins and back to the lungs. There, the blood absorbs more oxygen.

Digestive organs

Food must pass through the digestive system before the body can use it for energy. Food ends up in the stomach after being chewed and swallowed. Chemicals in the stomach convert the food into a soupy substance that passes to the small intestine. There it is turned into sugars and fatty acids by juices sent from the liver and pancreas. The digested materials pass into the bloodstream to help the body function. Undigested food passes into the large intestine and out of the body. The liver makes safe the

THE SENSE OF SOUND

Our eyes give us the sense of sight, and our ears give us the sense of sound. Our ears receive sound waves, which are passed from the outer ear to the inner ear. There they are changed into signals to be sent along the cochlear nerve to the brain. The brain interprets these messages as loud, soft, low- or high-pitched sounds.

toxins that are produced in the large intestine.

The human body has two kidneys. They filter waste products from the blood and excrete them as urine. The kidneys maintain the body's water and mineral balances.

The kidneys also help control blood pressure and produce red blood cells.

The nervous system

The brain controls the nervous system. This is made up of the nerves, spinal cord and all the sense organs. Messages from the brain are sent along the nerves to get the body to do things. The sense organs pick up information about the environment – sights, sounds, odours and temperature – and pass it back to the brain.

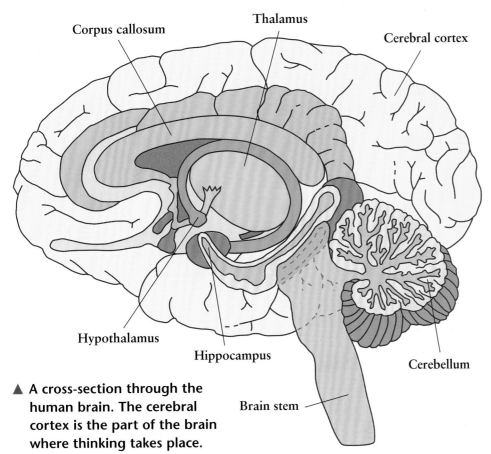

Corpus callosum

Thalamus

Cerebral cortex

Hypothalamus

Hippocampus

Cerebellum

Brain stem

▲ A cross-section through the human brain. The cerebral cortex is the part of the brain where thinking takes place.

GENERAL INFORMATION

● The body has a single liver, which processes digested food from the intestines, combats infections and controls the levels of fats, amino acids and glucose in the blood.

See also:

Human Body, Science of Life

SENSES & ORGANS

Q How do we breathe?

A Our bodies need oxygen, which they get from air breathed into the lungs. The lungs are made to expand by a big muscle called the diaphragm and smaller muscles fixed to the ribs. The diaphragm pushes downwards, while the other muscles lift up the ribcage. This draws air down into the lungs, where the oxygen is absorbed into the bloodstream (right).

Air breathed in through nose and mouth

Oesophagus

Lungs

Trachea

Bronchus

Diaphragm

Q Where does our food go?

A After the teeth chew the food, it is swallowed and goes down the oesophagus into the stomach (below). It is mixed with digestive juices, which break it down. In the small intestine, nutrients from the food are absorbed. Waste matter leaves the body through the anus.

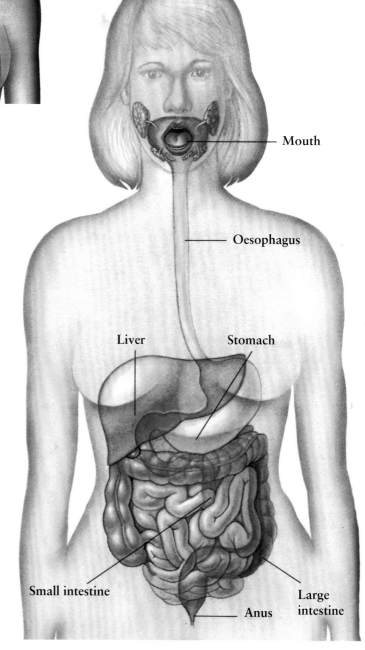

Mouth

Oesophagus

Liver

Stomach

Small intestine

Anus

Large intestine

Q How do our eyes see?

A When we look at something, light from it enters our eyes. The light is focused on the retina at the back of the eye by the lens. The optic nerves in the retina send a message to the brain, enabling us to 'see'.

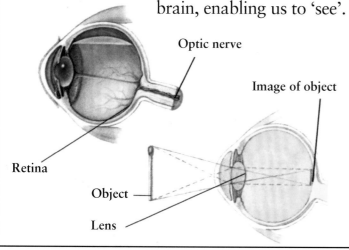

Optic nerve

Image of object

Retina

Object

Lens

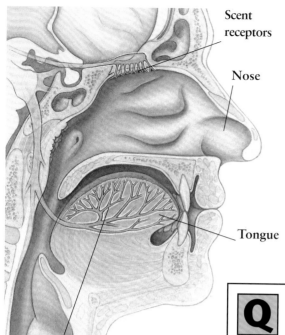

Scent receptors

Nose

Tongue

Taste receptors

Q How do we taste and smell?

A In the upper part of the nose are tiny scent receptors (left). When we sniff, molecules in the air are carried to these receptors. They sense what we are smelling. The tongue is covered with about 9,000 taste receptors, or taste buds. These sense what we are tasting. The taste buds are grouped in special areas on the tongue. Sweetness is tasted at the front, saltiness and sourness at the sides, and bitterness at the back.

Q How do our ears work?

A The outer ear collects sound waves, which pass through the eardrum and vibrate the tiny bones in the middle ear. These vibrations set the fluid in the cochlea in motion, shaking tiny hairs. Nerves attached to the hairs pass the message to the brain.

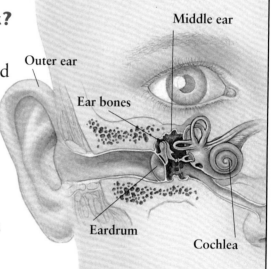

Outer ear

Middle ear

Ear bones

Eardrum

Cochlea

2 weeks

4 weeks

6 weeks

8 weeks

Umbilical cord

Baby

Uterus

Q How does a baby develop during pregnancy?

A A baby's life begins when a male sperm joins a female egg. The sperm travels from a man into a woman's body. It joins with the egg to form a single cell, and starts to grow. After a week, the single cell has multiplied to more than 100 cells. After eight weeks, the baby has all its major organs (such as heart, liver and lungs). The baby gets its food from its mother through the umbilical cord. After nine months, the baby is about 50 centimetres long (left). It is ready to be born.

SCIENCE OF LIFE

The science of living things (organisms) is called biology. It studies how they work, their structure and the way they interact with other life forms.

KEY FACTS

Number of species: in 2012 biologists estimated that there were about 8.7 million species of organisms; most of these have yet to be discovered

▼ To find out whether global warming is killing corals, biologists sometimes take photographs of them.

All living things – from animals and plants to simple bacteria – are made of cells. Most cells are so small they can be seen only under a powerful microscope. Some organisms, such as bacteria, consist of just a single cell, while others have billions.

All organisms need energy to live. Animals get energy from food. Green plants and some small life forms get their energy from sunshine, through photosynthesis. Organisms create new individuals of the same type to replace those that die, a process called reproduction. As they get older, animals and plants generally grow

▲ **People who study biology are called biologists. Here, a biologist is checking the health of a chick.**

and change shape. For example, an acorn looks nothing like the mature oak tree that grows from it.

Adapt to survive

All forms of life experience changes in their environment. If they are to survive they must be able to sense changes and respond to them. So, for example, a bird that spends the summer months in the tundra of Siberia can sense the shortening days in autumn. It responds by building up its fat reserves so it can make the long flight south to warmer places. If it did not do this, it would starve during the winter.

Likewise, plants produce flowers at the times of year when those animals that

pollinate them – usually insects – are active. If they flowered at a different time of year they would not be pollinated and so would not be able to reproduce.

Who does what?

The science of life is divided into many fields. Biologists who study plants are called botanists, and those who study animals are zoologists.

Some zoologists study particular types of animals. For example, herpetologists study amphibians and reptiles, and ornithologists study birds.

Some biologists study specific parts of animals. Biochemists study chemical reactions in plants and animals. Geneticists study genes, which determine the qualities that organisms inherit from their parents. Ecologists study how life forms relate to each other and their environment.

▲ This biologist, high in the canopy of a tree, is collecting invertebrates in a net. He is looking for new species.

ASEXUAL REPRODUCTION

The two kinds of reproduction are asexual and sexual. In organisms that reproduce asexually, such as slime moulds (left), the offspring come from a single parent. The offspring inherit the genes of that parent only. Single-celled life forms such as bacteria and many plants and fungi reproduce in this way.

GENERAL INFORMATION

- In organisms that reproduce sexually, the offspring come from two parents, so they inherit genes from both. Animals reproduce sexually and most plants can reproduce sexually or asexually.
- Species that are able to adapt more quickly to changes in their environment have a better chance of survival.

See also:

Animal Behaviour, Plant Life

SCIENCE OF LIFE

Plant cell

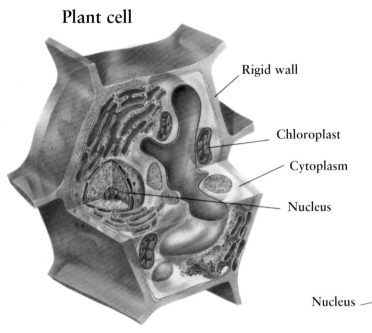

Rigid wall

Chloroplast

Cytoplasm

Nucleus

Animal cell

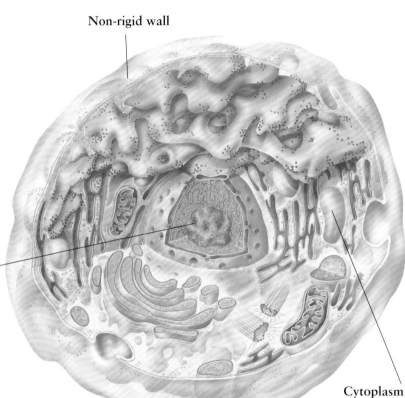

Non-rigid wall

Nucleus

Cytoplasm

Q **Why do animals of the same species fight?**

A Animals fight others of their species for several reasons. They may be arguing over territory or the right to be leader of their herd. Although many animals have powerful weapons, such as teeth, horns or claws, few are ever killed in these contests. These two klipspringer antelopes are jabbing at each other with their sharp horns.

Q **What is a cell?**

A A cell (above) is the basic building block of almost every living thing. Plant cells have a rigid wall made from a material called cellulose. Animal cells do not have a rigid wall. Inside all cells is a fluid called cytoplasm, containing the nucleus and other small bodies. The nucleus is the cell's control centre. The chloroplasts in plant cells help trap the energy from sunlight. The energy is used to turn carbon dioxide and water into food for the plant.

Q How do plants make seeds?

A Plants have male and female parts that join together to make seeds. A pollen grain travels from the male anther of one flower to the female stigma of another (right). The pollen is usually carried by an insect or the wind. It fertilises an egg in the ovary, which becomes an embryo and then a seed. The seed will grow into a new plant.

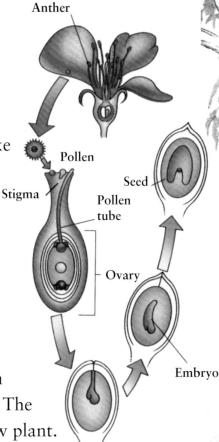

Anther

Pollen

Stigma

Pollen tube

Seed

Ovary

Embryo

Q How do racing pigeons find their way home?

A Racing pigeons and many other species of birds probably use more than one way of navigating. They can find their direction from the position of the Sun by day and the stars by night. They can also detect changes in the Earth's magnetic field as they fly over it. This tells them whether they are flying north, south, east or west. Some birds find their way by smell.

Q Do animals live in families?

A Some animals live together in herds or flocks, but others live in small family groups. This is a family of tamarin monkeys (above). The older brothers and sisters carry and help groom the babies.

Q How do birds fly?

A These pictures (below) show a duck beating its wings once as it flies. The downstroke (left) lifts the bird up and propels it forward. On the upstroke (right) the feathers are opened to let air through.

CHEMICALS AND MATTER

Everything around us is made of chemicals and matter. And all the matter exists in one of three forms: as a liquid, a solid or a gas.

KEY FACTS

Most dense element: the metal osmium (symbol Os) weighs 23 grams per cubic centimetre

Lightest element: the gas hydrogen (symbol H) weighs just 0.00009 grams per cubic centimetre

Most common element: hydrogen

▼ The Guggenheim Museum in Bilbao, Spain, is a spectacular building. The shiny effect is created by panels of the metal element titanium (symbol Ti).

Matter can change from one form to another, such as when solid ice-cream melts and becomes liquid. All matter is made of elements. An element cannot be reduced to a simpler substance. And all elements are made of tiny particles called atoms. Each element has a symbol of one or two letters. For example, chemists write oxygen as O, iron as Fe and aluminium as Al.

Different elements

When two or more atoms join together they form a molecule. A substance can be made of molecules of the same element or of lots of different elements. For example, a gold bar is made of the metallic element gold (chemical symbol Au) and nothing else. A brass object, however, is a mixture of copper (Cu) and zinc (Zn).

▲ Plants grow when carbon dioxide and water react to form sugar. This is called photosynthesis.

CATALYSTS

Chemists have to be able to control which reactions happen and how quickly they happen. They use catalysts to do this. Catalysts are substances that control the rate of a chemical reaction while not being changed themselves.

▲ Fireworks explode when heat is added to a mixture of chemicals, which burn in different colours.

Atoms and molecules combine in different ways to form solids, liquids and gases. These three types are called states of matter. For example, water is made up of two elements, hydrogen (H) and oxygen (O), whose atoms join to form water molecules. Water can exist as a solid (ice), a liquid (water) and a gas (steam).

States of matter

Solids have a definite shape and volume. Liquids have a definite volume, but not a definite shape. A liquid takes the shape of the container it is poured into. Gases change their shape and volume. They spread out to fill any container they are put in and can easily be squeezed into a smaller space, unlike a liquid or a solid.

Chemical reactions

A chemical reaction is any process that changes one chemical into another. Some examples of chemical reactions include the human body turning food into energy, iron becoming rusty and fireworks exploding in the night sky. Thousands of reactions are taking place all the time. Some look dramatic, but we do not even notice that others are taking place.

GENERAL INFORMATION
- All the elements are arranged in a chart called the periodic table.
- Of these, 98 elements occur naturally. The others do not occur in nature: they can only be made by chemists in a laboratory.

See also:

Atoms and Molecules, Materials

STATES OF MATTER

Molecules in a solid are packed closely together in a regular pattern

Molecules in a liquid are quite close but not in a regular pattern

Molecules in a gas are well spread, with no regular pattern

CHEMICALS & MATTER

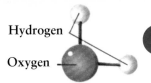

Hydrogen

Oxygen

Water molecule

Oxygen atoms → Oxygen molecule

 What are molecules?

A molecule (above) is the simplest part of a substance that can take part in chemical reactions. It is a group of two or more atoms linked together. The atoms may be the same or different. For example, a molecule of water is made of two hydrogen atoms linked to an oxygen atom. An oxygen molecule is made of two oxygen atoms linked together.

What is the difference between a mixture and a compound?

If iron filings and sulphur (1) are mixed together (2), there is no chemical reaction and they can be separated again by removing the iron with a magnet (3). When iron filings and sulphur are heated (4), they combine and change into iron sulphide, a compound.

 What chemicals are used in fire extinguishers?

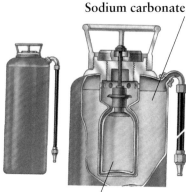

Carbon dioxide extinguishers send out a jet of carbon dioxide gas. Dry powder extinguishers blanket a fire with powder. Soda-acid extinguishers (right) mix sulphuric acid with sodium carbonate, making carbon dioxide gas which forces out a jet of water.

Sodium carbonate

Sulphuric acid

How do soaps and detergents work?

Soaps and detergents are made from long molecules that are water-loving at one end and grease-loving at the other end. When they go to work on a dirty cloth, they surround each droplet of greasy dirt stuck to the fibres of the cloth with their grease-loving tails plugged into the grease droplet (below). The coated droplet then floats off the cloth into the water and is washed away.

Grease

Cloth

Q How are chemicals made?

A The chemical industry makes chemicals by processing raw materials with heat, pressure and chemical reactions. Sulphuric acid is made from sulphur in a series of stages (right) that change sulphur into different compounds, ending with sulphuric acid.

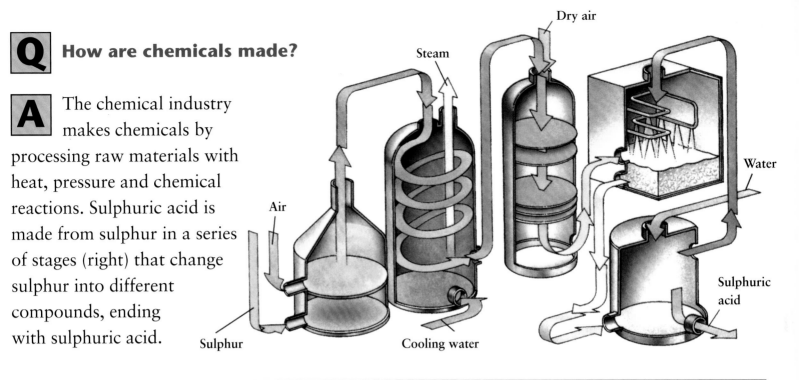

Steam

Dry air

Air

Sulphur

Cooling water

Water

Sulphuric acid

Q What are crystals?

A Crystals are solid pieces of material with flat faces set at angles to each other. All crystals of the same substance have the same angles between their faces. Crystals form in this way because their atoms always lie in the same regular patterns. Salt, sugar and quartz are crystals. Minerals can sometimes be identified by the shape of their crystals.

Q What is chemical analysis?

A Chemists use chemical analysis (right) to find out what an unknown substance contains. There are several methods. Volumetric analysis involves reactions in solutions. Gravimetric analysis involves weighing. In gas-liquid chromatography gas carries the sample through a column of moist powder. The sample separates into simpler compounds, which are recorded on a chart as they leave the column.

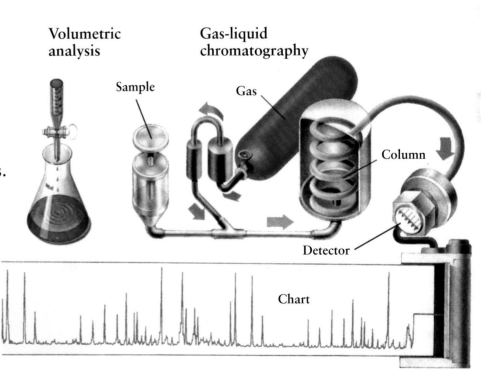

Volumetric analysis

Gas-liquid chromatography

Sample

Gas

Column

Detector

Chart

ATOMS AND MOLECULES

The building blocks of matter are called atoms, which are far too small to see. Atoms join up with other atoms – either of the same element or of other elements.

When atoms group together, they make a structure called a molecule. Every substance is made of molecules. Each type of molecule gives a substance its distinctive properties – how hard or soft it is, for example.

Inside an atom

In the 20th century scientists realised that atoms were made of even tinier particles, called protons, neutrons and electrons. The inside of an atom is mostly empty space but at its centre is a core, or nucleus. The nucleus contains protons and neutrons. Protons have a positive charge, and neutrons have no charge.

Electrons are the third kind of particle in an atom, and they move around the nucleus. Electrons have a negative charge. Since opposite charges attract one another, the electron does not move away from the nucleus but orbits around it. The number of electrons in an atom is the same as the number of protons. If there are several electrons, they will form shells around the nucleus. A hydrogen atom has just one electron, but other atoms have two, three, four or five electron shells.

Ionic bonding

Molecules can form as a result of ionic bonding or covalent bonding. Ionic bonding is when an electron moves from one atom to another. For example, a molecule of salt (sodium chloride) is made up of atoms of sodium and chlorine. There is one electron in the outer

◀ **Water is the most abundant compound on Earth. A compound is made of more than one element.**

▲ The fuel burnt to lift hot-air balloons is propane. Propane molecules are made up of carbon and hydrogen atoms.

shell of a sodium atom. And there is room for one more electron in the outer shell of a chlorine atom. The outermost sodium atom fills this gap, giving the sodium atom a negative charge and the chlorine atom a positive charge. The negative and positive atoms attract each other to form a salt molecule.

Covalent bonding

Covalent bonding occurs when two atoms share their electrons. Instead of one electron moving into the outer shell of another atom, the shells overlap to share the electron. One example is the way water molecules (below) form from two atoms of hydrogen and an atom of oxygen. A hydrogen atom has one electron and room for one more in its shell. Each hydrogen atom shares its electron with the oxygen.

GENERAL INFORMATION

● The gas responsible for global warming is carbon dioxide. It is made up of molecules with one atom of carbon and two of oxygen and has the formula CO_2.

See also:

Chemicals and Matter, Materials

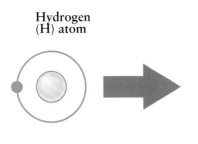

Hydrogen (H) atom

Oxygen (O) atom

Hydrogen (H) atom

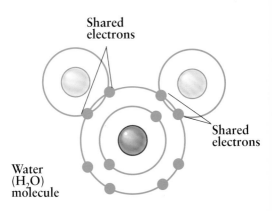

Shared electrons

Shared electrons

Water (H₂O) molecule

▲ An example of covalent bonding: two hydrogen atoms bond with an oxygen atom to form a water molecule.

ATOMS & MOLECULES

Uranium nucleus

Q What is inside an atom?

A An atom is made up of three kinds of tiny particles. Protons have a positive electric charge, and neutrons have no charge at all. Protons and neutrons cluster together at the centre of the atom, making up the nucleus. Around them travel electrons, which have a negative electric charge. An atom contains equal numbers of electrons and protons.

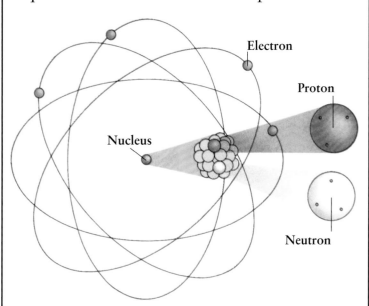

Electron

Proton

Nucleus

Neutron

Q How are atoms split?

A The atoms of different substances have different numbers of protons. Hydrogen has only one, but uranium has 92. All these protons jostle about, and make uranium very unstable. If extra neutrons are fired into the atom's nucleus, they are absorbed. This splits the nucleus in two, releasing energy as heat, and extra neutrons (right).

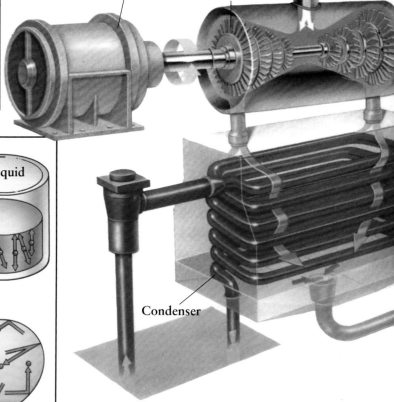

Generator

Turbine

Condenser

Q What happens when molecules are heated?

A If a solid object (1) is heated, its molecules vibrate strongly. If it gets hot enough, the solid melts into a liquid (2). Greater heat makes the liquid turn into gas (3).

1 Solid object

2 Liquid

3 Gas

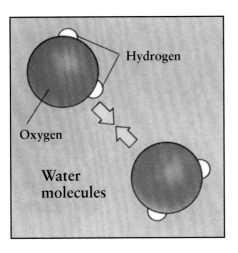

Hydrogen

Oxygen

Water molecules

Q What is a molecule?

A A molecule is the smallest part of a substance. Its atoms are linked chemically. Two hydrogen atoms and one oxygen atom make a water molecule (left).

Q How can we use the energy from atoms?

A When a uranium atom is split, it releases neutrons which shoot off into surrounding atoms and split them, too. This splitting carries on in what is called a chain reaction. It gives out a lot of energy in the form of heat, which can be used to generate electricity in a nuclear power station (left). Rods of uranium are placed inside the reactor. Control rods made of boron are put between the uranium rods to control the reaction. Water is pumped through the reactor under pressure and absorbs the heat. This water is carried to the steam generator, where its heat is used to boil a separate supply of water into steam. The steam is fed to a turbine. It spins the turbine, which turns the generator and so produces electricity. The used steam then travels to the condenser, where it is turned back into water and fed back to the steam generator to be reused.

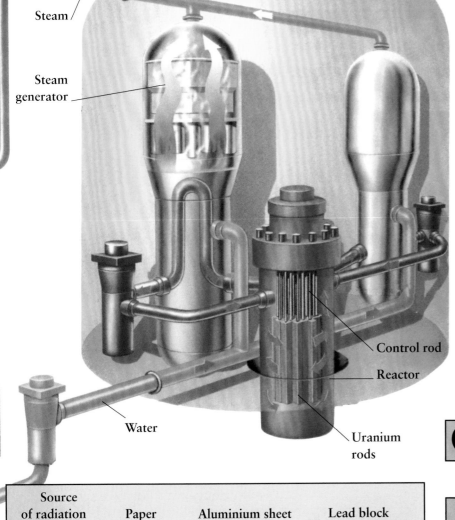

Steam

Steam generator

Control rod

Reactor

Water

Uranium rods

Q What types of radiation are there?

A There are three types of radiation – alpha, beta and gamma. Alpha particles are the least powerful. They cannot pass through paper. Beta particles cannot pass through thin metal, such as aluminium, and gamma rays cannot pass through lead (left).

Source of radiation

Paper

Aluminium sheet

Lead block

Alpha particles

Beta particles

Gamma rays

MATERIALS

Everything – from houses and clothing to cars, computers and footballs – is made of materials. Different materials are suited to different jobs.

In nature, some materials are hard and others are soft. Some are heavy and others are light. When choosing the material to make something, a designer has to decide what is most suitable. So, a car tyre has to be flexible to give the passengers a smooth ride but tough so as not to burst easily. The supports for a tall building have to be strong enough to support enormous weights. A yacht's sides

▼ Diamonds are a very hard material because of the special arrangement of their carbon atoms.

need to be both strong and light, so waves do not crush the vessel and it does not sit too low in the water. A child's cuddly toy needs to be soft and light.

Metallic materials

The simplest materials are those made of just one element. A gold bar is made of the metallic element gold and nothing else.

Alloys are another type of metallic material. They are a mixture of two or more different elements. Steel is an example of an alloy. It is composed mostly of iron, but it is stronger than iron. Steel also contains elements such as carbon, manganese and nickel.

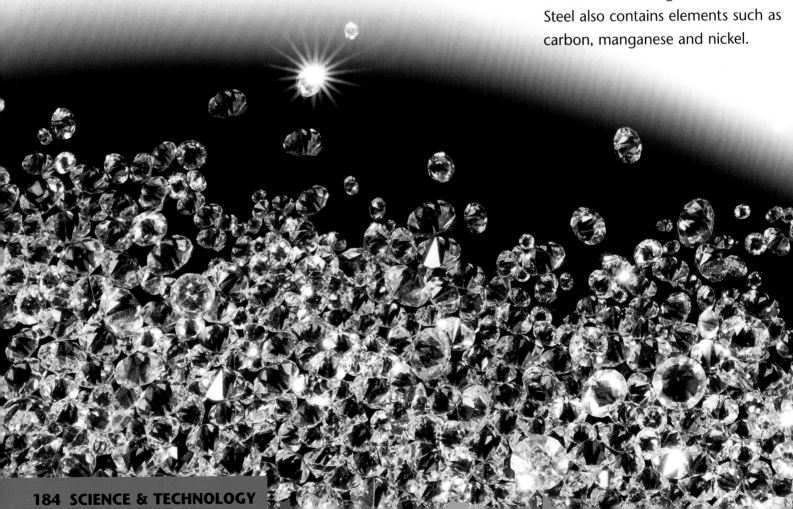

▲ A gold bar is heavy, very valuable and made of just the element gold.

in ceramics are minerals found in the natural world, such as quartz (silicon dioxide, SiO_2), periclase (magnesium oxide, MgO) and hematite (ferric oxide, Fe_2O_3). When ceramics are manufactured, these materials have to be heated to a great temperature, then cooled again. Glass is a particular kind of ceramic material that is often transparent and so ideal for making windows.

Plastics

Plastics are usually made from chemicals that do not occur naturally. They are called synthetics and have to be made by chemists, usually from the products of oil. Plastics can be moulded into every possible shape. Some are bendable and others are sturdier, and most are tough. Televisions, computers, games consoles, cars and mobile phones all have parts made of

▲ Many canoes are made from fibreglass, which is a strong and light material.

plastic components. Composite materials contain two or more different kinds of materials. The hull of a boat, for example, may be made of fibreglass, which is both strong and light. Fibreglass has fine fibres of glass embedded in a plastic material. Car brake pads are made of a soft metal with hard ceramic particles mixed in.

Brass is another alloy. It is a shiny yellowish metal, which is often used for decoration. Brass is a mixture of copper and zinc. Bronze is an alloy that is made of copper and tin. And nickel coins are made of copper and nickel.

Ceramics

Ceramics are different again. Cups and plates are examples of ceramics. The main chemicals used

ORGANIC MATERIALS

Organic materials come from living or once-living plants or animals. So wood comes from trees, and coal and oil come from the fossilised remains of plants and tiny animals. Natural rubber comes from the milky secretions (latex) of the rubber tree, *Hevea brasiliensis*. The latex is allowed to dry, then ground and dissolved in a solvent. Other chemicals are then added to stiffen or colour the rubber.

GENERAL INFORMATION
- **The hardness of a material is measured with the Mohs scale. It ranges from 1 (soft) to 10 (hard).**
- **There are many types of plastics, including polythene, which is used to make plastic bags and clingfilm.**

See also:

Atoms and Molecules, Chemicals and Matter

MATERIALS

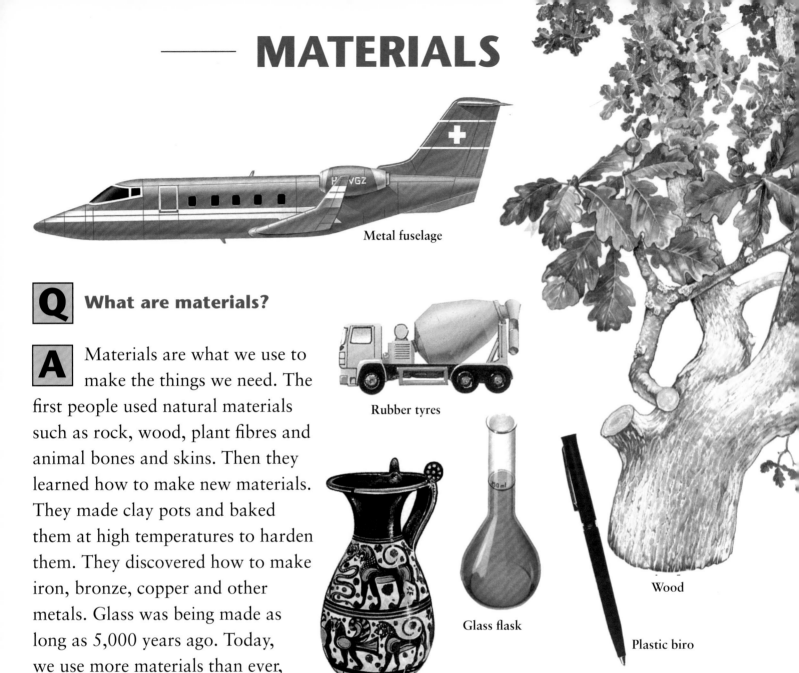

Metal fuselage

Rubber tyres

Pottery vase

Glass flask

Wood

Plastic biro

Q What are materials?

A Materials are what we use to make the things we need. The first people used natural materials such as rock, wood, plant fibres and animal bones and skins. Then they learned how to make new materials. They made clay pots and baked them at high temperatures to harden them. They discovered how to make iron, bronze, copper and other metals. Glass was being made as long as 5,000 years ago. Today, we use more materials than ever, including a wide range of plastics.

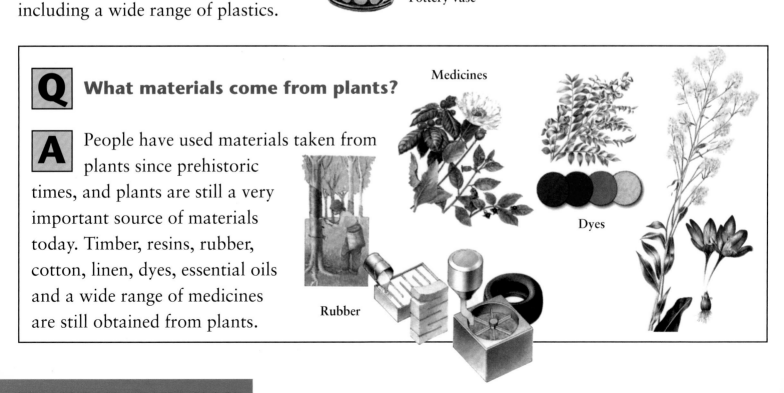

Medicines

Dyes

Rubber

Q What materials come from plants?

A People have used materials taken from plants since prehistoric times, and plants are still a very important source of materials today. Timber, resins, rubber, cotton, linen, dyes, essential oils and a wide range of medicines are still obtained from plants.

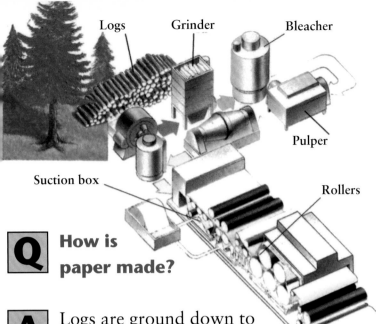

Logs Grinder Bleacher

Pulper

Suction box

Rollers

Q How is paper made?

A Logs are ground down to form a watery pulp. The pulp is poured on to wire mesh. Water is sucked and rolled out, leaving a thin film of paper. The process is continuous. Pulp is fed into one end of the machine (above) and paper comes out at the other end.

Paper

Q What do we get from crude oil?

A Crude oil is separated into materials ranging from bitumen for road-making to fuels such as petrol and gas. Crude oil is heated inside a tall fractionating tower (right). Gas and light fuels evaporate and collect near the top of the tower, leaving heavier oils and bitumen to settle at the bottom.

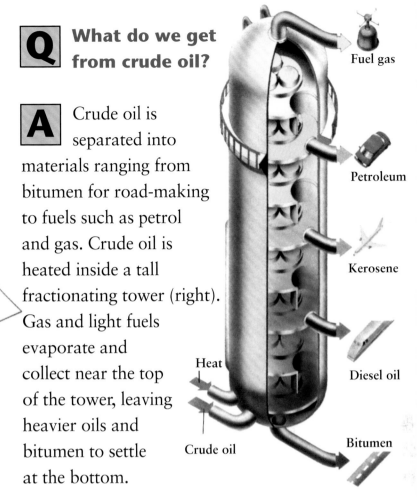

Fuel gas

Petroleum

Kerosene

Heat

Diesel oil

Crude oil

Bitumen

Q How is plastic recycled?

A Waste plastic is loaded into a furnace (below) and heated. The gas given off is then separated in a distillation column. Wax and tar collect at the bottom, while lighter gases collect further up. Some of the gas is fed back to fuel the furnace.

Q What are composites?

A Composites are materials made by combining two or more materials. Many kinds of boats (above) are made by laying mats of glass fibres into a mould and then soaking the mats in liquid plastic. The plastic sets hard and is reinforced by the fibres to make a smooth, tough, lightweight hull.

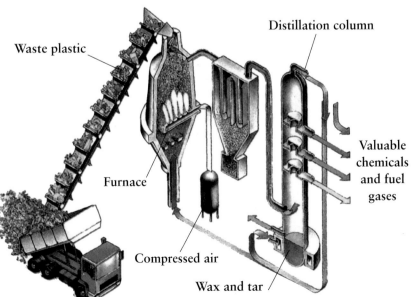

Distillation column

Waste plastic

Furnace

Valuable chemicals and fuel gases

Compressed air

Wax and tar

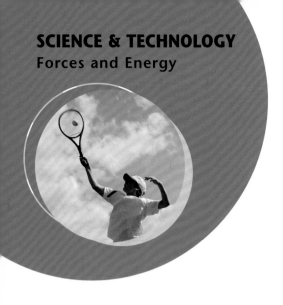

FORCES AND ENERGY

Force is a push or pull on an object. A force moves a stationary object or changes the direction or speed of a moving one. Energy makes things happen. There are several kinds of energy.

KEY FACTS

Unit of force: newton (N). This is the amount of force needed to accelerate an object with a mass of 1 kg by 1 m per second, every second.

Unit of energy: joule (J). This is the amount of energy need to apply a force of 1 newton over a distance of 1 m.

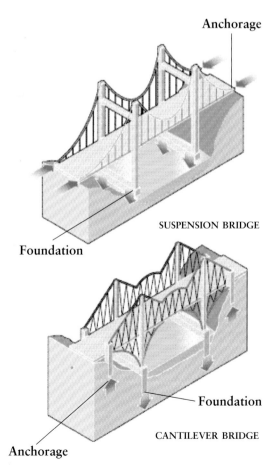

Anchorage

SUSPENSION BRIDGE

Foundation

Foundation

CANTILEVER BRIDGE

Anchorage

Forces can make things slow down, speed up or change direction. All these changes involve energy.

For example, a bullet in a gun is not moving, but when an explosive charge is detonated, it will apply a powerful force to the bullet. It will get faster (accelerate) very quickly and fly out of the gun barrel. When the bullet hits a wall, another force will act on the bullet and slow it to a complete stop.

◄ The red arrows show where forces act as each bridge pushes down on to its foundations and pulls at its anchors on land.

▲ Two hurdlers running at the same speed but in opposite directions. Their velocities are different because velocity is a combination of speed and direction.

Moving objects have kinetic energy. For example, waterwheels use the kinetic energy of moving water to perform mechanical tasks. A moving waterwheel is producing mechanical energy.

A ball balanced on a wall has potential energy, or the energy of position. When someone pushes the ball and it falls towards the ground, its potential energy is converted to kinetic energy.

CIRCULAR MOTION

When people spin around a carousel at a fair, their direction of motion is changing all the time. So they are constantly accelerating even though their speed may not change at all. Forces that cause circular motion are called torques. They pull objects around a central point. If the torque force stops acting on the object, it will fly off in a straight line.

A can of petrol has latent energy. The petrol is not doing any work, but if it is put in a car, and the engine is started, it will start doing work – driving the engine. The burning petrol in the car is producing heat energy.

Other types of energy

There are other types of energy, apart from mechanical and heat. They include electrical, chemical, sound, light and nuclear energy. Electrical energy is the energy produced by an electric current to light a bulb, for example. When the bulb lights up, the electrical energy changes to heat and light energy. Likewise, an electric guitar converts electrical energy to sound energy.

Energy conservation

When one type of energy is converted to another – for example, when electrical energy changes to heat and light in a bulb – the total amount of energy stays the same. This is called the law of conservation of energy.

GENERAL INFORMATION

- The unit of force, the newton, is named for the pioneering scientist Isaac Newton (1642–1727).
- Newton explained that any object moving in a straight line continues to move in a straight line unless a force acts on it.
- The unit of energy, the joule, is named for the English physicist James Prescott Joule (1818–1889).

See also:

Cars, Electricity and Magnetism, Heat and Light, Machines, Sound

▼ The different forces that can be applied to a ruler.

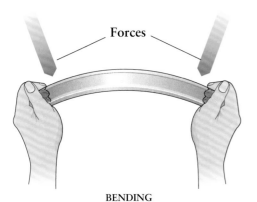

BENDING

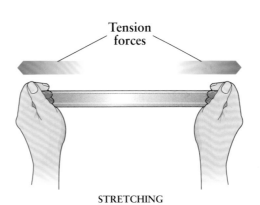

STRETCHING

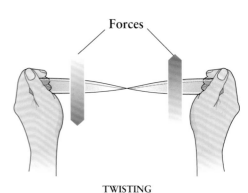

TWISTING

FORCES & ENERGY

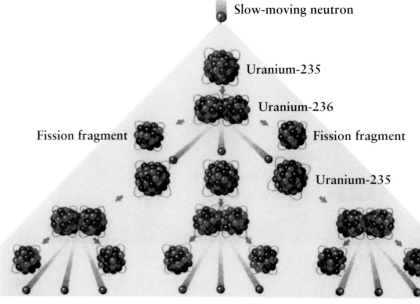

Slow-moving neutron

Uranium-235

Uranium-236

Fission fragment

Fission fragment

Uranium-235

Q What is gravity?

A Gravity is the force that pulls everything to Earth. Galileo showed that gravity makes all objects fall equally fast. When he dropped a light ball and a heavy ball from the leaning Tower of Pisa (above), they hit the ground at the same instant.

Q What is an Archimedes' Screw used for?

A The Archimedes' Screw (below) was invented by Archimedes in ancient Greece. It is used for lifting water. One end of the screw is dipped into water. By turning the handle, the water is raised up inside the tube until it spills out of the top.

Q How is energy released inside a nuclear reactor?

A A slow-moving neutron is made to hit an atom of uranium-235 (above). It combines with the nucleus at the centre of the atom, forming uranium-236. This splits into two particles called fission fragments, releasing a burst of energy and three more neutrons, which split more uranium atoms.

Q What forces act on an aeroplane in flight?

A Four forces act on an aeroplane. Its weight acts downwards. The thrust of its engines pushes it forwards. Lift created by its wings acts upwards. Drag tries to slow it down. Thrust must overcome drag, and lift must overcome weight, if a plane is to fly.

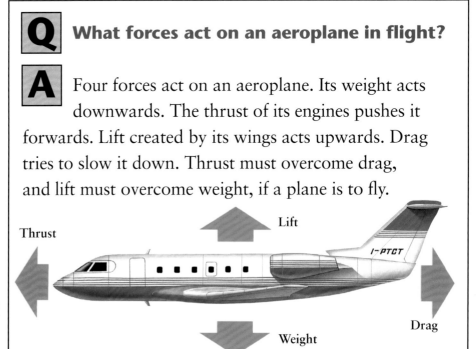

Thrust

Lift

I-PTCT

Drag

Weight

Q How does a space rocket work?

A A rocket motor propels a rocket by burning fuel mixed with an oxidiser. The oxidiser contains oxygen, which is necessary for burning. The Ariane V rocket (below) burns hydrogen fuel with oxygen. The hot gas produced rushes out of the motor nozzles, forcing the rocket upwards.

Fuel tank

Booster rocket

Oxidiser tank

Rocket motor

Motor nozzle

esa

Q What is a force?

A A force is something that changes an object's speed or direction. Forces always exist in pairs acting in opposite directions. When a rifle is fired (below right), the rifle kicks back as the bullet flies forwards. A heavier football player running faster applies a greater force than a lighter, slower player (below left).

Q What is friction?

A Friction is a force that stops surfaces sliding across each other easily. Sometimes friction is helpful. It allows our shoes to grip the ground. Without friction walking would be impossible. But friction can also be a problem because it wears out the moving parts of machines.

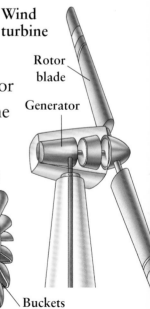

Q How does a turbine work?

A A turbine (right) is a machine that uses gas or liquid to make a shaft turn. Water hitting the buckets of a Pelton wheel drives the buckets round and turns the shaft. Wind spins the blades of a wind turbine. Wind and water turbines often drive electricity generators.

Wind turbine

Rotor blade

Generator

Pelton wheel

Water jet

Shaft

Buckets

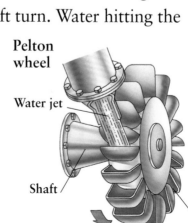

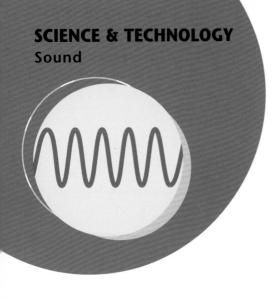

SOUND

Sound travels through air, water and even solid materials such as metals. It travels in waves. When the waves reach a person's ears, the brain turns the vibrations into sounds that can be heard.

KEY FACTS

Unit of sound frequency: hertz (Hz). This is the number of sound waves registered per second. 1,000 Hz is the same as 1 kilohertz, or kHz.

Unit of loudness: decibel (dB)

When something vibrates in air, the air molecules next to it are pushed together, then pulled apart. The molecules bump into the ones next to them, and they do the same. The vibrations spread further and further from the vibrating object. This is how sound travels, like a wave.

Sound cannot travel if there are no molecules to vibrate. So it will not move through a vacuum. It travels faster through a solid than it does through a liquid, and faster through a liquid than through a gas. In air at normal room temperature, sound travels at 1,224 kilometres per hour. Through steel it moves much faster – at 21,600 kilometres per hour.

Volume

Sounds may be loud or soft. When someone rings a large church bell, it sounds much louder than a squeaking mouse. Loudness, which is measured in decibels (dB), depends on the energy of the sound wave. The wave's energy

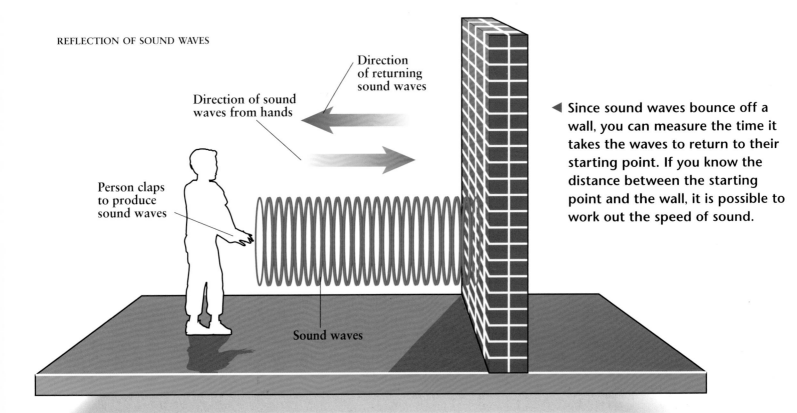

REFLECTION OF SOUND WAVES

Direction of returning sound waves

Direction of sound waves from hands

Person claps to produce sound waves

Sound waves

◀ Since sound waves bounce off a wall, you can measure the time it takes the waves to return to their starting point. If you know the distance between the starting point and the wall, it is possible to work out the speed of sound.

depends on lots of things – for example, how hard the church bell is struck.

Pitch

A squeaking mouse makes a high-pitched sound. A large bell being struck makes a low-pitched sound. Pitch is measured in hertz (Hz) and depends on the number of vibrations passing through the air each second. This is also called

the frequency of the sound. Most people can hear sounds as high-pitched as 20,000 vibrations per second (20,000 Hz, or 20 kilohertz; kHz) and as low as 20 vibrations per second (20 Hz).

Echoes

If you shout into an empty room or a cave, you hear the echo of your own voice a few moments after you shout. Echoes are sound waves that have been reflected off walls and other objects.

Refraction

Sound waves can also be bent away from their original path if they pass from one substance to another – for example, from air to water. This is called refraction.

◀ A woman's voice usually has a frequency between 165 and 255 Hz, while a man's is typically from 85 to 180 Hz. Bats make high-pitched sounds up to 100 kHz.

GENERAL INFORMATION

- The study of sound is called acoustics.
- A soft whisper 2 m away registers 30 decibels (dB). Every time the volume of the sound is doubled, the loudness increases by 10 dB. A person speaking very close is 70 dB. A jet aircraft taking off 60 m away is 120 dB.
- Units of sound frequency are named for the German scientist Heinrich Hertz (1857–1894).
- Sound bends around objects – as long as the objects are not very large. This is called the diffraction of sound.

See also:

Atoms and Molecules, Forces and Energy, Materials

SOUND

Direction of wave ▶

Q What is sound?

Rarefaction   Compression   Rarefaction

A Sound is a form of energy. Sound is made when something vibrates in air. The vibrations push against the surrounding air molecules, forming a sound wave. First the air molecules are squeezed (this is called compression), then they are stretched (this is called rarefaction). It is easiest to think of sound waves moving in the same way as a wave of energy moves along a coiled spring if one end is repeatedly pushed and pulled (above).

Q How do we hear sounds?

A When sound waves reach us, the outer ear channels them inside the ear, where they make the eardrum vibrate. The vibrations are magnified 20 times by the hammer, anvil and stirrup bones, causing liquid to vibrate inside a tube called the cochlea (right). Nerves in the cochlea pass messages to the brain, enabling us to recognise the sound.

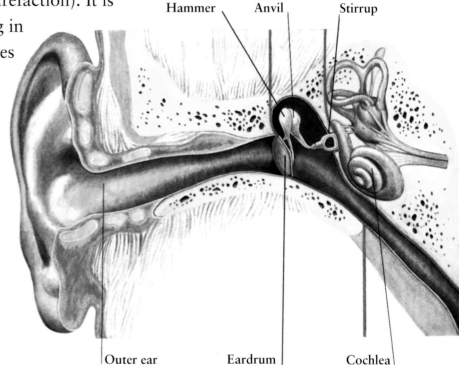

Hammer   Anvil   Stirrup

Outer ear   Eardrum   Cochlea

Q How fast does sound travel?

A Sound travels through solids, liquids and gases at different speeds. Its speed depends on the density of the material. It travels faster through dense materials like steel than through less dense materials like air (below).

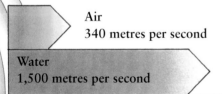

Air
340 metres per second

Water
1,500 metres per second

Concrete
5,000 metres per second

Steel
6,000 metres per second

The speed of sound in different materials

Q How is loudness measured?

A Loudness depends on the amount of energy carried by a sound wave. Loudness is measured in decibels (dB). Sounds louder than 120 dB can damage the ears. Sounds louder than 130 dB cause pain. Some animals, like bats, make sounds that we cannot hear at all (below).

Decibels 140   Pain threshold   130   100   70   40   0

Q Why does the sound of a racing car engine change as it drives past us?

A As the racing car (right) approaches, the sound waves in front of it get squashed together. These short sound waves make the engine's noise sound high pitched. As the car moves past, the sound waves become stretched out behind it. The longer waves make the engine's note sound lower.

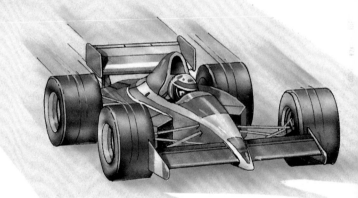

Q How does sound travel down telephone wires?

A A microphone in the mouthpiece converts the sound pressure waves of the caller's voice into electrical signals. These flow along wires (below) to the telephone at the other end. The magnet in the earpiece converts the signals back into sound pressure waves.

Magnet

Microphone

ELECTRICITY AND MAGNETISM

Electricity is the name given to anything that happens because of the presence or movement of charged particles. Magnetism is a force that draws some metals together, or pushes them apart.

Most people use electricity every day – to light homes, start cars and operate computers and machinery.

Electricity comes from charged particles that are too small to see. Everything is made of atoms, and these are made up of even smaller particles called neutrons, protons and electrons. Protons contain a small positive electrical charge and electrons have a small negative charge. Usually, the number of protons and the number of electrons inside an atom are the same. The charges balance. If atoms lose some of their electrons, they become positively charged. If they gain electrons, they develop a negative charge.

Static electricity

Particles with a positive charge attract those with a negative charge. If you rub a plastic ruler with a cloth, some of the electrons on the atoms from the ruler will rub off onto the cloth. The ruler will gain a positive charge, and the cloth a negative charge. The cloth and the ruler will attract each other and stick together for a few seconds. This is static electricity.

Electrical current

In the 19th century, scientists managed to get electrons to flow

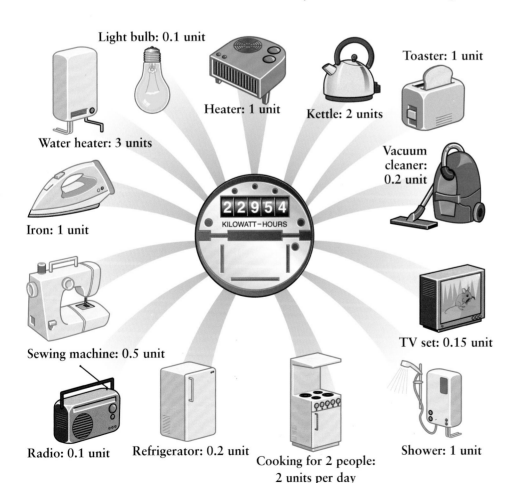

Light bulb: 0.1 unit

Heater: 1 unit

Kettle: 2 units

Toaster: 1 unit

Water heater: 3 units

Vacuum cleaner: 0.2 unit

22954
KILOWATT−HOURS

Iron: 1 unit

Sewing machine: 0.5 unit

TV set: 0.15 unit

Radio: 0.1 unit   Refrigerator: 0.2 unit

Cooking for 2 people: 2 units per day

Shower: 1 unit

◀ **The diagram shows the number of units of electrical energy typically used by household appliances in one hour. Information such as this can help people reduce their energy usage.**

See also:

Atoms and Molecules, Heat and Light

GENERAL INFORMATION

- American inventor Thomas Edison (1847–1931) built the world's first electrical power station in 1882.
- Earth has its own magnetic field. It is this that directs the needle on a compass.
- Magnets were once made from iron or nickel. The strongest magnets are now made from metals such as cobalt.

◄ Modern electromagnets are strong enough to lift loads of scrap metal.

along wires. This flow is called electric current and it works by electrical conduction. It allowed the use of many types of electrical machinery that used current generated in power stations.

Magnetism

Magnetism is the force that holds a magnet to a refrigerator and works a compass. Magnetism and electricity work together to make a force called electromagnetism.

Every electrical current creates its own magnetic field. And every magnet can create an electrical current. Electricity can be used to make very powerful magnets called electromagnets.

CONDUCTORS AND INSULATORS

Some materials are better at conducting electrical current than others. They are called conductors. Metals are good conductors. Plastics, rubber, glass and wood are poor conductors. They are called insulators. Plastic insulation is placed around wires to keep the charge from escaping.

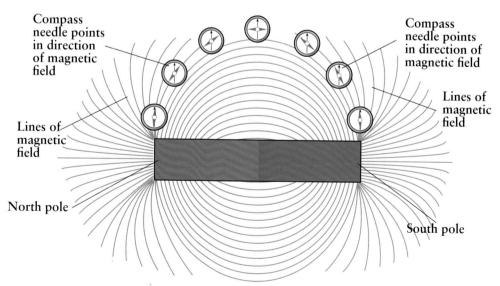

▲ The area influenced by a magnet is called its magnetic field. It is this that directs the needle on a compass, as shown on this diagram.

ELECTRICITY & MAGNETISM

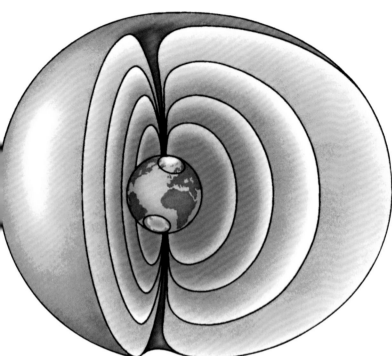

Q How do electric vehicles work?

A An electric car (above) works by using electricity stored in batteries to power an electric motor connected to the car's wheels. Electric trains are supplied with electricity from wires above the track or a third rail beside the track. It powers electric motors that turn the wheels.

Q What is a magnetic field?

A A magnetic field is a region of forces that exists around a magnet. The field can be drawn as a series of curved lines, called lines of force, joining the magnet's north and south poles. The Earth behaves like a magnet. Its magnetic field (above), caused by electric currents inside the liquid part of its core, stretches thousands of kilometres into space.

Q How are magnets made?

A An iron bar contains molecular magnets pointing in all directions. If the bar is placed inside a coil carrying an electric current, the molecular magnets line up with the coil's magnetic field. The bar has now become a magnet (right).

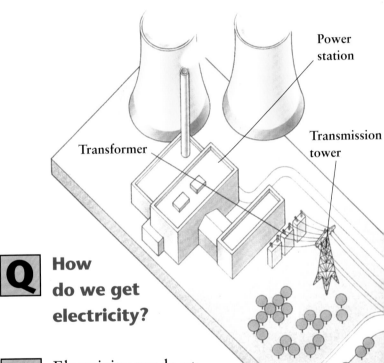

Power station

Transmission tower

Transformer

Q How do we get electricity?

A Electricity made at power stations (right) is distributed along cables at a very high voltage. The cables cross the countryside, strung between tall transmission towers. Electricity is distributed inside towns by underground cables. Before it can be used, its voltage must be reduced. The final voltage varies from country to country.

Q How do electric motors work?

A An electric motor is made of a coil of wire inside a magnet. The coil is free to turn. When an electric current flows through the coil, it magnetises the coil. This magnetic field pushes against the magnetic field produced by the surrounding magnet and this makes the coil spin.

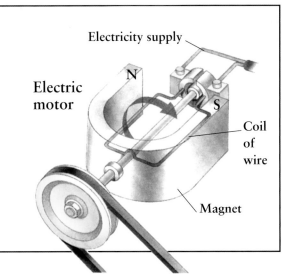

Electricity supply

Electric motor

N

S

Coil of wire

Magnet

Q How does a door bell work?

A When the bell push (below) is pressed, the coil becomes magnetised. The iron rod shoots out of the coil and strikes the short chime. When the bell push is released, the rod swings back into the coil and hits the long chime.

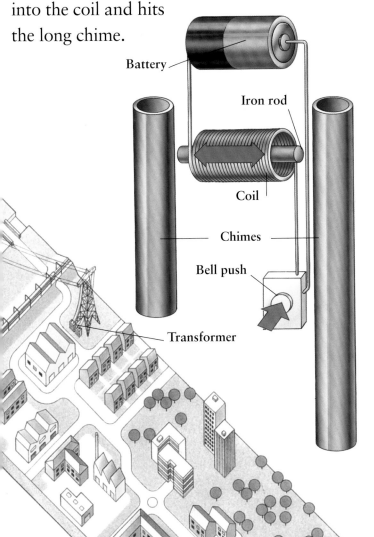

Battery

Iron rod

Coil

Chimes

Bell push

Transformer

Q What is inside a battery?

A Cars and lorries use a type of battery called an accumulator (below). It contains flat plates of lead and lead oxide dipped in sulphuric acid. When the battery is connected to a circuit, a chemical reaction between the plates and the acid makes an electric current flow round the circuit. An accumulator is recharged by passing an electric current through it.

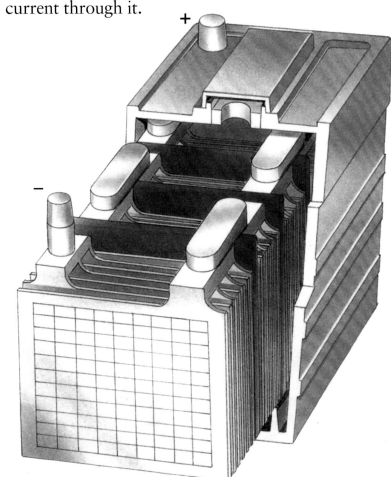

+

−

HEAT AND LIGHT

Heat and light are forms of energy. Heat is produced by the movement of the tiny particles that make up all matter. Light is made up of waves of electric and magnetic vibrations.

KEY FACTS

Heat: is measured in joules (J)
Temperature: is measured in degrees Celsius (°C) or Fahrenheit (°F)
Light: is measured in several different ways

When heat energy is added to any material, its molecules vibrate faster and faster. This is true of the air around us on a summer day or the water in a boiling kettle. Heat naturally flows from hotter objects to cooler ones. Some of the energy of motion in the molecules in the hotter object is given to the molecules in the cooler one.

Making heat

Heat can be produced in many ways. For example, when an electrical current flows through a wire, the current makes the atoms of the wire move faster, and the wire gets hot. When two surfaces rub against each other at speed, both surfaces will become hot

▲ This furnace for making glass is giving off light and heat energy.

▶ When an object is cool its molecules vibrate only slowly. As it is heated, they vibrate more and more.

because their molecules are vibrating faster. This is called friction. When sunshine beats down on a road, the infrared radiation within the sunlight excites the road's molecules. They vibrate faster and get hot.

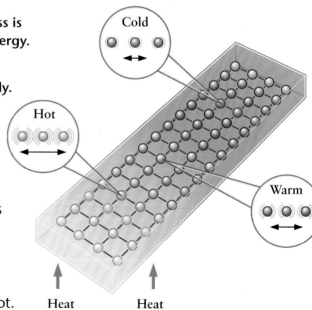

Light

The main source of light is the Sun. During the day, we see objects because they reflect sunlight into our eyes. Light is made up of moving waves of electric and magnetic energy. Light travels at 300,000 kilometres per second. Scientists think that nothing travels faster than light.

Visible light cannot travel through everything. Non-visible wavelengths, such as X rays, can pass through more substances.

Refraction and reflection

When light waves travel from one material to another, they bend, or refract. This is what happens when you hold a rod in water. The part of the rod above the water appears to be at a different angle

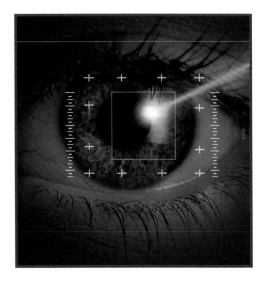

▲ A laser focuses light in a very narrow beam, producing heat. This can be used to cut through soft tissues in eye surgery.

from the part below the surface. Different substances bend light rays by different amounts. Light waves cannot travel through a mirror but they reflect off the silvery surface behind the glass so you see a reversed image of yourself.

GENERAL INFORMATION

- Heat is not the same as temperature.
- Temperature is the word used to describe how hot something is. The temperature of something is not the same as how much heat it contains.
- The coldest temperature possible is called absolute zero. It is 0 Kelvin (K), or –273.15°C. No one knows what the hottest possible temperature is.
- Nearly every material gets bigger, or expands, when it heats up and gets smaller, or contracts, when it cools down.

See also:

Forces and Energy, Materials, Molecules and Atoms

VISIBLE LIGHT SPECTRUM

When sunlight passes through a special block of glass called a prism (right) it splits into different colours, called a spectrum. We see the rainbow colours of the visible spectrum: red, orange, yellow, green, blue, indigo and violet. Our eyes cannot see light of higher or lower wavelengths. Rays that are just longer than red light are called infrared and are felt as heat. Rays that are just shorter than violet light are called ultraviolet.

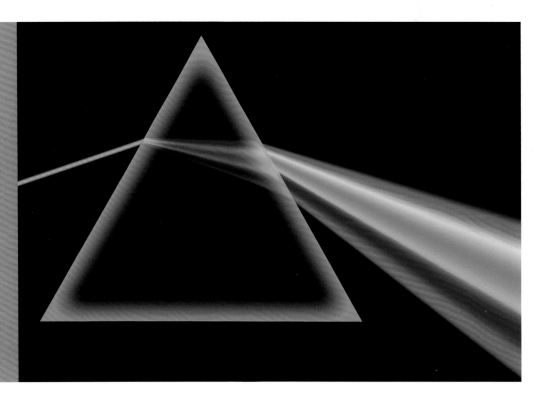

HEAT & LIGHT

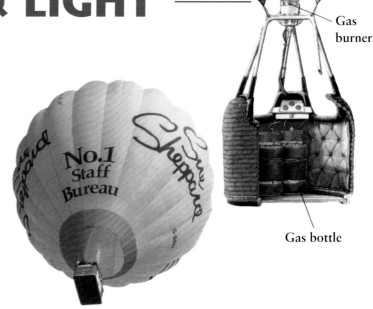

Gas burner

Gas bottle

Q What is light?

A Light is a form of energy. It is composed of waves of electric and magnetic vibrations that our eyes can detect. The different colours (below) are produced by light waves of different lengths. We are unable to see waves shorter than blue light and longer than red.

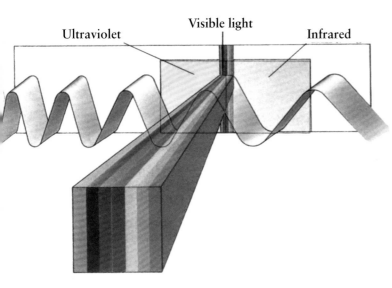

Ultraviolet   Visible light   Infrared

Q How does a hot-air balloon rise?

A A gas burner supplied with gas from bottles in the balloon's basket (above) heats the air inside the balloon. As the air warms up, it expands. The thinner air inside the balloon is lighter than the surrounding air, so the balloon floats upwards.

Q How fast does light travel?

A The speed of light is 300,000 km/s, faster than anything else in the Universe. Light takes roughly 8.5 minutes to travel from the Sun (below) to the Earth. Looking at distant objects allows us to look back in time. When we look at a remote galaxy, we see it as it was when the light left it.

Q How does a laser work?

A Light is normally composed of different wavelengths (colours) mixed at random. A laser produces an intense beam of high-energy light in which all the light is of the same wavelength. The process is started by an electric current or a flash of light from a flash tube, which causes a gas or ruby rod (below) to send out the laser beam.

Mirror

Laser beam

Mirror

Ruby rod

Flash tube

Q What are thermals?

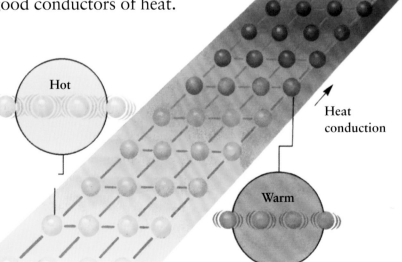

Bird's flight path

Thermal

A Birds can often be seen gliding in tight circles, being carried upwards by rising columns of air called thermals (right). Ground heated by the Sun warms the air above it. The warm air rises, sucking cool air in below it. That, too, is warmed and rises up. Glider pilots use thermals. They circle and climb inside one thermal, then glide to the next (below).

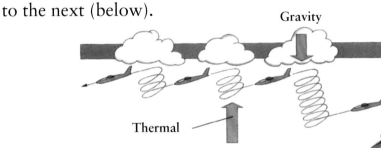

Gravity

Thermal

Q How does a fluorescent tube work?

A A hot wire inside the tube sends out particles called electrons, which crash into atoms of mercury gas. The mercury atoms give out invisible ultraviolet radiation. The white phosphor coating inside the tube (below) changes this into bright visible light.

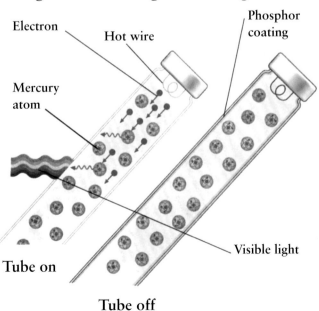

Electron

Hot wire

Phosphor coating

Mercury atom

Visible light

Tube on

Tube off

Q How does heat move along a metal bar?

A When something is heated, its atoms vibrate. If one end of a metal bar is heated, the atoms at that end vibrate more than the atoms at the cold end. The vibration spreads along the bar from atom to atom. The spread of heat in this way is called conduction. Metals are good conductors of heat.

Cold

Hot

Warm

Heat conduction

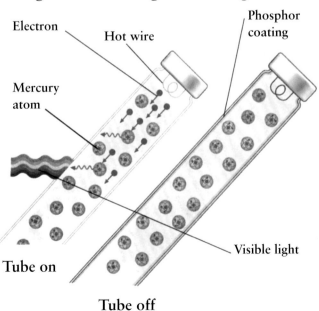

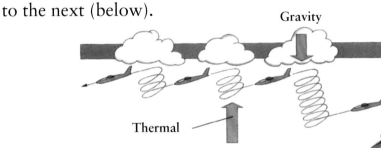

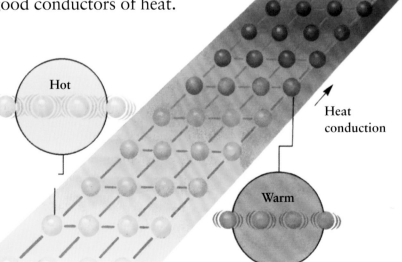

EVERYDAY SCIENCE

Think for a few moments about the things around you at home and in your school. Hardly anything does not work on the basis of scientific principles.

KEY FACTS

Everyday appliances that use electric motors: computer fan, electric toothbrush, food blender, tin opener, hairdrier, microwave fan, refrigerator, washing machine and vacuum cleaner

Everyday appliances that use electromagnetism: electric door bell, electric fan and electromagnets in a television

Appliances, tools and modes of transport are all around us. Even the simplest things work because of scientific processes. For example, if energy is used to push a pencil across a sheet of paper, it leaves a pattern, which we read as writing.

And we rely on complicated processes, too, at home and in school. Many, such as computers, rely on electrical processes. Others, such as taps, depend on mechanical processes.

◄ **The motor that turns the drum in a washing machine is driven by a combination of electricity and magnetism.**

▲ **Science makes a lovely barbeque! Heat from burning charcoal passes through air to cook the meat and vegetables.**

Kinetic energy

Simple human effort drives many simple machines but it is science all the same. For example, a manual food mixer does its job because someone turns the handle quickly. As the handle turns, kinetic energy is transferred to the spinning mixer blades and produces cake mixture. Cycling to school is another example: the kinetic energy of legs and feet turning the pedals drives the bicycle wheels around.

Excited molecules

Other things work because heat flows from one substance to another. This is called conduction. Molecules vibrate and knock into others. In turn, those molecules vibrate and move those next to them. In this way a hot gas flame or electric filament in an oven will heat the air around it. Then the hot air will heat the food in the oven.

Vacuum flasks work in the opposite way: heat from a hot drink cannot escape because there is a vacuum (with no molecules to become excited) around it. And heat from warm surrounding air cannot pass through the vacuum to warm an iced drink.

Electromagnetism

Appliances as different as trains, washing machines and power tools rely on electromagnetism.

This works because an electric current passing through a magnetic field experiences a force. If the wire carrying the current is bent into a loop, the two sides of the loop experience forces pushing in opposite directions. These forces produce a turning effect, and the rotating motion drives the machinery around.

Computers

Many modern appliances, from the timer on a washing machine to the satellite navigation system in a car, a digital camera and a mobile phone, rely on computer systems.

▼ **The picture on an LCD (liquid-crystal display) TV screen is created by electromagnetism and chemistry.**

ELECTROMAGNETIC RADIATION

Electromagnetic radiation travels at the speed of light. It makes lots of everyday items work. TV pictures and sounds, and radio sounds are carried by low-frequency electromagnetic radiation. Mobile phones use them to receive and transmit. And microwave ovens (above) depend on the microwave part of the electromagnetic spectrum.

GENERAL INFORMATION

● Liquid crystal displays are used in TV screens, computer monitors, clocks and calculator screens. Light shines on a liquid crystal solution. Each crystal either lets light pass through or blocks it. This creates the digital displays or moving images that we see.

See also:

Atoms and Molecules, Computers, Electricity and Magnetism

EVERYDAY SCIENCE

Q How does a digital clock work?

A Tiny quartz crystals inside the digital clock (right) vibrate at a steady rate when an electric current from a battery is applied. A silicon chip picks up the vibrations and turns them into regular pulses. The pulses are displayed as numbers on the liquid crystal display (LCD) on the clock face.

LCD

Vibration

Battery

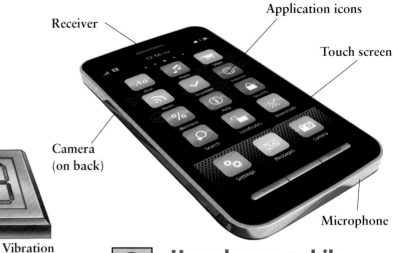

Receiver

Application icons

Touch screen

Camera (on back)

Microphone

Q How does a mobile phone work?

A When someone speaks on a mobile phone, their voice is converted into radio waves. These are sent to the nearest phone mast and forwarded to the person they are calling. When the radio waves reach the receiver's phone, they are changed back into a human voice.

Fan

Electric motor

Elements

On/off switch

Q How do hairdriers blow out hot air?

A A hairdrier (above) uses electricity in two different ways. When you switch it on, a small electric motor turns a fan inside. The fan sucks in air from the back of the hairdrier, and blows it out at the front. As the air travels through the hairdrier, it passes over a set of wire coils called elements. These are heated by the electricity, warming the air as it passes.

Q How does a vacuum flask keep liquids hot?

Cup

Stopper

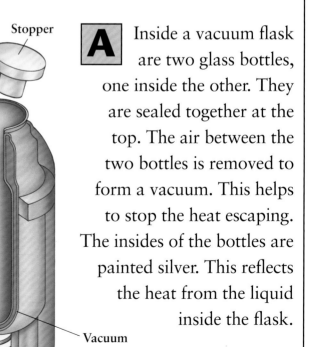

A Inside a vacuum flask are two glass bottles, one inside the other. They are sealed together at the top. The air between the two bottles is removed to form a vacuum. This helps to stop the heat escaping. The insides of the bottles are painted silver. This reflects the heat from the liquid inside the flask.

Vacuum

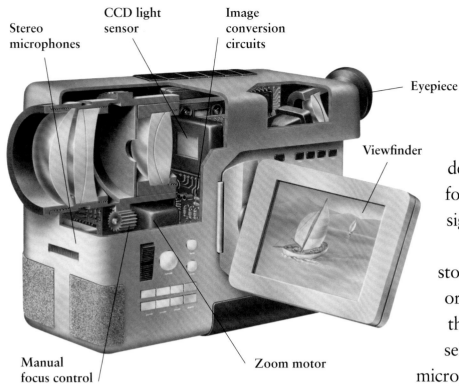

Stereo microphones

CCD light sensor

Image conversion circuits

Eyepiece

Viewfinder

Manual focus control

Zoom motor

Q What is inside a camcorder?

A Inside a camcorder, a single charge coupled device (CCD) chip converts the image formed by the lens into a colour video signal, which is recorded as a series of bytes (1s and 0s). These can then be stored as moving images in a computer or on a CD. An infrared beam focuses the lens automatically, or the user can select manual focus. At the same time, microphones pick up and store the sound.

Q Why do bicycles have gears?

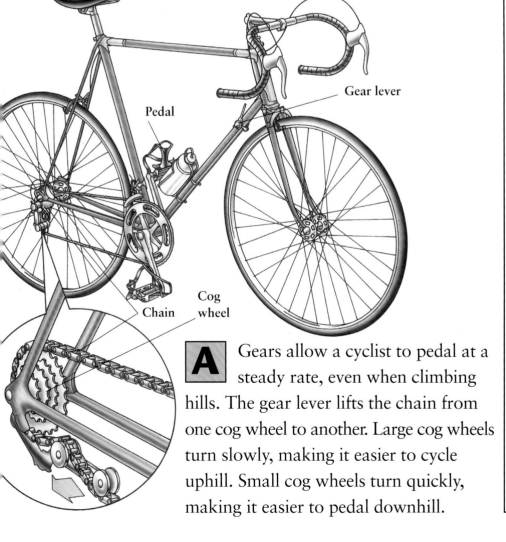

Gear lever

Pedal

Chain

Cog wheel

A Gears allow a cyclist to pedal at a steady rate, even when climbing hills. The gear lever lifts the chain from one cog wheel to another. Large cog wheels turn slowly, making it easier to cycle uphill. Small cog wheels turn quickly, making it easier to pedal downhill.

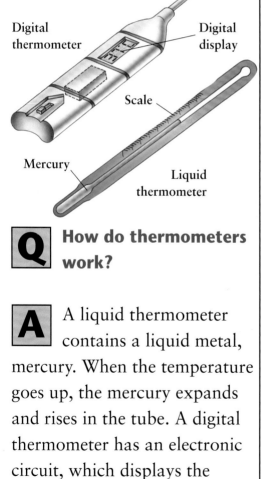

Digital thermometer

Digital display

Scale

Mercury

Liquid thermometer

Q How do thermometers work?

A A liquid thermometer contains a liquid metal, mercury. When the temperature goes up, the mercury expands and rises in the tube. A digital thermometer has an electronic circuit, which displays the temperature digitally.

INDUSTRY

Most of the things around us, from clothes to cars, have been made in factories. Factories are a crucial part of industry but not the only one. Shops and transportation are also industries.

Industry can be divided into the primary, secondary, tertiary and quaternary sectors. Primary industries produce raw materials and include agriculture (arable and livestock), logging, fishing, coal mining and oil extraction. The raw materials are then sent to factories or processing plants.

Manufacturing

Secondary (or manufacturing) industries process or refine the products of primary industry. Examples include timber mills, dairies, metal and oil refineries, car and clothes factories and mobile phone manufacturers.

▲ Cars move along a conveyor belt. More and more parts are added as they move along.

Manufacturing industry grew quickly in the Industrial Revolution, which happened in the 18th and

KEY FACTS

Countries whose factories make the most products: the United States and China each make 15 per cent of the world's total production. The next biggest producers are Japan, Germany, Russia and Brazil.

Biggest assembly plant: the Foxconn factory in Shenzhen, China, has more than 200,000 workers. They build mobile phones and cameras.

▼ High explosives blast rock from a quarry. The rock will be used for road construction. This is an example of a primary industry.

19th centuries in Europe and North America. Later, manufacturing industry developed in virtually every country in the world.

Transport and retail

Tertiary industries provide services. These include the transportation that moves manufactured goods to the shops where they are sold. These shops may be in other parts of the world. Research and development into new techniques and new products is a fourth (quaternary) sector of industry.

Automotive industry

A good example of industry at work is the manufacture of vehicles. The automotive industry makes cars, lorries and buses, and it depends on all four industrial sectors. It needs primary industries for the aluminium, iron, silica

INDUSTRY AND TRADE

Industry depends on trade between countries. The raw materials in a mobile phone, for example, are mostly metals, plastics and ceramics. Some of the metal ores come from Africa, and the plastics are from refined oil from the Middle East. The phone's circuit board might be put together in China, and the finished phone might be made in Japan. Phones are then sent around the world.

▲ Manufactured goods are packaged before being sent to a warehouse for storage.

and plastics that go into a car's bodywork, engine, glass and electrical insulation. The raw materials are processed and turned into car parts, which are put together in a car assembly factory. The assembled cars are transported to car showrooms around the world, and they also have to be advertised for sale. Meanwhile, technicians are constantly working on designs for new models of cars.

A range of industries

Industries can also be divided according to the type of things they make or the services they provide. Some examples include the chemicals, construction, ceramics, food processing,

automotive, electronics, paper-making and publishing industries.

The countries whose factories make the most products (called the gross domestic product, or GDP) are the United States and China.

GENERAL INFORMATION

- Trade between countries is made up of exports (when things are sent abroad) and imports (when things are brought in from other countries).
- The countries that send the most products abroad are China, Germany and the United States.
- The name for everything that a country produces is its gross domestic product (GDP).

See also:

Everyday Science, Transport

INDUSTRY

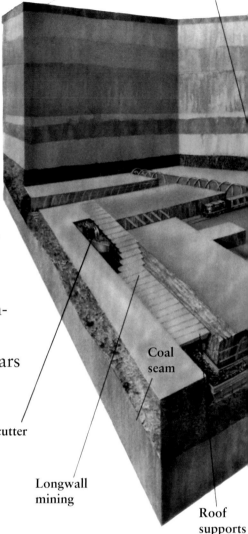

Coal seam

Coal cutter

Longwall mining

Roof supports

Q How is plastic made into shapes?

A In blow moulding, a piece of hot plastic tubing is placed in a mould. Air is blown into the tube, pushing it out into the shape of the mould.

Blow moulding

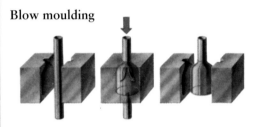

In vacuum moulding, plastic is placed over a mould and heated. Air is removed, and the vacuum pulls the plastic into the mould.

Vacuum moulding

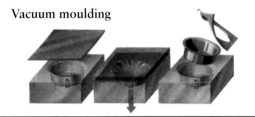

Q How is coal mined?

A Most coal is mined by either the 'longwall' or 'room-and-pillar' method (right). In longwall mining a giant coal cutter runs down the coal face removing coal as it goes, In room-and-pillar mining the coal is removed from chambers, but pillars of coal are left behind to support the roof.

Q What is paper made from?

A Most paper is made from wood (left). The wood is ground up or mashed into pulp using chemicals. The pulp is beaten so that the tiny wood fibres separate and soften. Then it passes on to a belt of wire mesh. The water drains through the mesh, and the pulp (now called the web) is squeezed first between heavy rollers and then between heated rollers. The dried and finished paper is wound on to reels.

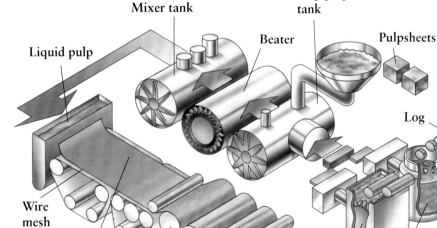

Mixer tank

Pulp preparation tank

Liquid pulp

Beater

Pulpsheets

Log

Wire mesh belt

Paper web

Steam-heated rollers

Grinding wheel

Chemical solution

Paper reel

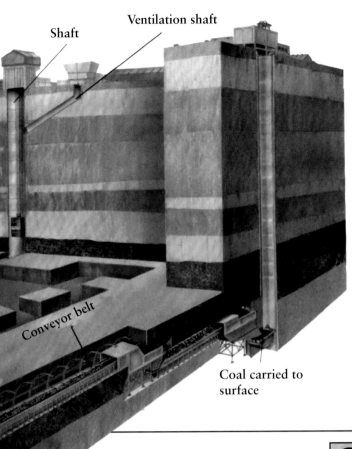

Shaft

Ventilation shaft

Conveyor belt

Coal carried to surface

Q How is cloth made on a loom?

A A loom is a machine that joins together two yarns (long threads) in a criss-cross pattern to make a cloth. The warp yarn is strung along the loom (below). The threads are raised and lowered, forming a gap, or 'shed'. Then a shuttle carrying the weft yarn is passed through the shed. Yarns can be woven into many different patterns.

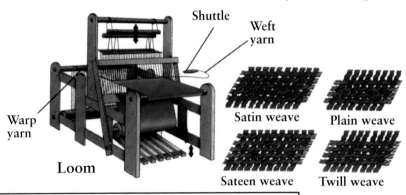

Shuttle

Weft yarn

Warp yarn

Loom

Satin weave

Plain weave

Sateen weave

Twill weave

Q How is a newspaper printed?

A Each page is made into a metal plate and wrapped around a cylinder. Where there are letters, chemicals allow ink, not water, to stick. A plate cylinder is inked and wetted, and the letters are printed on a roll of paper.

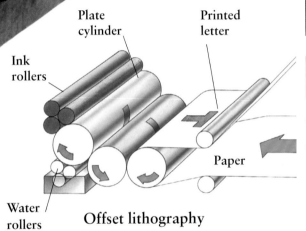

Plate cylinder

Printed letter

Ink rollers

Paper

Water rollers

Offset lithography

Q How is iron extracted from iron ore?

A Iron ore contains other substances as well as iron. The iron is extracted in a tall tower called a blast furnace (right). The ore, mixed with limestone and coke, is fed through the top. Then very hot air is blown in through pipes at the bottom of the furnace. The iron melts, and the other materials rise to the top as slag. The iron is drained off from the bottom.

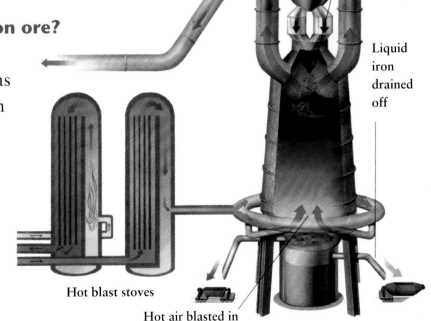

Iron ore mixed with limestone and coke

Liquid iron drained off

Hot blast stoves

Hot air blasted in

TRANSPORT

From the earliest times people have moved from place to place in search of food and shelter, to trade goods with other people or simply out of a sense of adventure.

KEY FACTS

Busiest rail station: Shinjuku in Tokyo, Japan, 1,350 million passengers every year

Busiest airport: Hartsfield-Jackson, United States, 89 million passengers every year

Busiest ferry: Star Ferry in Hong Kong, China, 26 million passengers every year

Transport has progressed from oxen carrying loads at walking pace to supersonic jet flights and even space travel. Modern modes of transport include trains, cars, lorries, aircraft, ships, canal barges, motorcycles, bicycles and spacecraft.

Modern transport

People are always seeking ways to move themselves and their goods more quickly and easily. Fast highways, with carefully designed intersections to avoid traffic queues, now link most large cities. Some six-lane and eight-lane motorways carry up to 500,000 vehicles per day. Super-fast trains connect many large cities, often in different countries.

Modern transport requires fixed installations for vehicles to travel on

◄ Barges on a canal in Amsterdam, Netherlands. The city's canals were built in the 17th century.

▲ Travelling by donkey is still a common mode of transport for people and goods in many parts of the world.

– railways, roads, aircraft runways and canals, for example. Even at sea, in the busiest waters shipping lanes have to be marked clearly to avoid collisions. Many stretches of road are lit at night to avoid accidents.

The need for speed

Transport has not always been so easy. It was slow and often hazardous until the 19th century, when the development of steam engines allowed fast rail travel.

Then, in the early 20th century, the internal combustion engine, assembly lines and better roads led to a big increase in car ownership.

Modern cities now have public transport – scheduled train, bus and ferry services, as well as taxis. People expect shelter and comfort while they wait, so bus and rail stations, airports and ferry terminals are provided.

Freight transport

Freight transport involves the movement of goods and animals by land, sea or air. The volume and speed of freight carried by sea

▲ Modern highway intersections are designed to keep cars and lorries on the move.

increased when the Suez Canal in Egypt was opened in 1869. This was a quicker route from Europe to Asia. Ships could pass from the Mediterranean to the Indian Ocean. Before, they had to sail around the southern tip of Africa.

The invention of containers and container ships made it possible to move greater volumes of freight by sea. Shanghai, China, handles 506 million tonnes of freight each year, making it the world's busiest port.

AIR FREIGHT TRANSPORT

There has also been an increase in the amount of freight carried by air. Air cargo can travel in special aeroplanes, such as the giant Russian Antonov 225, or in the holds of passenger planes. Cargoes include anything from food and books to medicines and electrical equipment.

GENERAL INFORMATION

● The Silk Road was one of the great transport routes of ancient times. It connected China, India and Persia (now Iran) with Europe and North Africa. Trade in silk and other fabrics, perfumes, spices, medicines and slaves began in the time of the Chinese Han Dynasty (206 B.C.–A.D. 220) and lasted until the late 15th century.

See also:

Flight, Land Travel, Ships

▶ A passenger aircraft takes off from a major international airport.

TRANSPORT

Q What is a maglev train?

A Maglev trains are the trains of the future. They have been designed without wheels and use the principle of magnetic levitation to raise them off the track. With friction almost eliminated, they can be propelled forward at speeds of up to 580 km/h. Commercial maglev train services now run in Shanghai, China, and Tobu-kyuryo, Japan. In 2011 work started on a new route in Beijing, China, and others are planned.

Q How big is an oil tanker?

A Oil tankers (right) carry crude oil and oil products. Supertankers can carry hundreds of thousands of tonnes of oil. The largest supertanker was over 458 metres long and 69 metres wide. When it was fully loaded with petroleum, 25 metres of its hull were under water. Supertankers are difficult to steer, and so heavy that they can take up to 5 kilometres to stop completely.

Tug used to help tanker dock

Q What is an articulated lorry?

A An articulated lorry (right) is one that consists of two separate parts. At the front is the part called the tractor unit, which contains the diesel engine, the controls, the fuel tank and the driver's cab. It has very powerful brakes and some have more than 20 gears. The tractor unit pulls the part called the trailer, which carries the cargo.

Q Is there a 'supersonic' airliner?

A Supersonic means faster than the speed of sound. The speed of sound is measured as 1,200 km/h at sea level. Concorde (left) and the Tupolev Tu-144 have been the only airliners capable of flying at supersonic speed, but neither carries passengers any more. Other commercial aircraft are not designed to fly at such speeds.

Q Who built the first steam railway locomotive?

A In 1804, Englishman Richard Trevithick built the first successful steam engine to run on rails. It hauled trucks of coal along a tramway in South Wales, UK. Trevithick later built a locomotive called *Catch Me Who Can*, which travelled at up to 16 km/h.

COMPUTERS

A computer is a system of electronic components that work together to store, obtain and process information. Modern computers can be small enough to fit into a mobile phone.

KEY FACTS

Binary system: the language used by computers to work out problems and store information. It is based on long series of the two numbers 0 and 1.

Computers have a bigger influence on our lives than we probably think. At supermarket checkouts, computers scan the barcodes on food packaging. On factory assembly lines, they direct the robots that place components on machinery and cars. They control the focussing mechanism in digital cameras. Computers link schools, businesses, governments and people around the world.

Computer hardware

People sometimes talk about computer hardware and software. Hardware is the actual machine

▲ Laptops and mobile phones are both types of computer.

– the keyboard and monitor of a laptop, for example. Computer hardware includes a central processing unit (CPU) and input and output devices. A keyboard is an input device, and so is a mouse. Output devices include monitors and printers. The CPU is the heart of the machine. It uses digital data – lots of information expressed in binary form – to make its calculations. Binary data are a series of 1s and 0s.

Information that has to be processed is given to the CPU via the keyboard or mouse. The answers (output) are displayed on a monitor, printed on paper, put on

▼ An industrial robot performs a task that a worker would once have done on a factory production line.

a disk or sent to another computer. A computer has a memory that stores data and can be read later.

Computer software

A computer needs instruction programs to tell it what to do and how to do it. One computer may have lots of different programs. They are the computer's software.

The first computers

Since ancient times people have used machines to count and calculate. The simplest of these were abacus counting machines such as those used by the Babylonians in 1000 B.C. However, it was not until the early 19th century that the English mathematician Charles Babbage (1791–1871) built what many people consider to be the first true computer.

▼ Computers at automated supermarket checkouts read bar codes on items.

COMPUTERS AND ROBOTS

Computer technology allowed the rapid development of human-like robots such as ASIMO, which was first introduced by the Japanese car manufacturer Honda in 2000. ASIMO can run at 9 kilometres per hour and reacts to moving objects, sounds and faces. It can judge distances and directions, shake hands, pour drinks and recognise ten different faces, addressing them by name. More dramatic advances in robotic technology are expected in the future.

GENERAL INFORMATION

- The first personal computers (PCs) were invented in the 1980s.
- Early computers were mechanical. When people found out how to use electricity, computers became much faster.
- The first computers to share information between different locations were built in the 1950s. They were for military use only. Later, this network spread far beyond the military to form the Internet. Millions of computers and mobile phones are now connected to the Internet.
- Wireless communication between computers is now commonplace.

See also:

Electricity and Magnetism, Industry

COMPUTERS

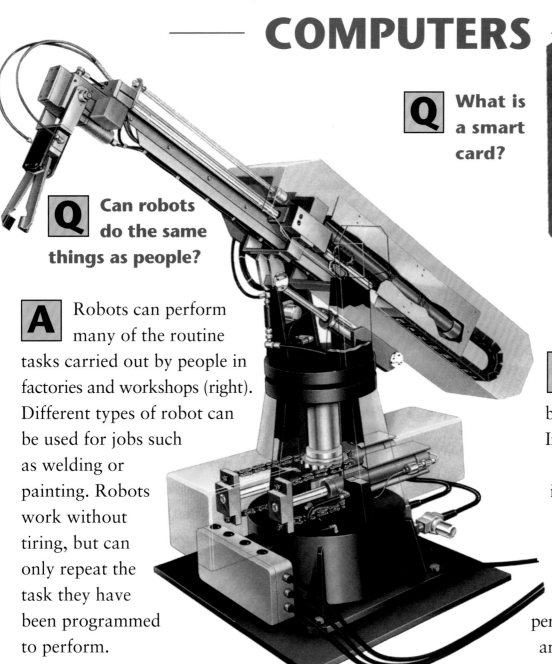

Pick-and-place robot

Q **What is a smart card?**

Micro circuit

Q **Can robots do the same things as people?**

A Robots can perform many of the routine tasks carried out by people in factories and workshops (right). Different types of robot can be used for jobs such as welding or painting. Robots work without tiring, but can only repeat the task they have been programmed to perform.

A Smart cards (above) are used by banks and other organisations. Inside the small piece of plastic is a micro-circuit on which information is stored. A smart credit card, for instance, has money values stored in it that are reduced every time a purchase is made. Cards that permit travel on public transport are another form of smart card.

Q **What is virtual reality?**

A Virtual reality is a computerised fantasy world that seems like the real thing. To enter it, the user wears a helmet with a computer screen inside (right). As the user moves his/her head, different parts of the 'world' appear within the screen. In some virtual reality programs the user moves a joystick to make the images move on the screen. Sometimes sensors attached to the body enable the user to 'touch' things. The science of virtual reality is developing very quickly. Simulators used to train aircraft pilots and tank commanders use a form of virtual reality.

Printer

CD or DVD

External hard drive

Laptop computer

Wireless mouse

Virtual reality glove and helmet

Smartphone

Audio headphones

Q What are computer peripherals?

A Peripherals (left) are devices that input or output information to or from a computer. The computer itself (the one illustrated is a laptop) consists of a case with electronic circuits inside. All other equipment is peripheral, meaning that it is outside of or extra to the computer. A mouse or a keyboard is most commonly used to input instructions, and a screen and printer to output them. Information is stored on the hard disk (in the computer itself) or on CDs or DVDs. Virtual reality devices, audio headphones and picture scanners can be attached to the computer. A smartphone carries out many of the functions of a computer and is even more portable.

Q What is computer-aided design?

A Computer-aided design (CAD) is often used in industry. Details of a new product design are fed into a computer. The computer displays a model that designers can look at from all angles. They can test out new ideas on the model. For instance, the addition of a more powerful engine may require wider tyres. Here (right) a computer model is being used to test air flow over a car design. This shows that the addition of a small spoiler on the rear of the car will give better road holding.

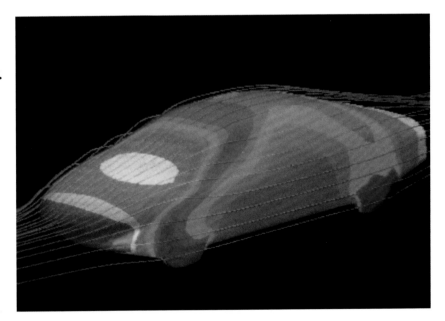

MACHINES

Machines use power to do a job of work. The machine can be simple – for example, a hand-held lever. Many modern machines, however, are very complex, such as the engine of a jet plane.

The first machines were little more than simple tools. They included wooden levers and rollers made of tree trunks, which were used to move rocks. Thousands of years of innovation were needed to advance from these to today's machinery. Many revolutionary inventions came during the Industrial Revolution. Modern machinery includes extraordinarily complex computer-controlled robots and ultra-powerful jet engines and water-driven turbines.

Many different kinds of machines perform every conceivable task. Some of the

KEY FACTS

Biggest machine: the Large Hadron Collider in Cern, Switzerland, is used for physics experiments and is 27 km long
Biggest digging machine: the Bagger 288 is 95 m tall and 215 m long

▼ An old flour mill in the United States. The mill ground grain into flour for bread making. Power was provided by a flowing stream, which turned the waterwheel and the grinding apparatus.

▲ A radio telescope is a combination of many different machines.

components used in modern machinery are basically the same as those used centuries ago, such as axles, gears and bearings. However, many more sophisticated machines do harder work more efficiently.

Electrical machinery

Electrical machinery either converts mechanical energy to electrical energy (electric generators) or electrical energy to mechanical energy (electric motors). The electric generators in power stations are some of the biggest machines of all. They produce almost all the electricity we use. In coal-fired, oil-fired and nuclear power stations, the mechanical energy is provided by steam

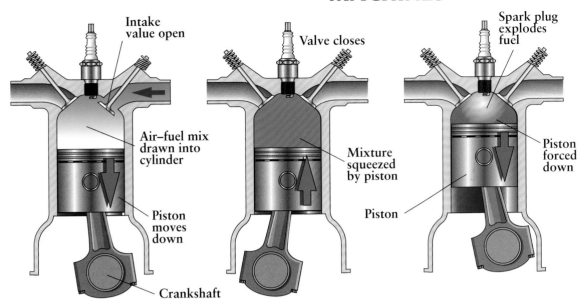

Intake valve open

Air–fuel mix drawn into cylinder

Piston moves down

Crankshaft

STROKE ONE: PISTON DROPS

Valve closes

Mixture squeezed by piston

STROKE TWO: PISTON RISES

Spark plug explodes fuel

Piston forced down

Piston

STROKE THREE: PISTON DROPS

Exhaust

Piston pushes gases out of cylinder

STROKE FOUR: PISTON RISES

▲ Petroleum and air are ignited in a car's internal combustion engine. The high-pressure gases produced move pistons and turn the car's wheels.

turbines. The power of flowing steam turns the turbines, which then produce electricity. In a hydro-electric power station the power comes from water flowing through a dam. Wind turbines operate using the same principles, except that air rather than water is the power source. The electricity that is produced provides the energy for factories, schools and homes. Most of this electricity drives electric motors inside millions of machines.

Engines

Internal combustion engines are another everyday type of machine.

They operate by burning a mixture of petroleum or diesel and air and are found in cars and lorries, and many aircraft and boats. The largest are the diesel-powered engines in some supertankers.

GENERAL INFORMATION

- The first steam engine was designed by Hero of Alexandria in the 1st century A.D.
- In 1826 the English inventor Samuel Brown used an internal combustion engine to power a vehicle for the first time.
- The world's biggest internal combustion engine is used to power supertankers and giant container ships. Ignition of the diesel fuel takes place in 14 huge cylinders. These engines are nearly 30 m long.

PUMPS AND COMPRESSORS
Pumps are devices that move gases or liquids – for example, removing oil from the ground (left) or keeping a mine dry. Heat pumps move heat from one area to another, something that is vital in refrigerator technology. Compressors increase the pressure of a gas by reducing its volume. They are used in many types of machinery, including jet engines.

See also:

Industrial Revolution, Land Travel

MACHINES

Q When was the first locomotive invented?

A On 21 February 1804, Richard Trevithick demonstrated his latest invention at the Penydarren mining railway in Wales. It was the world's first railway locomotive (right). It made a journey of 16 kilometres in four hours, pulling 10 tonnes of iron on which 70 men sat.

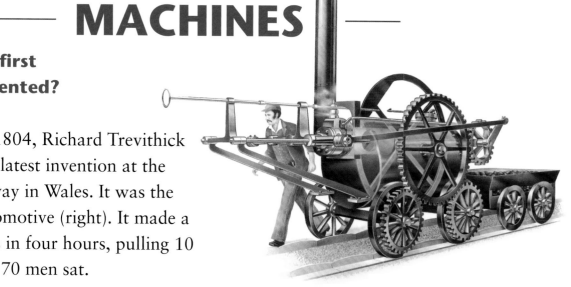

Q What is a bulldozer?

A A bulldozer is a machine used mainly on building sites to shift earth. It has caterpillar tracks to grip soft ground and a blade at the front that can be raised or lowered. To scrape the ground level, the bulldozer drives forwards with the blade lowered.

Q How does a hovercraft work?

A A hovercraft (below) travels over land and water by floating on top of a cushion of air. Powerful fans inside the hovercraft suck air down underneath it. A flexible rubber skirt around the edge of the hovercraft holds the air in as the craft rises. Propellers above the deck spin round to push the hovercraft forward.

Air   Fan

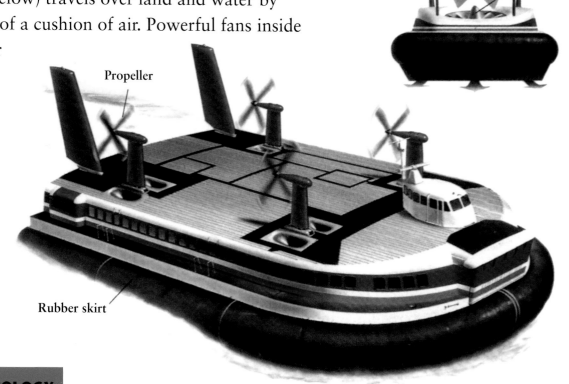

Propeller

Rubber skirt

Jib — **Driver in cab** — **Weight to balance load**

Q How does a tower crane work?

A A tower crane (right) moves materials on a building site. A hook is suspended from a trolley that can move along the jib. The jib can also swing round. The hook is raised by a motor that winds a cable around a drum. The open frame of the tower and jib saves weight.

Q How do machines study the Earth?

A Satellites orbiting the Earth are observing our planet all the time. Seasat (below) bounced radar signals off the sea to carry out oceanographic research. Other satellites measure the temperature of the sea and land, wind speed and direction, the height of waves and pollution. They also measure forest clearance, iceberg movements, volcanic eruptions and the ocean floor.

Q How does a robot arm work?

A Robot arms are used in industry for cutting, drilling, welding and painting. Their joints are driven by motors that are controlled by computer. Different tools can be fitted to the arm's mechanical hand and then its computer can be programmed to make it carry out different jobs.

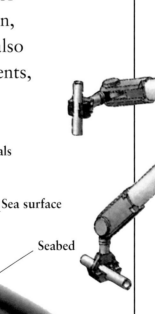

Radar signals

Sea surface

Seabed

SHIPS

For thousands of years people have used ships to trade goods, explore the world and fight their enemies. Many modern ships and boats are used simply for pleasure.

KEY FACTS

Largest cruise ship: *Oasis of the Seas* carries 6,000 passengers and weighs 225,000 tonnes

Largest cargo ship: TI Class supertankers *Africa*, *Asia*, *Europe* and *Oceania* weigh 518,000 tonnes when fully laden with oil

Fastest ship: *Spirit of Australia*, a jet-powered speedboat, reached 464 km/h in 1978

▼ Dug-out canoes, powered by people with oars, have remained largely unchanged for thousands of years.

A ship is a watertight vessel, usually powered by sails, oars, steam turbines or internal combustion engines. Smaller craft are usually called boats, and these range from motor cruisers and yachts to open rowboats and racing dinghies.

The first boats were probably built around 8000 B.C. They were constructed from hollowed-out logs, bundles of reeds and rafts made with animal skins. The ancient Egyptians are known to have built boats with streamlined hulls in 3000 B.C. Around this time, sails were first used on boats in Mesopotamia. At last, human effort was not required to move a boat – as long as there was some wind.

▲ Modern submarines are powered by nuclear reactors.

The age of sail

From the 13th century onwards, larger ships were built to carry more cargo over greater distances and explorers to distant parts of the world. Instead of one mast with a single sail, ships had numerous sails on two or three masts. Many ships had several decks built on top of each other. Passenger transport came later: the first scheduled sailing-ship service across the Atlantic Ocean, between New York, USA, and Liverpool, England, ran in 1817.

Steam power

Steam power took over from sail in the later 19th century. It was more reliable than sail since it did not depend on winds. Other important developments followed. Strong

▲ In the 19th century, bigger areas of sail on multi-masted clippers increased sailing speeds.

iron hulls replaced easily damaged wood. Screw propellers replaced paddle wheels. High-speed turbine engines were developed, and diesel engines replaced steam in the early years of the 20th century. The age of giant cruise liners and mighty battleships had arrived.

Ships today

Most of the world's international trade is carried on 35,000 large commercial ships. These include container ships – large flat-decked craft that can be stacked high with sealed freight containers – and oil-laden supertankers, which weigh up to 518,000 tonnes. Trawlers spend long periods fishing at sea. There are also countless leisure craft: cruisers, dinghies and yachts.

▲ Luxurious cruise liners are like floating hotels and are popular with people wishing to take an ocean holiday.

GENERAL INFORMATION

- Submarines enabled underwater travel but they are used for military use only. Nuclear-powered submarines were built in the late 20th century. They can stay under water for months and do not need refuelling during their 25-year lifespan.

See also:

Great Explorers, Transport

UNUSUAL CRAFT

Some ships have unusual designs. Hydrofoils (right) and hovercraft are used for fast, short-range passenger services. Hydrofoils skim over the water on ski-like struts, so their hulls lift clear of the water at high speeds. Hovercraft sail on a cushion of air a few centimetres above the water's surface.

SHIPS

Q What was the largest ship ever built?

A The world's largest ships are cargo vessels. The largest of these are the supertankers that carry oil around the world (left). The largest one ever built was the oil tanker *Knock Nevis*. It was 458 metres long and 69 metres across. Its cavernous hull extended 25 metres below the waterline. When full of oil, it weighed 565,000 tonnes.

Q How does a lifeboat work?

A When a distress message is received, a lifeboat is quickly on its way. It may be launched from a carriage, down a slipway, or from a permanent mooring that the crew reaches by small boat. Lifeboats are designed to operate in rough seas. Most can turn themselves the right way up if they capsize.

Q What is inside a submarine?

A A submarine (below) contains a pressurised compartment where the crew lives and works. The space between this and the outer hull contains a series of fuel, oil, water, waste and ballast tanks. When the ballast tanks are flooded with sea water, the submarine becomes heavier than the surrounding water and sinks. When air is pumped into the tanks, forcing the water out, the submarine becomes lighter and rises.

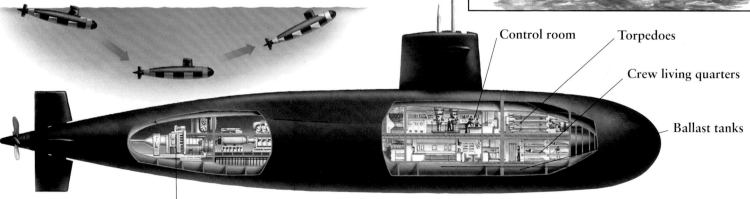

Control room

Torpedoes

Crew living quarters

Ballast tanks

Engine room

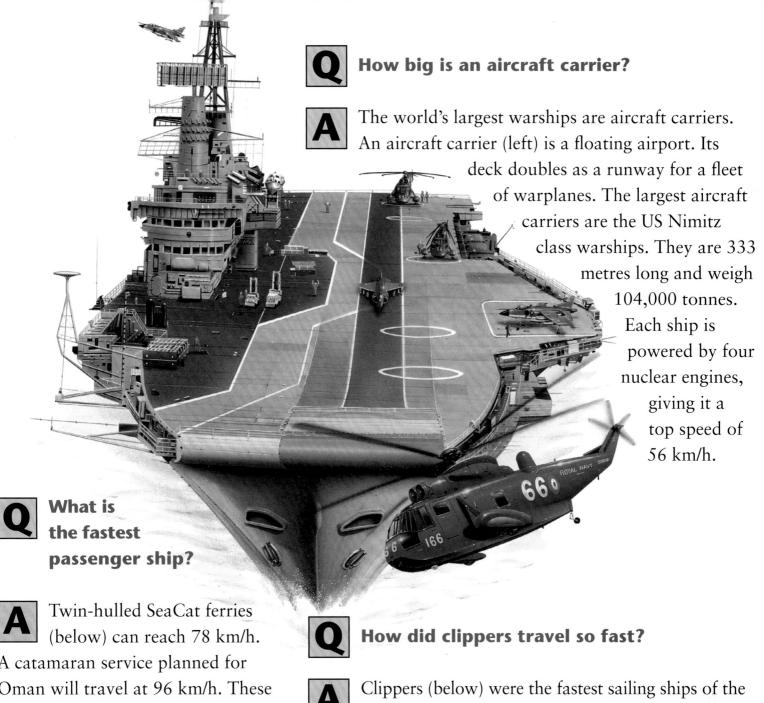

Q How big is an aircraft carrier?

A The world's largest warships are aircraft carriers. An aircraft carrier (left) is a floating airport. Its deck doubles as a runway for a fleet of warplanes. The largest aircraft carriers are the US Nimitz class warships. They are 333 metres long and weigh 104,000 tonnes. Each ship is powered by four nuclear engines, giving it a top speed of 56 km/h.

Q What is the fastest passenger ship?

A Twin-hulled SeaCat ferries (below) can reach 78 km/h. A catamaran service planned for Oman will travel at 96 km/h. These ships are powered by water-jet engines. Instead of propellers, they pump water backwards at great speed to propel the ship forwards.

Q How did clippers travel so fast?

A Clippers (below) were the fastest sailing ships of the 19th century. Their narrow hulls slipped through the water easily. They carried a large sail area to catch as much wind as possible. The fastest clippers, such as the *Cutty Sark*, carried almost 3,000 square metres of sail and could reach a speed of just over 31 km/h.

UNDERSEA EXPLORATION

Undersea exploration investigates the water below the ocean surface, the life it contains and the seafloor beneath. It has given scientists a better understanding of ocean biology.

KEY FACTS

First major dive: William Beebe and Otis Barton in *Bathysphere* in 1930

Deepest dive: Challenger Deep, 10,916 m by Jacques Piccard in *Trieste* in 1960 and James Cameron in *Deepsea Challenger* in 2012

People have always wondered what lies far beneath the waves, but the ocean depths were dark and so hard to explore. The British *Challenger* expedition (1872–1876) was the first major undersea survey. It searched for life by dragging the ocean bed and trawling the waters, mapped ocean temperatures and saltiness, and made depth measurements, or soundings.

The soundings provided the first strong evidence that the ocean floor was not all the same. Relatively shallow continental plains descend steeply along continental slopes to the very deep and relatively flat abyssal plain at 4,300 metres. Mid-ocean ridges rise up from this, but in places there are much deeper ocean trenches.

HYDROTHERMAL VENTS

In 1979–1980, off the coast of Ecuador in South America, scientists found cracks in the ocean floor that were spewing out super-hot water and plumes of chemicals. They called the cracks 'hydrothermal vents'. The water from the vents can be as hot as 300°C. Around the cracks are animals that live nowhere else in the ocean.

The need to dive

To get more information, people had to dive. The pressure of the water column and the need to carry oxygen supplies meant that divers could not dive very deeply. Before the 1930s, the deepest humans could safely descend in diving suits was 30 metres. Submarines had gone deeper but they had no windows, making them useless for seeing anything.

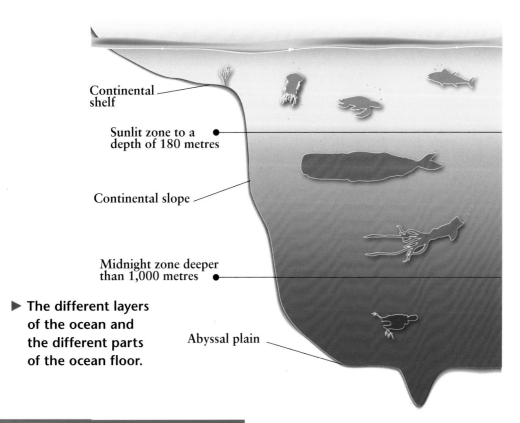

Continental shelf

Sunlit zone to a depth of 180 metres

Continental slope

Midnight zone deeper than 1,000 metres

▶ **The different layers of the ocean and the different parts of the ocean floor.**

Abyssal plain

In 1930 the explorers William Beebe and Otis Barton dived to 435 metres in a submersible they called the *Bathysphere*; later they took this craft down to 1,370 metres. They saw animals that had never been seen before.

Voyage to the depths

The invention of sonar allowed scientists to accurately chart the depth of the ocean. Inspired by Beebe and Barton, Jacques Piccard in 1960 organised an expedition in the submersible *Trieste* to the bottom of the Marianas Trench, east of the Philippines. The deepest point *Trieste* reached (Challenger Deep) was 10,916 metres. James Cameron returned there in 2012 in *Deepsea Challenger*.

▲ The submersible *Alvin* at work.

Crewed submersibles such as *Alvin* could be directed more easily than earlier underwater craft. *Alvin* had bright spotlights to light up its surroundings and robotic arms to collect samples. *Alvin* can descend to 4,500 metres. In 1974 it explored the Great Rift Valley of the Mid-Atlantic Ridge near the Azores islands. It found evidence that new sea floor was being created along the mid-ocean ridge. Since then, submersibles have made many exciting discoveries.

▼ The *Bathysphere* enters the ocean near Bermuda at the start of its record-breaking dive in 1930.

NEW YORK ZOOLOGICAL SOCIETY BATHYSPHERE

GENERAL INFORMATION

- Five nations have sent expeditions to depths greater than 3,500 m. They are: United States, France, Russia, Japan and China.
- The submersible *Alvin* can take a crew of three to a depth of 4,500 m. Between 1964 and 2012 it made 4,400 dives.

See also:

Great Explorers, Planet Earth, Ships

UNDERSEA EXPLORATION

Q How did early diving suits work?

A Early diving equipment made in the 1600s and 1700s worked by pumping air down a hose from the surface into a metal helmet over the diver's head (right). The pressure of the air inside the helmet stopped water from rising up inside.

Q How does a pressurised diving suit work?

A A pressurised diving suit (below) is supplied with air pumped from the surface through a hose. The diver can alter the air pressure inside the suit by adjusting a valve in the helmet. Heavy metal boots help to keep the diver weighted down on the seabed.

Q What is an atmospheric diving suit?

A An atmospheric diving suit (below) is a watertight suit of armour used for the deepest dives. The diver breathes air at atmospheric pressure, which is that of surface air. The heavy metal suit with watertight joints stops the huge water pressure 300 metres below the surface from crushing it.

Q What is an aqualung?

A An aqualung (above) is a device that enables divers to move around freely under water without any connection with the surface. The diver breathes air from tanks worn on the back.

Q Why are shipwrecks explored?

A Sunken ships can tell us a lot about the sailors who sailed them and the world they lived in. The ship's timbers may be all that is left, but sometimes the divers who explore shipwrecks (right) find tools, weapons and some of the sailors' belongings.

Q What animals have been found in the ocean depths?

A Light does not reach the bottom of the ocean. Many of the fish that live there make their own light. They catch smaller fish by dangling a glowing lure over their mouth. Smaller fish swim towards the lure and straight into the fish's mouth.

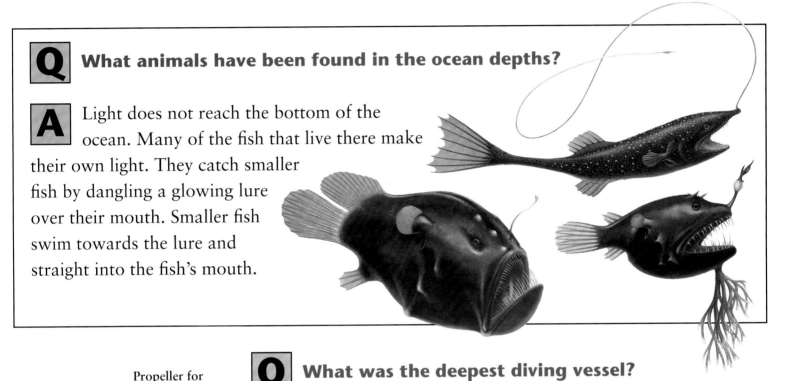

Q What was the deepest diving vessel?

A On 23 January 1960, the submersible *Trieste* (left) descended 10,916 metres into the deepest part of the Marianas Trench in the Pacific Ocean. No one has dived deeper. *Trieste*'s crew of two were protected inside a thick metal sphere beneath a large float partly filled with petrol. When sea water flooded into the float, *Trieste* sank. To return to the surface, it dropped metal weights.

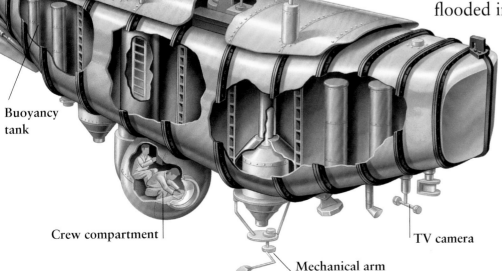

Water ballast tank

Propeller for manoeuvring

Buoyancy tank

Crew compartment

TV camera

Mechanical arm

LAND TRAVEL

People provided the earliest means of transport, carrying goods on their backs. Horses and oxen could carry heavier loads, including people.

With the invention of the wheel and the development of carts, even bigger loads could be moved, generally following rough dirt tracks. Early civilisations such as those in Mesopotamia (in modern-day Iraq) paved their major roads to speed movement between towns. The ancient Romans developed road-building technology even further, building straight roads with only gentle slopes and drains.

KEY FACTS

Bicycles: about 1 billion worldwide
Electric bicycles: 40 million in China
Motorcycles: about 160 million worldwide
Cars: about 600 million worldwide
Lorries: more than 200 million worldwide

▼ Decumanus Street, in the ancient Roman city of Thamugadi, Algeria. The Romans built paved and well-drained roads so horse-drawn traffic could move more quickly.

▲ Shinkansen trains carry 150 million passengers a year at great speed between major cities in Japan.

Steam powers the way

Until the Industrial Revolution, travel by land was generally slow. Several inventions in the 18th and 19th centuries changed the way people travelled. The first of these was the steam engine. When used to turn wheels, running along two parallel tracks, a steam locomotive could pull much heavier loads than a team of horses ever could. The Stockton and Darlington Railway in England carried 600 passengers at 16 kilometres per hour on its first journey in 1825.

More powerful locomotives followed, and in the 20th century fast diesel- and electric-powered trains replaced steam. Modern high-speed trains pick up electric current from overhead power lines. For example, the Shinkansen trains in Japan travel at up to 320

▲ A cheap method of transport: in the back of a lorry in India.

kilometres per hour. Magnetic levitation (maglev) technology will power a German train even faster.

Internal combustion

The invention of the internal combustion engine in the early 19th century paved the way for automobile transport towards the end of the century. Today, internal combustion engines power most cars, buses, lorries and motorcycles. However, like the early trains, the first generation of cars was slow and unreliable. More efficient engines and smoother, straighter roads reduced journey times dramatically in the late 20th century. In many parts of the world the car is the most popular method of transport. Most are fuelled by petroleum or diesel, though biofuels and electric cars are becoming more popular.

TWO-WHEELED TRANSPORT
In much of the world bicycles (right) were the most popular mode of transport in the 20th century. They are relatively cheap to buy and do not require fuel. Bicycle use declined as car ownership became more common. For example, in China, one-third of all journeys were made by bicycle in 1995, but 15 years later that figure had fallen to one-fifth.

GENERAL INFORMATION
● Most major cities are linked by highways for cars and lorries. These roads have two sets of lanes so traffic going in different directions is kept apart. Vehicles travelling at different speeds use separate lanes.

See also:

Cars, Machines, Transport

Q How are heavy loads carried by road?

A The largest and heaviest loads are carried on a special low trailer pulled by a powerful tractor unit (right). This vehicle has six axles to spread the load. The tractor unit has six sets of wheels. Four of them are driven by the engine to give maximum power.

Trailer

Tractor unit

Q How does a refrigeration lorry keep its cargo cold?

A Cargoes that have to be kept cold are transported in a refrigerated lorry (below). The insulated trailer has a refrigeration unit on the front. Liquid coolant flows through pipes in the trailer and absorbs heat from the cargo. The coolant returns to the refrigeration unit and gives up its heat to the outside air. It is then compressed to turn it back into a cold liquid and re-circulated through the trailer.

Refrigeration unit

Q Which were the largest ever steam trains?

A The largest steam locomotives ever built were five giants called Big Boys. They were built in the 1940s for the US Union Pacific Railroad. The locomotive and its coal tender (right) were almost 40 metres long, 3 metres wide and 5 metres high. They each weighed 600 tonnes. They pulled up to 4,000 tonnes of freight in the Rocky Mountains.

Q Can the Sun power vehicles?

A Sunshine can be turned into electricity by solar cells. A vehicle covered with solar cells can produce enough electricity to drive an electric motor. A solar-powered bicycle crossed Australia at an average speed of 50 km/h. In 2011 *Sunswift Ivy* (right) set a new world speed record for a solar-powered car – 89 km/h.

Q What is the fastest train?

A The world's fastest train in service today is the Chinese CRH 380A (right), which operates on several high-speed rail links around Shanghai. This train has a cruising speed of 350 km/h and a maximum operating speed of 380 km/h, though it can travel much faster. In 2010 it began to serve the route between Shanghai and Nanjing.

Q What is a supercar?

A Supercars are the super saloons and super sports models of the car world. They are fast, powerful and very expensive. The Ferrari F40 (right) is certainly a supercar. One of the world's fastest production cars, it can reach a top speed of 325 km/h. One special feature is that the engine is behind the driver.

CARS

Cars are rubber-tyred vehicles that run on roads rather than rails. Most cars are powered by internal combustion engines using petrol or diesel for fuel.

A Frenchman, Nicolas Cugnot, built the first self-powered road vehicle in 1769. It was a three-wheeled steam engine designed to pull cannons, but it was never used. Modern car design began to take shape in the late 19th century. German engineers Gottlieb Daimler and Karl Benz both created engine-driven cars in 1886. A few years later Frenchman Emile Levassor built a car with spring suspension (for a smoother ride) and gears.

Car engines

The heart of a car is its internal combustion engine. Petrol or diesel

▲ The Model T Ford was the first mass production car. Its top speed was 72 km/h.

and air are ignited in a combustion chamber and hot expanding gas pushes pistons. The motion of the pistons turns the car's axles, and these turn its wheels.

A transmission system (gearbox) uses gears to match the engine's speed to the desired road speed. The clutch, which may be manual or automatic, controls the transmission. Oil protects the various engine parts from rubbing against each other, and a cooling system keeps the engine from overheating. The exhaust removes

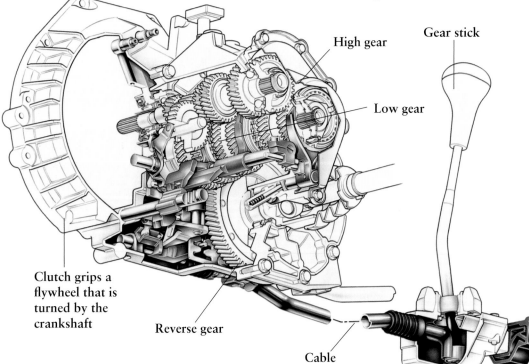

High gear

Gear stick

Low gear

Clutch grips a flywheel that is turned by the crankshaft

Reverse gear

Cable

◀ A manual gearbox (transmission) of a car. The diagram shows the clutch, the different gear wheels and the gear stick, which the driver operates to change gear.

SOME FEATURES OF A MODERN CAR

Modern cars have comfortable seats and safety features such as airbags. Car makers devote huge sums of money to improved style and greater engine efficiency. Many cars now have computers to control in-car temperature and humidity, satellite navigation (sat-nav) systems (right) to direct drivers to specified locations and high-quality sound systems for music players and radios.

waste gases. The suspension is a set of springs and shock absorbers that soften unevenness on the road and help the vehicle take corners easily.

Mass production

The American Henry Ford (1863–1947) began a revolution in car manufacture. He developed the assembly line that made mass production possible around 1913.

Cars that were being assembled moved slowly along a conveyor belt. Each worker had a few simple tasks to perform on each car, over and over, many times each day. Many more cars could be produced in a day, and so Ford could sell them more cheaply than other car models. By 1927, 15 million of Ford's Model Ts had rolled off the production line.

More efficient cars

By the 1960s the huge increase in car use was causing pollution problems. Manufacturers began to make cars smaller and more efficient. To reduce our reliance on oil, biofuels (made from vegetable oils, for example) are now used instead in some cars. Also, battery-powered cars have been developed to protect Earth's resources.

▶ An electric car has its battery recharged by the roadside in Oslo, Norway.

GENERAL INFORMATION

- Car ownership varies greatly from nation to nation. In the United States there are more than 800 cars for every 1,000 people, and in Japan the figure is 600. In Bangladesh, however, there are only two cars per 1,000 people.

See also:

Land Travel, Transport

CARS

Q **How is a modern car built for safety?**

A A modern car has complex machinery and structures built into the bodywork so that it is safe (right). A strong body frame is designed to protect the occupants in a crash. An anti-lock braking system (ABS) enables the car to brake without skidding by releasing and reapplying the brakes many times every second. The steering column is made in sections that will collapse in the event of a crash.

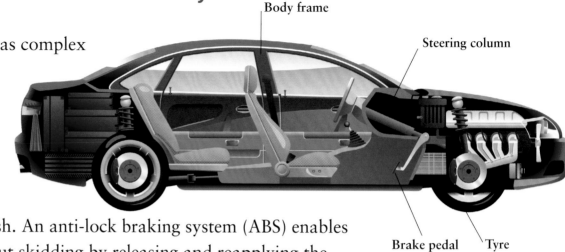

Body frame

Steering column

Brake pedal   Tyre

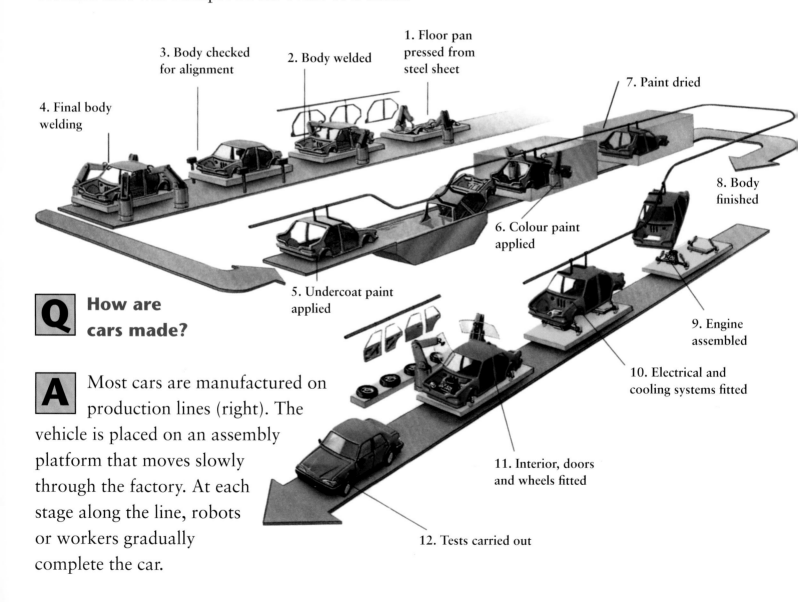

3. Body checked for alignment

2. Body welded

1. Floor pan pressed from steel sheet

7. Paint dried

4. Final body welding

8. Body finished

6. Colour paint applied

5. Undercoat paint applied

9. Engine assembled

10. Electrical and cooling systems fitted

11. Interior, doors and wheels fitted

12. Tests carried out

Q **How are cars made?**

A Most cars are manufactured on production lines (right). The vehicle is placed on an assembly platform that moves slowly through the factory. At each stage along the line, robots or workers gradually complete the car.

Q Why do car engines need oil?

A As a car travels, many of its parts move against each other. The different parts of the engine (right) move at high speed. Oil is pumped from the sump to lubricate the bearings, pistons and other components, allowing the metal parts to move without causing wear or generating heat through friction. Some vehicles use special oils if they are to be used in very cold conditions.

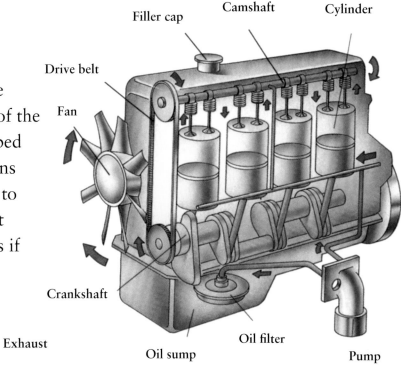

Filler cap · Camshaft · Cylinder · Drive belt · Fan · Crankshaft · Oil sump · Oil filter · Pump

Q What is fuel injection?

Fuel in · Injector · Air in · Spark plug · Exhaust · Cylinder

A Car engines burn fuel in closed cylinders. A fuel injection system pumps a precise amount of fuel into the cylinders as air is sucked in (above). The mixture is then ignited by a spark plug and the waste gases flow through the exhaust.

Q What did the first cars look like?

A The first cars were built in the 1880s. To begin with, engines were built into carriages normally pulled by horses. These 'horseless carriages' had simple controls.

Q How are racing cars designed to go fast?

A Most modern cars are designed for comfortable travel. Racing cars (right), however, are designed for speed. They are very light but strong, and the powerful engines are designed to accelerate extremely fast. The tyres are wide so they grip the road extremely well. The bodywork is designed to reduce air resistance, and special fins are added to improve handling and road holding.

Engine · Extra wide tyres

FLIGHT

Even before the ancient Greek myth of Icarus – who flew on wings of wax and feathers – people have wanted to fly. That wish has become reality only in the last 200 years or so.

KEY FACTS

Passenger aircraft cruising height: around 12,000 m

Passenger aircraft cruising speed: around 900 km/h

Biggest passenger aircraft: Airbus A380 seats up to 850 passengers on two decks

Fastest aircraft: Lockheed SR-71 'Blackbird', 3,530 km/h in 1976

Three forces act on an aircraft when it is airborne. Since a plane is heavier than air, it can fly only if air flows over its wings fast enough to produce an upward force called lift. This force has to be stronger than the force of gravity if the plane is to stay in the air. A third force – thrust – is produced by the aircraft's engines and drives the plane forwards. Thrust must be stronger than drag, the resistance of the air, for the plane to fly.

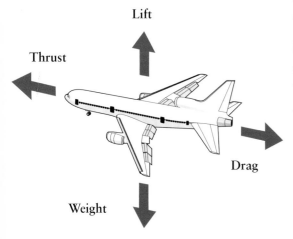

Lift

Thrust

Drag

Weight

◀ The four different forces that act on a plane as it is flying.

▲ Modern jet aircraft carry hundreds of passengers, for thousands of kilometres, without refuelling.

Early flight

The earliest form of air transport was by hot-air balloon. The first manned flight took the pilot about 8 kilometres near Paris in 1783. However, this was a slow and unreliable means of transport, being completely dependent on the wind.

Pioneers such as George Cayley (1773–1857) and Otto Lilienthal (1848–1896) experimented with engine-less gliders. However, controlled, powered flight was mastered only in 1903 when an internal combustion engine and reliable propellers allowed Orville and Wilbur Wright to fly 36 metres. Improvements followed, and the first commercial flights began after World War I (1914–1918).

Jet engines

Until the outbreak of World War II, in 1939, planes had engines that drove propellers. These converted engine power into thrust. Ideas for a jet engine, which could increase flying speeds, emerged independently in England and Germany in the 1930s. Fans inside a jet engine suck air through them. As the air is forced out of the back of the engine, it pushes the aircraft forwards.

The German He 178 was the first jet plane, making its maiden flight in 1939. The need for faster warplanes during World War II accelerated the development of

jet technology, and better planes followed. After the war, jet engines were used increasingly to power passenger aircraft, from the de Havilland Comet in 1952 to the world's first supersonic passenger plane, the Concorde. Concorde flew between London, New York

▲ Not all flight is powered. Hangliders make the most of breezes to stay airborne.

and Paris between 1976 and 2003, cruising at 2,140 kilometres per hour. Even faster planes have been built for military use.

HELICOPTER FLIGHT

The first operational helicopter flew in 1936. Full-scale production started in the United States three years later. The thrust and lift in a helicopter is provide by engine-driven rotor blades above the craft. Although they were first used for military roles, helicopters now also carry passengers and deliver food aid in emergency relief operations.

GENERAL INFORMATION

● The longest ever flight was made in a propeller-driven Cessna plane. Americans Robert Timm and John Cook kept it airborne for 65 days in 1957–58. The Cessna was refuelled in flight.

See also:

Everyday Science, Transport

FLIGHT

Q How does an aeroplane stay in the air?

A Aeroplanes (left) can fly because of the shape of their wings. The top of the wing is more curved than the bottom. Air rushing over the top of the wings travels further and faster than the air flowing underneath. This produces lower air pressure above the wings than below them (below), causing the wings to lift.

Jet of hot air

Airflow

Q How does a jet engine work?

A A large spinning fan at the front of the engine (above) sucks in air. The air is then compressed and heated by burning fuel in the combustion chamber. This makes the air expand quickly. A jet of hot air rushes out of the back of the engine and pushes the aeroplane forwards.

Fan

Combustion chamber

Q What happens before take-off?

A An airliner (below) is carefully prepared for each flight. The passenger cabin is cleaned. Meals and luggage are loaded. The fuel tanks are filled. Engineers check the plane and the crew make their pre-flight checks.

Q What did the first aeroplane look like?

A The first aeroplane, called *Flyer 1* (right), flew in 1903. It was made from wood. It had two wings covered with fabric, one above the other, and the pilot lay down on the lower wing to fly it.

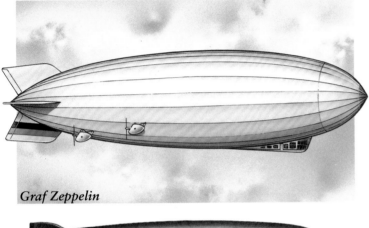

Graf Zeppelin

Hindenburg 245 metres

Concorde 62.1 metres

Q What is a Zeppelin?

A A Zeppelin (left) is a giant airship named after its inventor, Count Ferdinand von Zeppelin. The Zeppelins were built in Germany between 1900 and the 1930s. The biggest passenger-carrying Zeppelins were the *Graf Zeppelin* and the *Hindenburg*. They carried passengers across the Atlantic Ocean. Zeppelins could fly without wings because they were filled with hydrogen gas. This is lighter than air and made the airships float upwards.

Q Which aircraft can carry the largest cargo?

A The Airbus Super Transporter A300-600ST Beluga has the largest cargo of any aircraft. It can carry up to 47 tonnes of cargo in a hold that is 37 metres long and up to 7.4 metres wide. Belugas are built from Airbus A300 airliners. They replaced the Super Guppy transporter (below). The Super Guppies were built to transport parts of the giant Saturn V moon rockets.

AIRBUS SKYLINK

STRUCTURES

As well as roofed buildings, people erect structures that are every bit as important for society to function. They include bridges, tunnels and dams.

Structures are important for transport, generating energy, communications and the extraction of raw materials. Some of the earliest structures were monuments to honour gods and dead kings.

Transport

Transport structures include highways, railways, canals and docks. Modern roads are built with speed in mind. Overpasses and underpasses are built at intersections. Tunnels and bridges are constructed to straighten road and rail routes through mountainous areas. Roads and railways cross over or tunnel under wide rivers and inlets of the sea.

Canals are narrow artificial waterways, along which barges can travel. Ocean-going cargo ships and ferries are loaded and unloaded at docks. Where the water is too shallow for the ships to approach the land, long piers and jetties are built into deeper water.

Dams and reservoirs

Since ancient times people have built dams across rivers to hold back reservoirs for drinking water and irrigation. The earliest of these is the Jawa Dam, Jordan, built of stone and earth around 3000 B.C.

KEY FACTS

Longest bridge over water: Lake Pontchartrain, United States, 38 km
Longest tunnel: Seikan, Japan, 54 km
Tallest dam: Nurek, Tajikistan, 300 m
Tallest chimney: Ekibastusz power station, Kazakhstan, 420 m

▼ The Akashi-Kaikyo Bridge carries a highway over the Akashi Strait, Japan. There is clearance beneath for large ships to pass.

◀ Three Gorges Dam, China, which controls flooding on the Yangtze River and produces electricity.

Hydro-electric power stations are usually attached to modern dams. The water rushing through the dams turns turbines that generate electricity. Some modern dams are immense: the Nurek Dam in Tajikistan is 300 metres high.

Drilling and mining

There are special structures where raw materials are being extracted from the ground: oil derricks where there is drilling for oil on land; oil rigs standing on the ocean floor where the drilling takes place at sea; and winding gear at the top of lift shafts that takes miners to deep deposits of coal, copper or gold.

Bridge design

The ancient Romans were great bridge builders, constructing long, arched constructions in stone and brick. However, they could not span very long distances. It was not until the 19th century that new designs made this possible. In a suspension bridge, the deck (carrying the roadway) is hung from very strong cables that run through tall supporting towers. The longest suspension bridge in the world today is the Akashi-Kaikyo Bridge in Japan: its main span is 1.9 kilometres long.

ANCIENT STRUCTURES

There are more than 130 pyramids in Egypt, built as resting places for the pharaohs from 2630 B.C. onwards. Many other cultures had smaller chambered tombs for burials – for example, the chambered long barrows of north-west Europe. No one knows why some structures were built – for example, the Great Sphinx of Giza, Egypt (right), which was sculpted in about 2500 B.C., and the standing stones of Stonehenge, England.

GENERAL INFORMATION

- The oldest known religious structure is the temple at Gobekli Tepe, Turkey. It was built around 10,000–9000 B.C.
- The Eiffel Tower in Paris is a unique lattice structure. It was built for an exhibition in 1889. The wrought-iron tower weighs 7,300 tonnes and is 300 m tall.
- Wind turbines harness the energy of wind and turn it into electricity. Collections of wind turbines, called wind farms, are sometimes built in shallow offshore waters.

See also:

Buildings, Land Travel, Transport

STRUCTURES

Q How long did it take to build the Great Pyramid?

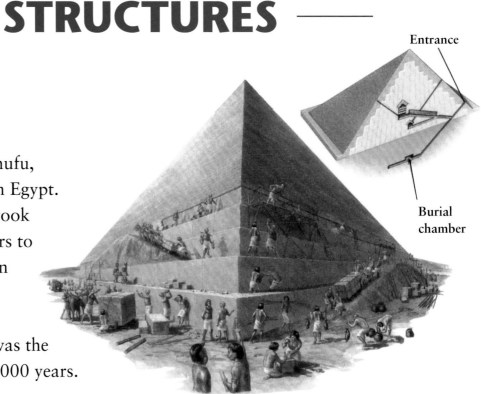

Entrance

Burial chamber

A The Great Pyramid was built as a tomb for King Khufu, also called Cheops. It is at Giza, in Egypt. Work began in about 2575 BC. It took thousands of people about 25 years to assemble it (right) from 2.3 million blocks of stone. It weighs over 6 million tonnes and is today 138 metres high. The Great Pyramid was the tallest building in the world for 4,000 years.

Q What type of bridge is the Sydney Harbour Bridge?

A The Sydney Harbour Bridge in Australia is a steel arch bridge spanning 503 metres. It is not the longest steel arch, but it is the widest. It carries two railway tracks, eight traffic lanes, a cycle lane and a footpath. It was opened in 1932.

Q What is the Eiffel Tower?

A The Eiffel Tower (right) in Paris is one of the most famous French landmarks. Designed by the engineer Alexandre-Gustave Eiffel, it was built in 1889 to celebrate the 100th anniversary of the French Revolution. It stands 300 metres high, and is a slender pyramid made from 7,300 tonnes of iron girders.

Q How was the space shuttle moved to its launch pad?

A The space shuttle (left) was prepared for launch inside a building at the Kennedy Space Center in Florida, USA. It was moved to the launch pad 6 kilometres away by the world's largest crawler transporter. This giant is 40 metres long and weighs 2,700 tonnes. It travels on four double caterpillar tracks. The tracks are moved by electric motors driven by generators powered by diesel engines.

Q What is an oil platform?

A Oil platforms are offshore drilling rigs that stand on the seabed. The tallest is the Baldpate platform in the Gulf of Mexico. It stands in 580 metres of water. The Gullfaks C platform (above) in the North Sea stands on concrete pillars and supports production equipment, loading derricks and a helicopter pad.

Q How does a flood barrier work?

A The Thames Barrier (right) was opened in 1984 to protect London from flooding. It consists of eight gates each weighing 3,700 tonnes. They normally lie on the river bed. If there is any danger of flooding, the gates are rotated to raise them up against the flood water.

Gate raised

Gate lowered

BUILDINGS

Houses, flats, churches, schools and factories are all buildings. The first buildings would have been simple structures made of stone, thatch, wood, reeds and animal skins.

KEY FACTS

Biggest building: Boeing's factory at Everett, United States, has a volume of 13 million m³ and an area of 400,000 m²

Tallest building: Burj Khalifa, Dubai, 830 m

Oldest building: walled entrance to a cave near Kalambaka, Greece, 21,000 B.C.

BURJ KHALIFA

The Burj Khalifa in Dubai is the tallest building in the world, at 830 metres. It has more than 160 floors, which are serviced by 57 fast lifts. The building has 26,000 glass panels and a spectacular observation deck.

▲ Beijing's Bird's Nest stadium was built for the 2008 Olympic Games. Around the stadium is an unusual steel lattice structure.

From the time of the first permanent settlements around 10,000 B.C. to the Industrial Revolution in the 18th century, buildings were made from materials that could be found locally. These materials were mainly wood where there were forests; stone where it could be quarried; and brick where there was clay.

The exceptions were especially important buildings. So palaces and cathedrals often used high-quality stone, such as marble. After the Industrial Revolution, new materials such as cast iron and steel became generally available. Cranes, strong scaffolding and tough concrete enabled much taller buildings to be erected.

Early buildings

The earliest buildings were single-storey homes. For thousands of years, building design was influenced by the local climate. In cold regions, homes were built with thick walls of wood or stone, and relatively small windows, so heat was retained. In hotter parts of the world, walls were usually thinner and windows larger.

As settlements grew bigger and more crowded, space became a problem. Taller homes were constructed. There were probably 10-storey apartment blocks in ancient Rome, for example.

Early religious buildings were often very large. The Great Buddha Temple in Nira, Japan, is the largest building made entirely from wood. It was originally built in the 8th century. Many religious structures from the Middle Ages are still standing. Enormous Christian cathedrals, Muslim mosques and Buddhist temples were built throughout much of Europe, Asia and Africa.

Modern buildings

In the centre of most modern cities, space is limited and land is expensive so people often live in high-rise flats of steel, reinforced concrete and glass. People often

▶ The mud-brick tower houses of Shibam, Yemen, were built in the 16th century. Shibam has been called the oldest skyscraper city.

work in multi-storey offices of the same materials. Central heating, air conditioning and insulating building materials allow the climate to be controlled inside modern homes, offices and factories.

Factories, schools, office blocks, train and bus stations, and large housing complexes are usually mostly concrete. Glass, stone, brick, wood and steel are also important components. Sports stadiums are built to seat huge crowds in comfort. Architects produce unique designs for the most important buildings.

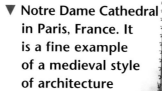

▼ Notre Dame Cathedral in Paris, France. It is a fine example of a medieval style of architecture called Gothic.

GENERAL INFORMATION

- The most common building materials are stone, concrete, brick, wood, glass and steel. Unusual materials include titanium metal, straw, toughened cardboard and tyres.

See also:

Ancient Rome, Early Civilisations, Middle Ages, Structures

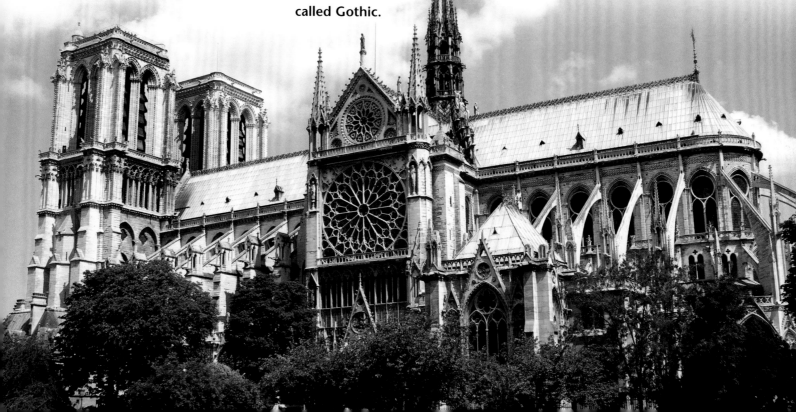

BUILDINGS

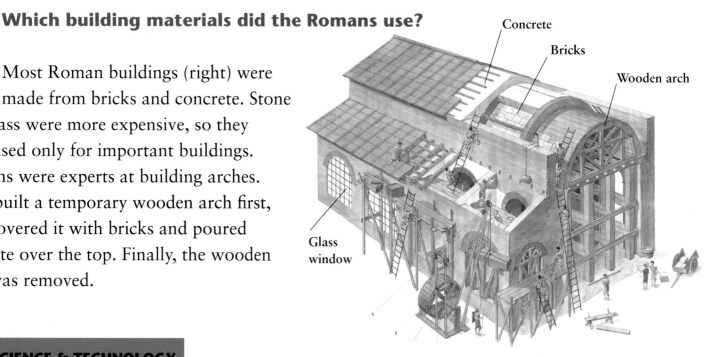

Q Why was the Great wall of China built?

A The Great Wall of China (right) was built by Chinese emperors to keep out invaders. Most of it was built by the emperor Shih Huang Ti between 221 B.C. and 204 B.C. The wall finally reached a length of over 6,000 kilometres. Much of the wall is still standing.

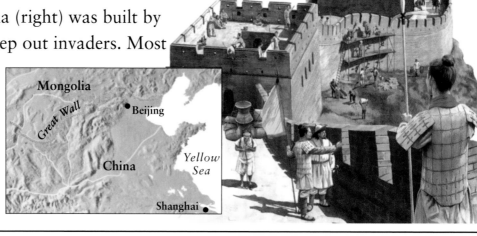

Q What is Abu Simbel?

A Abu Simbel is a place in Egypt where the Egyptian king Ramesses II built two temples in about 1,250 B.C. They were cut into blocks and rebuilt on higher ground in the 1960s when the rising waters of Lake Nasser threatened to cover them.

Q Which building materials did the Romans use?

A Most Roman buildings (right) were made from bricks and concrete. Stone and glass were more expensive, so they were used only for important buildings. Romans were experts at building arches. They built a temporary wooden arch first, then covered it with bricks and poured concrete over the top. Finally, the wooden arch was removed.

Concrete

Bricks

Wooden arch

Glass window

Q Why were castles built?

A Castles were built to protect the people who lived in them. They were often built on hilltops or surrounded by water to make them easier to defend. Bodiam Castle (right) was a manor house in Sussex, England, that was strengthened to resist French attacks in the 1300s.

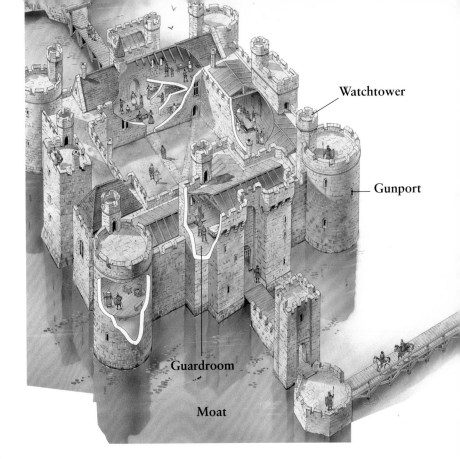

Watchtower

Gunport

Guardroom

Moat

Q Why was the Statue of Liberty built?

A The Statue of Liberty (above) stands on an island at the entrance to New York Harbor. It was a gift from France to the USA in 1886 to celebrate the American Revolution. It is made from copper sheeting, and with its base stands 93 metres high. Its rusting iron skeleton was replaced by stainless steel in the 1980s.

Q What is a skyscraper?

A A skyscraper is a very tall building supported by a steel frame inside it. The world's most famous skyscraper is the Empire State Building in New York, USA (below). Built in 1931, it stands 381 metres tall. The tallest skyscraper today is the Burj Khalifa building in Dubai. It stands 830 metres high, 530 metres taller than the Eiffel Tower in Paris, France, which was itself the tallest building in the world until 1930.

Eiffel Tower

Empire State Building

Burj Khalifa

INDEX

INDEX